ACHIEVING
SUCCESS
for New and Aspiring
SUPERINTENDENTS

To superintendents and those aspiring to the position.
Their leadership and the success of their students are essential to
maintaining the strength of this country and our democratic process.

ACHIEVING SUCCESS

for New and Aspiring

SUPERINTENDENTS

A PRACTICAL GUIDE

MARY FRANCES CALLAN
WILLIAM LEVINSON

CORWIN
A SAGE Company

For information:

Corwin
A SAGE Company
2455 Teller Road
Thousand Oaks, California 91320
(800) 233-9936
Fax: (800) 417-2466
www.corwin.com

SAGE Ltd.
1 Oliver's Yard
55 City Road
London EC1Y 1SP
United Kingdom

SAGE Pvt. Ltd.
B 1/I 1 Mohan Cooperative
  Industrial Area
Mathura Road, New Delhi 110 044
India

SAGE Asia-Pacific Pte. Ltd.
33 Pekin Street #02-01
Far East Square
Singapore 048763

Printed in the United States of America

Library of Congress Cataloging-in-Publication Data

Callan, Mary Frances.
Achieving success for new and aspiring superintendents: a practical guide / Mary Frances Callan, William Levinson.
     p. cm.
Includes bibliographical references and index.
ISBN 978-1-4129-8896-4 (pbk.)

    1. School superintendents—In-service training—United States. I. Levinson, William. II. Title.

LB2831.72.C35 2011
371.2′011—dc22   2010037119

This book is printed on acid-free paper.

10   11   12   13   14   10   9   8   7   6   5   4   3   2   1

Acquisitions Editor:	Arnis Burvikovs
Associate Editor:	Desirée A. Bartlett
Editorial Assistant:	Kimberly Greenberg
Production Editor:	Veronica Stapleton
Copy Editor:	Trey Thoelcke
Typesetter:	C&M Digitals (P) Ltd.
Proofreader:	Dennis W. Webb
Indexer:	Sheila Bodell
Cover Designer:	Michael Dubowe
Permissions:	Karen Ehrmann

Contents

Foreword

Prior to becoming a partner in a national consulting firm, I served twenty-four years as a suburban school superintendent. In my current position, I have worked with almost 300 boards of education in urban, suburban, and rural settings, assisting them in finding superintendents to lead their districts. I also provide governance training to superintendents and boards in a number of districts.

My background gives me a unique perspective on the role of the superintendent. Today that work is more complex than when I was one. Superintendents still work with a broad constituency composed of students, staff, parents, elected and appointed officials, and the tax-paying citizenry. But there are fewer available resources and greater student needs and staff demands. Often the community, while supportive, does not think through solutions they offer to address district issues. As a result their responses fail to identify or anticipate unintended consequences.

Superintendents also work in a society marked by technological advances that have resulted in 24/7 communications and rapidly expanding information. This influences what is taught and how students learn. In addition, anyone can say anything, irrespective of the facts, and have it appear in the mass media. Examples abound on community blogs. This makes it more difficult to find solutions to school community problems. Add to this an expectation of instant responses to e-mails or text messaging.

The greatest challenge is providing exceptional instructional leadership. Every day, superintendents must address state and national accountability, standards-based instruction, and a greater diversity in the student population. The superintendency today requires educators who understand the complexity of the work and embrace these challenges.

In this context, *Achieving Success for New and Aspiring Superintendents* could not be more timely or needed. In a clear, straightforward format, authors Mary Frances Callan and Bill Levinson provide guidance that helps ensure the success of superintendents. This book contains useful information on how to seek, assume, execute, and reflect on the work of a superintendent. The tips proffered throughout this book are based on the authors' experiences as successful superintendents. They also include examples from other superintendents working in a variety of settings. This book will assist readers in assessing the most appropriate response to situations they encounter.

Effectively leading school districts is both a *science* and an *art.* As one pages through this book, the material presented contributes to a deeper understanding of the science of leadership. Guidance is provided on everything from the application process through negotiating a contract; transitioning to the position; working with staff, the board, and unions; communications; and the challenges facing superintendents in years two and beyond. The scenarios and examples illustrate the art of leadership. They underscore that the art of leadership is learned only by having a thorough understanding of its science.

Superintendents who labor daily to make this a better world for their students, as well as aspiring superintendents who are seeking an opportunity to make their mark on public education, will find this book to be an effective guide. It will help them be successful in an increasingly challenging, yet rewarding profession.

Bill Attea

Retired superintendent, Glenview Public Schools (IL)

Founding partner and chair, board of directors, Hazard, Young, Attea & Associates, Ltd.

September 1, 2010

Preface

Public education is the cornerstone of democracy. Its mission is to transmit the knowledge and skills needed for children to become productive and contributing members of society. Given the growing number of students who live in poverty, as well as a growing number of students whose first language is not English, this mission is even more critical.

To meet it requires effective public school leadership that understands the relationship between high expectations, quality teaching, student learning, and accountability. This leadership also needs to know how to develop systems that encourage students to think, create, and contribute. Further these leaders need to see the connection between the success of our public schools and the economic, political, and democratic success of our nation.

The need for effective leadership is compounded by the large number of superintendent openings across the country. There are more than 15,000 school districts in the United States, many led by baby boomers close to retirement. School administrators, who traditionally form the pool for superintendent applicants, also are retiring. Add to this teachers and other school staff who are retiring and taking with them years of experience. While this presents a unique opportunity for restructuring, filling these positions with capable and competent educators is a daunting task.

Due to the large number of vacancies, more people are hired with little or no experience as a superintendent or even as a district office administrator. Once hired, many receive little or no mentoring or coaching. Some new superintendents view asking for assistance as a sign of weakness, while school boards are often reluctant to include the cost of coaching in the district budget.

In other situations, highly competent administrators fail to achieve their goal of serving as superintendent because they lack an understanding of how to prepare for the position. Some have no idea what to do once they are selected, failing to achieve a successful transition from their current position to that of superintendent. Still others lack an understanding of how to work with boards or unions, or to communicate with their constituents. The end result is that qualified people fail to become superintendents or fail to perform once hired.

The complexity of the work and the loneliness of the position often come as a rude awakening for new superintendents. Some do not make it past their second year. Those who master the complexity of the role and do well are frequently recruited to better performing or higher paying districts, often with as little as two or three years of experience. This turnover, whether due to failure or success, causes a lack of stability as districts must again seek new superintendents.

A growing number of aspiring and new superintendents recognize this and are asking for assistance. We decided to write this book after receiving numerous requests for assistance from new and aspiring superintendents. In reviewing those requests, we were intrigued that the majority did not focus on the theory of leadership or effective instruction but rather on how to put the theory into practice. As the noted Italian painter Giorgio Morandi wrote, "Nothing is more abstract than reality."

OUR PURPOSE AND APPROACH

We present this book as a practical guide to effective practice, covering a wide range of topics important for the success of a superintendent. Included is information on how to prepare for the superintendent position, guidance in succeeding during the first several years, and help determining if and when you should seek a new position. What makes our approach unique is that we believe talented people who aspire to become a superintendent are far more likely to accomplish that goal and achieve success on the job if they understand the totality of the position. It is like being an artist who has a vision of the completed work and the tools necessary to accomplish it.

School districts are complex organizations. Providing effective leadership to these organizations requires mastery of a wide array of leadership and organizational skills. Superintendents with vision and motivation who understand the inherent challenges of the position have a great advantage over those who do not. Our goal is to provide this advantage to our readers and help them be successful.

The authors of this book collectively worked more than seventy-five years in public education. Thirty-seven of those years were spent as superintendents in districts ranging in size from 1,000 to 13,000 students. While we wrote this book for aspiring and new superintendents in districts of 500 to 20,000 students, the information contained in the book can be used by those serving any district. Calling on our own experiences and those of others, we included examples to illustrate the points being made. These examples are composites of situations that we experienced or that were shared with us. No example is an actual representation of a particular individual.

Finally, we wrote this book because of our belief in the mission of public education. We have seen the positive effect of good leadership on students. We know such leadership is essential to meeting the diverse needs of the students we serve. It is our hope that this book contributes to good leadership practices and assists the wonderful women and men drawn to the superintendency.

USER GUIDE

This book is a how-to primer for aspiring and new superintendents. Use it as a guide, not a set of instructions. If you are thinking of becoming a superintendent, read the entire book before submitting your first application. This will provide a broad understanding of the superintendent position and what leadership skills and knowledge are required for success. It will help you make decisions about what you need to do to prepare for this position.

Throughout this book we emphasize that the primary responsibility of the superintendent is to ensure the highest levels of teaching and learning. But this is not a guide on instructional leadership. Rather it assists the reader in developing the systems necessary to be an effective instructional leader. For it is the structure of the district and the effective use of its resources that allow superintendents to meet the educational needs of students.

Few books are all comprehensive. This book is no exception. For each subject we cover there are numerous books or articles that delve more deeply into theory, subject matter, and practice. Some of these sources are included in the resources section at the end of the book. Readers may use these resources, as well as classes and seminars, to deepen their understanding of all aspects of district leadership.

CHAPTER OVERVIEW

Throughout the book, topics are introduced and revisited depending on the context. For example, information about working with school boards appears in every chapter. Teaching and learning and communications are other topics frequently discussed.

Chapter 1 "Becoming a Superintendent" presents information on understanding the roles and responsibilities of a superintendent: academic preparation, preparing for and completing the application process, the interview process, and achieving a fair employment contract.

Chapter 2 "Transitioning to Your New District" discusses leaving your current position, learning about your new district, setting up your office, working with your new administrative assistant, and addressing issues that affect your personal life.

Chapter 3 "Getting Started: Organizing to Lead" offers information on establishing needed systems, including meeting groups, schedules, and agendas; conducting effective meetings with your management team, teachers, and staff; managing extracurricular school activities; and working with consultants and legal counsel.

Chapter 4 "Moving the District Forward" covers decision making, mastering the district budget, leading teaching and learning, goal setting and accountability, and superintendent and administrator evaluation.

Chapter 5 "Completing Year One, Planning Year Two: A Continuous Cycle" discusses how to develop legacy goals, as well as successfully complete year one and effectively plan for year two.

Chapter 6 "Working With a School Board" includes information on the basics of working with a board, informal and formal board communications, and preparing and managing board meetings.

Chapter 7 "Working With Employee Groups" covers establishing relationships, an overview of the collective bargaining process, and issues affecting the collective bargaining process.

Chapter 8 "Negotiating Agreements" discusses how to build on your knowledge about working with unions to be successful at the bargaining process. It covers what occurs at the bargaining table, from the preparation of openers through the ratification of contracts.

Chapter 9 "Communicating: Enhanced Decisions" covers communication with parents and the public, working with the media, as well as communicating with staff, students, and other groups essential to the district. It includes how to address emergencies and the importance of customer relations.

Chapter 10 "Looking Ahead" presents information on preparing for twelve challenges of years two and beyond, including factors to consider in determining whether to remain or leave the district.

Resources. This section provides a listing of organizations, books, and resources that can support superintendents in their work.

Every superintendent will have different experiences and different needs. We wish you the best as you begin your work to become a superintendent. In our opinion, no job is more crucial to the success of students and the continuance of public education in our country.

Acknowledgments

It would be impossible to list everyone who influenced our understanding of the skills needed to succeed as a superintendent. Throughout our long careers we have been fortunate to work with many outstanding instructional leaders. Each contributed to our knowledge. We thank them all.

We also want to acknowledge the guidance, support, and inspiration received in the writing of this book from many outstanding educators. Foremost among them is our publisher Corwin and Arnis Burvikovs, our editor. He assisted us in refining the book and strengthening its concepts.

In addition we owe a debt of thanks to the following individuals. We list them in alphabetical order. Each knows the special role he or she played in our careers and the development of this book. Thank you.

- Jennifer Abrams, author of *Having Hard Conversations* and national educational consultant
- Barbara Austin, CEO, College Quest
- Dr. Bill Attea, Hazard, Young & Attea
- Mary Jane Burke, Marin County Superintendent of Schools, CA
- Dr. Susan Cota, former chancellor, Chabot-Las Positas Community College System, CA
- Dr. Donn Gilbert, retired assistant superintendent and chief financial officer, Gilroy Unified School District, Gilroy, CA
- Dr. Martha Kanter, Under Secretary, U.S. Department of Education
- Dr. Dale Mann, author and president of Interactive, Inc.
- Kathleen Ruegsegger, administrative assistant to the superintendent, Palo Alto Unified School District, CA
- Dr. Gail Uilkema, AASA National Superintendent of the Year

We also thank the many aspiring and new superintendents who reviewed chapters of our manuscript and provided invaluable comments and suggestions.

Finally, to our family and friends, in particular Judy and Pat, a very special thank you.

PUBLISHER'S ACKNOWLEDGMENTS

Corwin gratefully acknowledges the following individuals for their editorial insight and guidance:

Kenneth Arndt, Superintendent
Community Unit School District 300
Carpentersville, IL

Randel Beaver, Superintendent
Archer City ISD
Archer City, TX

Marie Blum, Superintendent
Canaseraga Central School District
Canaseraga, NY

Peter Dillon, Superintendent
Berkshire Hills Regional School District
Stockbridge, MA

Jill Gildea, Superintendent
Harrison School District #36
Wonder Lake, IL

Lynn Macan, Superintendent
Cobleskill-Richmondville CSD
Cobleskill, NY

Jill Shackelford, Superintendent
Kansas City Kansas Public Schools
Kansas City, KS

About the Authors

 **Mary Frances Callan, PhD,** recently retired after serving fourteen years of her career as superintendent of schools in Milpitas, Pleasanton, and Palo Alto, California. She now coaches aspiring and new superintendents, assists with superintendent searches, and is codeveloping a curriculum to train aspiring and new superintendents. Earlier in her career she was a teacher, counselor, and administrator in a number of states, as well as overseas.

Callan also serves on boards, including the school board of ICA Cristo Rey, the Board of Regents of Santa Clara University, and the Keenan Health Advisory Board. She is active with the Educational Records Bureau Board and other educational organizations, as well as a volunteer for local nonprofit organizations.

In addition to the above, Callan has presented numerous workshops and given speeches to various profit and nonprofit organizations. Among other writings, she has co-authored publications, including two handbooks for Phi Delta Kappa's Exemplary Practices Series on *Staff Development* and *Organization Development*, and a book published by McGraw-Hill, *Containing the Health Care Cost Spiral*.

She earned her undergraduate degree and master's in education from Santa Clara University and another master's and PhD from the University of California, Santa Barbara. She has attended summer institutes at both Columbia Teachers College and Harvard and is a member of the Association of California School Administrators and the American Association of School Administrators. Currently she resides in San Francisco, California, close to family and friends.

 **William Levinson, EdD,** recently retired after serving twelve years as the superintendent of the Tamalpais Union High School District, located in Marin County, California. He previously served eleven years as superintendent in three other California districts: Reed Union, Sonoma Valley, and Lafayette. His earlier career included elementary teaching and principal positions in New York, New Jersey, and California. He served as a Vista Volunteer in Florida, where he founded an after-school language development program for migrant laborer children using college students as tutors. Throughout his long career, he has presented workshops that assist teachers and administrators to further their careers.

Since retiring, Levinson works with a national search firm and has conducted numerous superintendent searches. He provides coaching support to principals, aspiring and new superintendents, and nonprofit executive directors. He is codeveloping a curriculum to train aspiring and new superintendents, and he serves on a number of community advisory boards.

He received his undergraduate degree and master's in special education from the University of Michigan and a master's degree in school administration and a doctorate from Teachers College, Columbia University. He is a member of the American Association of School Administrators and the Association of California School Administrators. He resides with his wife in Marin County, California.

Both authors may be reached at achievingsuccess1@yahoo.com.

Becoming a Superintendent

Success in seeking a superintendent position requires both personal commitment and professional preparation. More important, it requires a dedication to improving education and helping all students achieve at their highest level.

Most superintendents begin as teachers. Following success in the classroom, they obtain an administrative credential and move to a principal or district office position. Over time, based on their knowledge, skills, and interest, they are promoted to director or assistant superintendent. Often they start studying for a doctorate in educational administration. Some even enroll in superintendent preparation programs offered by state and national superintendent organizations. Others talk with colleagues and mentors about the possibility of becoming a superintendent.

At some point, they determine that the next step in their career is to seek a superintendent position. If you make that determination, you now need to take action to achieve your goal. Begin by asking yourself some questions.

Questions to Ask Yourself

- Is there an ideal career track for becoming a superintendent?
- Should I attempt to find a position even if I have never worked in a district office position?
- How big a district is too big for my first superintendent position?
- How many years should I serve as an assistant superintendent before seeking a superintendent position?
- How will I know I am ready to be a superintendent?

The truth is, there is no perfect test to determine when you are ready to become a superintendent. Much of it depends on your skills, interests, and passions. Some people determine they want to become a superintendent and find a position within a year. Others take two to three years of concentrated effort to secure their first superintendent position.

GETTING READY

Before moving forward on this journey, spend time reflecting on your decision. Be certain that becoming a superintendent is really what you want to do with your career and life. Not every successful administrator wants, or even should, be a superintendent. You may contribute more to education by staying in your current position, and it may be more enjoyable for you. Ask yourself these questions.

✓ Am I committed to improving education for all students?

✓ Do I have a clear vision of educational excellence with a broad background in teaching and learning?

✓ Do I want to be an instructional leader?

✓ Do I have expertise in school finance, budget, school construction, and state and national governance issues?

✓ Do I have good speaking and writing skills?

✓ Can I live with criticism and ambiguity and succeed without external affirmation?

✓ Am I intellectually curious?

✓ Can I work on several issues at the same time?

✓ Am I comfortable with hard work and isolation?

✓ Can I make difficult decisions and take responsibility? Do I make these decisions based on a consistent set of moral and ethical values?

✓ Do I have sufficient confidence in my skills and abilities to take on the huge responsibilities of the superintendent position?

✓ Do I have a history of successful collaborative leadership?

✓ Do I work well with people?

✓ Am I successful and respected in my current position?

✓ Are others, including my superintendent and search consultants, urging me to become a superintendent?

✓ Do I have the support of my family or support group?

If the answer to most of these questions is a resounding yes, it makes sense to proceed on your journey. If the answers are no, maybe, or not sure, hold off on moving forward and reconsider. School boards look for confident, talented, dedicated, and highly accomplished candidates. You are unlikely to obtain a superintendent position if you do not possess those qualities.

Anyone with little or no administrative experience should think twice before deciding to apply for a superintendent position. Rarely do these applicants get selected for interviews. In addition, those who have a career marked with jumping from district to district and position to position will have a difficult time being selected for an interview. This is not a position you should seek simply because you are unhappy in your current role. Rather it is a position to seek if you wish to use your talents and skills to make a difference for students.

Once you decide to become a superintendent, there are important practical steps to take that will lead to your success. A number of these steps can, and ideally should, begin at least two years prior to submitting your first application.

During this time, work with a mentor or an experienced administrator with whom you have a confidential relationship, and who will be honest with you concerning your aspirations. These individuals may be former professors, your current superintendent, or colleagues. Listen to their advice.

1. Superintendent's Role and Responsibilities

The roles and responsibilities of a superintendent include the following.

✓ Provide instructional leadership.

✓ Promote student learning.

✓ Recommend policy to the board.

✓ Implement board policy.

✓ Hire, supervise, support, and evaluate staff.

✓ Plan strategically.

✓ Set and implement goals.

✓ Manage district finances.

✓ Communicate with all constituents.

✓ Work effectively with employees groups.

✓ Understand collective bargaining.

✓ Implement applicable state and federal law.

✓ Set the tone for the district.

Learn more about what these entail through meetings, readings, and observations. Start by meeting with your superintendent to discuss your interest in becoming one. Most superintendents enjoy helping subordinates achieve their professional goals and will offer suggestions and even mentor your development. Observe your superintendent in various settings and situations. Ask yourself what you would or would not have done differently and why.

Attend board meetings in your district on a regular basis. Prior to the meeting, carefully read the board packet. Following the meeting, ask questions of your superintendent or other key staff about what occurred at the meeting.

Meet with key district office administrators, particularly assistant superintendents and directors, and ask them about their positions and responsibilities. Be attentive to how they describe their work in relation to student achievement and the support they need from the superintendent in doing this work.

Join state and national organizations that deepen your understanding of the superintendent's role. For example, the American Association of

School Administrators (AASA) is the national organization of school superintendents and provides assistance to aspirants.

Interview superintendents from other districts and gain their perspective on their roles and responsibilities. Be certain to interview superintendents from districts substantially different from your own experience. Compare and contrast what you learn from each superintendent. Assess the skills needed to lead different types of districts. Learn how the size of the district office and the amount of administrative support impact the role of the superintendent. All districts present challenges. Where can you make the most difference for students?

Observe how effective leaders set a positive tone within a district. Read about districts that have successfully done this. Examine the difference between the art and science of being a superintendent. Effective superintendents know not only what to do but when and how to do it.

Learn how superintendents in small districts, who have little or no district office support, manage their roles and provide effective leadership. Understand the role of superintendents who also serve as principals.

Of all the responsibilities of the superintendent, no matter the size of the district, the most important is that of educational leader. Effective educational leaders understand the link between high expectations for all students, high accountability, and student achievement. As superintendent you are responsible for ensuring that all students learn and improve academically each year.

Speak with superintendents and assistant superintendents in curriculum and instruction to better understand how superintendents can move the district's instructional agenda forward. Ask them how assessment data influences their decisions, how this data is used at the school sites, and what information is the most valuable to them as they make decisions about instruction. Learn how they set the instructional agenda and how they keep abreast of current research. Use this information to determine what additional classes, seminars, or books you need to pursue. This is addressed in more detail in Chapter 4.

Always follow each exploratory meeting, be it with a school board member, superintendent, or chief business official (CBO) with a thank-you note. Preferably this should be handwritten and on your own stationery, not district stationery.

2. Skills and Knowledge You Need

Broaden and deepen your knowledge and understanding of school district administration and leadership. Pay particular attention to the following.

Federal and State Student Achievement Accountability Systems and Expectations. Foremost among these is Race to the Top (RTT) and

No Child Left Behind (NCLB). The federal government considers these critical to the improvement of student performance in schools and districts across the country.

State and Federal Laws Governing Personnel Practices. Work with your district's human resources (HR) administrator to familiarize yourself with your district's personnel policies, practices, and procedures.

State Laws Governing the Collective Bargaining Process. Speak with your HR director and superintendent about the negotiations process for teachers, support staff, and, where applicable, administration. Speak with union leaders about their perspectives.

Use of Technology. Focus on technology in classroom instruction, human resources, instructional support, finances, and communications. Almost every superintendent interview now includes questions about the use of technology for student learning.

Difference Between School District Policy and Administrative Regulations. Review your district's policies. Understand how district policy is developed and implemented. Know which district policies are mandated by state law. Understand the importance of having fewer but more significant policies and learn why too many policies may actually impede the progress of a district. Learn how board policies can affect student learning and narrow the achievement gap.

District Budget and Finances. Ask your district's CBO to assist you with this. Attend fiscal conferences and workshops. Mastering the budget is an essential skill. It should reflect the district's goals and priorities with resources allocated to implement the district goals.

Role and Function of the School Board. The board is the superintendent's employer, establishes the district's mission, and sets long-term and short-term goals. Boards hire, support, monitor, and, when needed, replace the superintendent. They set policy, approve district budgets, and generally make decisions based on the values and expectations of the community they serve. Boards only have authority when they act as a body. This appears to be an easy concept. Learn why it is difficult in practice. Gather information on this topic from your superintendent, local school board members, and state and national associations like the National School Boards Association (NSBA). Due to the importance of this topic, Chapter 6 is devoted entirely to board-superintendent relationships.

3. Academic and Professional Preparation

Based on your investigation of the areas of knowledge mentioned above, assess where you need more development. Determine what workshops, academies, publications, and college or university courses will provide the knowledge you need and begin this work. Boards and search consultants review candidates' attendance at recent workshops. They want candidates who are current with the most recent trends. Boards also examine candidates' recent history of workshop presentations and publications to assess their teaching, writing, and research skills.

Review your recent evaluations to identify areas of growth. Ask your supervisor for feedback on your leadership and interpersonal skills. These skills are essential for the superintendent position. Ask the same of the people you directly supervise. One way to gain information on your leadership style is to conduct a *360 process.* This formal process normally involves a consultant who distributes a survey instrument that focuses on your leadership style to selected staff, parents, administrators, board members, community members, and, if appropriate, students. Anonymity is guaranteed to each respondent. The consultant then meets with you to interpret the results. This information may help you determine whether you have the leadership skills to be a superintendent or if there are areas for improvement.

Enroll in superintendent academies or preparation programs. These may be offered by your state administrative organization or local or national universities. In addition to the knowledge you gain, you will develop a network of colleagues in a similar stage of professional growth. Many of these people will become superintendents and lifelong professional colleagues. Frequently, search consultants contact program directors for the names of outstanding attendees. If funds are not available from your district for these courses, pay for them yourself. Invest in your future.

Earn the appropriate degrees needed for superintendent certification in the states in which you wish to work. Include coursework or internships relevant to school leadership positions. Focus on how to establish and assess effective teaching programs.

Pursue coursework that demonstrates academic rigor and commitment to lifelong learning. Consultants and board members review candidates' coursework and grades.

Do not assume you need a doctorate. While some boards prefer this degree, candidates are judged on the depth of their knowledge and their record of success. Boards want effective instructional leaders to run the district. Obtaining a doctorate may be appropriate if it deepens your leadership skills, confidence, and knowledge. It is important and probably essential if you plan on teaching or conducting research at a college or university during or after working as a superintendent.

Develop a broad network of colleagues who know your work and support you. Your network will grow as your proceed through your academic and work experiences. Maintain these relationships through e-mail, telephone calls, informal meetings, and conversations at conferences, courses, and meetings. Use your network to hone your professional skills and to assist in broadening your knowledge of the roles and responsibilities of the superintendent position.

THE APPLICATION PROCESS

Applying for a superintendent position requires focus and commitment. You may apply a number of times before you are granted an interview. Each application may require different information and have a different process. It is likely that one or two application processes will overlap each other, with interview dates conflicting with your work responsibilities. It is important to balance your job-seeking activities with your other responsibilities and obligations.

Before applying, recognize that it is your responsibility to demonstrate your competence and skills. If you want to be a superintendent, present yourself in an intelligent, deliberate, and purposeful way. In some ways, you are marketing a product, and that product is *you*. Preparing for the application process takes hard work and perseverance. As one superintendent put it, "Finding a job is a job in itself."

Continue performing at the highest level in your current position. Boards seek successful candidates. Success is measured by the impact of your work on student performance and the respect others have for you. Allowing your performance to slide while searching for a superintendent position severely limits your opportunities.

Inform your superintendent and key members of your network, who will be a part of your application effort, when you start looking for a superintendent position. But do not inform everyone you know. Maintaining confidentiality is important to you and to the districts where you are applying. The time to inform your entire universe of friends and acquaintances is when you become a superintendent.

1. Where to Apply

Use your network to learn of possible job openings, and keep your network informed about where you are applying. Seek and listen to their advice. Determine which vacancies are of interest to you. Your earlier work in exploring different types of districts is helpful here. Decide if you are willing to move from the state in which you currently reside. If so, have the appropriate certifications.

Other considerations include your family's wants and needs; your lifestyle; your values; where you can afford to live, especially if you must sell a home before moving; and the effect on your current pension and retirement contributions. It is inappropriate to actively apply for a position and then withdraw because you determine the district is not a good fit for you. Do your homework on the district before applying.

If you are unwilling or unable to move, pull out a map of your area and determine the furthest you are willing to commute to work. List all the districts that fall within your commuting range. Focus your energies on the districts within this radius that fit your skills and knowledge.

Another strategy is to find a district that may be too far for a daily commute but where it is possible to live during the week and return home to family on weekends. Most boards want a superintendent, especially a new superintendent, to be available for community events on weekends. Still, this commuting strategy works for some, especially in small rural districts that have difficulty attracting superintendents.

The more you focus on becoming superintendent in one district, to the exclusion of others, the less likely you are to obtain that position. For example, if you want to be a superintendent in a particular, high-performing affluent district five miles from your home, you may have to wait years until the position is vacant. Even when it does become vacant, another more qualified candidate may receive the appointment.

The more mobile you are, the more opportunities you have. However, if it appears you are applying everywhere and anywhere, you hurt your chances. Boards are looking for candidates who can demonstrate a meaningful reason for their application. Saying "I want to be a superintendent," is not the same as "I want to be the superintendent of your district. I grew up three miles from here, and have always wanted to return to this area to make a difference for the students. "

Some administrators seek a small school district where they can serve as both principal and superintendent. Their goal is to leverage the superintendent title and experience into a better position in a larger district. An upside to serving in a small district is that the superintendent assumes a variety of roles as there is little or no office support. This can deepen and broaden your administrative expertise. It also provides an opportunity for closer contact with students, staff, and parents.

The down side to this approach is that, even after three or four years, it can be difficult to transition to a larger district. Boards may not consider this experience relevant to a larger district. However, if you are more comfortable in smaller districts, this choice is an excellent one as it allows you to hone your craft while holding the title of superintendent.

Open Versus Closed Searches. Assess the impact of submitting an application in an *open* or *closed* search. An open search is one in which members of the community are involved in screening applicants and the interview process. Community members may include administrators, teachers, support staff, parents, students, and others. The role of the community is to advise the board. The board makes the final decisions.

The challenge for a candidate of an open search is loss of confidentiality. The greater the community participation, the greater the likelihood that confidentiality will be lost and your district will learn that you are seeking another position. If you do not want your district to learn of your application, it is better not to apply to districts using an open process.

Some states mandate that the entire interview process be open to the public. These are truly open searches, where all interviews are conducted in open forums, may include questions from the audience, and are frequently televised.

A closed search is one in which the public does not participate directly in the screening or interview process. In these searches the consultants typically meet with members of the community and ask for ideas concerning the strengths of the district and the challenges the new superintendent might face. The consultants also may inquire as to qualities desired in the new superintendent. A report summarizing the information is prepared and recommended to the board for approval. This information guides the selection process and takes the place of direct community participation. The role of search consultants is reviewed in depth later in this chapter.

Closed searches are now the norm in those states where they are permitted by law. Closed searches generate a deeper candidate pool as there is less risk of the loss of confidentiality. Candidates can move a long way through the selection process without risk of exposure in their current district. However, once finalists are selected, it is difficult to maintain absolute confidentiality, due to reference checking and site visitations.

Whether a search is open or closed, inform your superintendent if you are applying for a new position. The superintendent will determine when to tell the board president. In turn, the board president will determine if and when it is necessary to inform the full board. Do this before your first interview but no later than your return for a second interview, unless your contract includes a provision outlining when you must notify the superintendent or board. You may run some risk if you do not receive the position, but you run a larger risk of losing the respect of your current superintendent or board if you do not inform them.

Learn About the Position and the District. Learn as much as you can about the districts to which you might apply.

- ❑ Review district and individual school websites.
- ❑ Review state and national education websites for assessment, budget, and other data.
- ❑ Check local newspaper files online.
- ❑ Contact close friends or colleagues who may be familiar with the district.
- ❑ Visit the district, driving around to see the schools.
- ❑ Review the posted materials about the district and the vacancy.

Unless directed to do so through the application process, do not call the district and request information. If you need information you cannot obtain through other sources, request the information from the person heading the search.

If you know the current superintendent or the search firm recommends that you call this person, it is appropriate to do so. But do not call the current superintendent without first checking with the consultants. Most sitting superintendents are only too willing to answer questions about the district. Use this opportunity to listen and gain better insight into the district, not to try and uncover "skeletons in the closet."

Sometimes the consultants or the board may prefer that candidates not speak with the current superintendent. There may be a number of reasons for this, including the forced resignation or retirement of the current superintendent. In these situations it is best to gather information about the district in other ways.

Compensation Considerations. Explore all aspects of superintendent compensation, including your minimum compensation needs. Compensation includes not only salary but may also include health benefits, life insurance, long-term care insurance, tax-sheltered annuities, applicable state teachers retirement payments, vacation, moving allowances, car allowance, expense allowances, and housing allowances. Boards and communities, along with local unions, look at your *total compensation,* not just the salary. It is important to understand this difference. Also note that each state treats these issues differently.

Before they post a vacancy, boards determine the range of total compensation they are willing to offer a final candidate. They do this by comparing the total compensation of superintendents in similar, nearby districts, considering the district's financial ability to pay and community expectations, and estimating what will attract outstanding candidates. Once the range is determined, boards prefer not to exceed it. Determine if this range meets your needs. Even if the opening lists salary and compensation as "competitive and negotiable," the board has a range in mind. The consultant can tell you what it is.

Many candidates want to know the total compensation of the current superintendent. While superintendent salaries are considered public information in most states, obtaining that information can be challenging and even misleading. For example, the current superintendent's total compensation may be particularly high due to outstanding performance and longevity or it may be low due to the district's finances or the current superintendent's performance. Also, many superintendents and boards, especially those with highly compensated superintendents or superintendents with unusual forms of compensation, are reluctant to share this information and make it difficult to obtain the information.

Competitive compensation can and does differ substantially between states and even regions within a state. Some of this is driven by the higher cost of living in urban areas and affluent suburbs. This means that a generous offer in a high-wealth suburban area may be worth much less in purchasing power than a lower offer in a less affluent part of the same state.

Also become familiar with state law as it pertains to compensation issues. In particular be aware of the types of compensation that will or will not be counted toward your retirement. For example, in some states tax-sheltered annuities provided by a board may apply toward your retirement base. The same applies for car allowances, bonuses, and other forms of nonsalary remuneration. In other states this is not so. Often it is the wording of the compensation in the contract that determines its eligibility toward retirement. You are responsible for knowing this, not the search consultant or the board.

You should address all compensation issues and needs before seeking a particular superintendent position. It is not professional to participate in a search process and then not accept a position at the last minute because the total compensation was less than you needed or more than the board was willing to pay.

2. Superintendents' Contracts

Familiarize yourself with the issues pertaining to a superintendent's contract. This permits you to negotiate your contract from a position of knowledge and confidence. If you are applying in different states, learn the rules that govern superintendent contracts in those states. Many states have adopted legislation limiting certain aspects of these agreements, especially length of contracts, total retirement compensation, and payout provisions for early termination. This information can be found in a number of ways.

❑ Contact your state administrator organization as they may have retired superintendents or other employees who provide contract support.

❑ Confer with an attorney familiar with superintendent contract issues and ask to review an "ideal" superintendent contract. This may cost you an hourly fee but it is worth the cost.

❑ Attend annual superintendent conferences sponsored by state administrator associations as they frequently offer sessions on superintendent contracts that are presented by attorneys.

❑ Obtain and review sample superintendent contracts. In most states superintendent contracts are subject to public disclosure. If you cannot obtain copies from your state administrator association, contact individual school districts and request a copy of its super-intendent's contract. You may need to submit this request in writing and pay a copying and mailing fee. Avoid seeking this information from districts where you intend to apply.

❑ Become familiar with contract provisions. Provisions besides com-pensation include term, annual evaluation process, role and responsibilities including job descriptions, professional develop-ment, travel, and termination. Each contract may have these in different forms. Reading contracts helps you become familiar with the terms and legal language. The importance of this knowledge becomes evident as you negotiate a contract. This is discussed in greater length later in the chapter.

In researching superintendent contracts you may find the term *golden handcuff.* These are items placed in a contract to keep a superintendent in the district for a long period.

Example: One district provided a fully paid life-time annuity to a superintendent who agreed to stay five years and then retire from the district.

These are rarely given to first-time superintendents. In no way do these guarantee a trouble-free tenure. Sometimes superintendents even leave the district in spite of the provision. Further, unions and communi-ties often criticize them.

3. Hiring Process

Learn as much as possible about how boards hire superintendents. All boards have a number of options to use in filling the position. They can appoint an interim for a few months until the search is completed, promote from within, or conduct a broad-based search.

Not all districts retain a search firm or search consultants to manage the search. Many smaller districts manage their own superintendent search process. Others use the county office or the state school boards association. However a district proceeds, there will be a person designated to manage the search process. This person serves as a *consultant* to the board, making certain the search goes well and there is a broad range of qualified candidates from which the board can choose.

Superintendent positions are advertised at the local, state, and national level. Many state administrative organizations include job postings. There are state and regional online posting services. National publications like *Education Week* list job postings, with an online posting as well. Some search firms also list postings on their websites.

Search consultants often contact experienced superintendents in the county or state, perhaps even your superintendent, to request names of successful administrators who are ready and interested in seeking a superintendent position. Search consultants also contact superintendents placed by their firm for recommendations. Based on this information they call to actively recruit candidates. These practices have led to search consultants being called *head hunters.*

When working with a search firm or consultants, remember they work for the district and not for you. Be professional at all times and only ask questions for which answers are not readily available elsewhere. Consultants judge your independence and competence from the moment you meet or call them.

Consultants have long memories. Even if you are not selected for one position the consultants know who you are. They may conduct a future search for which you are qualified. You want to impress them with your professionalism. Search consultants and boards expect candidates to present themselves well. Candidates who treat search consultants as their "best friend" or confidant and need substantial hand-holding are less likely to be selected for an interview.

While some search firms have a "stable" of candidates they work to place, most of them treat each vacancy individually. Most consultants will encourage a familiar candidate to apply for a position if there appears to be a good fit.

Contact search firms active in your area and ask for an exploratory interview. Send an up-to-date copy of your resume. Use this interview to gain insights as to what the search firms look for and how they conduct a search. Following the interview, send the consultant a thank-you note. Occasionally, write or e-mail the consultant about your current job status and professional work. Search consultants assess your readiness and professional competence in all interactions. You want to make a positive impression.

4. Completing the Application

Before you start filling out applications, obtain and review sample applications. Do this through your state administrator association or by requesting applications for specific vacancies from districts and search firms. Avoid asking for applications from districts where you intend to submit an application. While each application varies in the information it wants, there are some materials and information that most require. Use your review of applications to prepare this information. It will make it easier when you start to fill out applications.

A Resume. Review and revise your resume. Structure it to emphasize your leadership qualifications and experiences. Provide a detailed record of your professional history and education. Include professional publications, workshops, and honors. Make sure it is up to date.

References. Identify those who can serve as references. They should be respected in their field or your community, familiar with your experience and leadership qualities, and supportive of your aspirations.

A Letter or Written Statement. While not required for most online applications, this is an important component of many application procedures. The letter is an opportunity to provide information that differs from information normally included in an application and resume. These letters are challenging to write and should be modified to address the expectations of each specific district. Having a prepared statement of why you are interested in becoming a superintendent and why you believe you are qualified will assist you.

You are now prepared to move to the next step in your journey: filling out applications. Obtain the application for each position in which you are interested. Request it from the person, district, or group that is identified in the advertisement for the position. Do not contact the district directly unless specifically directed to do so. Some search firms use an online, Web-based application process. These firms provide technical support to assist you with this.

When you call to obtain an application, or if you are called about applying for a position, there are a number of questions you may wish to ask. These questions should be directed to the search consultant. Following are some questions search consultants are prepared to answer.

Questions to Ask Search Consultants

- What is the board like?
- When do the board members' terms expire?
- Why is the current superintendent leaving?
- Is there an inside candidate?
- Is this a confidential (closed) search process?
- How will the process be conducted and what is the timeline?
- What is the proposed compensation range?
- What are the major challenges facing the district?

Gather Information. Before you start filling out the application, read what is required and gather the information you need. Frequently, districts provide a listing of board-approved qualifications and criteria for the position. Some districts provide a brochure with this information while others post the information on the district or search firm websites. Carefully analyze what the district is seeking in relation to your background, experience, skills, and knowledge. Prepare an outline of what you want to communicate about yourself to the district through the application process. You may use your introductory letter, resume, and application to convey this information.

The application also may require responses to open-ended questions. Examples of such questions follow.

- Why are you interested in serving as superintendent in this district?
- How would you describe your leadership qualities and accomplishments?
- What do you believe are the major issues facing K–12 education today?
- How would you address these issues?

Adjust your open-ended responses based on the specific questions asked in each application.

Select References. Determine which references you wish to use for the application. Contact each one, preferably by phone, and let all of them know you are applying for a position. Ask permission to include their names as references on the application. Let them know they may be contacted by the search consultant.

If the application requires it, ask your references to write a letter of recommendation. Usually the application provides room for an extensive list of references while requiring only three to five written reference letters. Offer to send all your potential references your resume and any other information you believe would assist them or that they request.

It is appropriate to inform your references if you would like them to address some aspect of your background or performance in a letter. For example, if the posting references technology expertise in teaching and learning and you have expertise in this area, ask a reference to address this in the letter.

As most professionals are busy, provide substantial advance notice of what you need. Inform your references of the due date. Where appropriate, provide preaddressed envelopes with the proper postage. As the application deadline approaches, contact your references to ensure their letters are sent in time.

Search consultants should let you know when they start contacting your listed references. This usually occurs prior to the first interview. They also may call as references people you have not listed. This usually occurs between the first and second interview. The consultant should inform you when these reference calls begin.

This deeper reference checking is a routine part of the search process for most reputable firms. The additional references they call may be members of your school board, union leaders or administrators with whom you previously worked, or even community members. This is a reminder of how important it is to build your career on a continuing foundation of hard work, integrity, and strong interpersonal relationships. You never know who will be called by a prospective employer to provide an overview of your competence and integrity.

The Final Steps for Completion and Common Errors. Complete the entire application as requested. This is very important. Many candidates are eliminated from consideration because they fail to follow directions or fail to realize the importance of accuracy and style. The following are major errors to avoid.

1. *Failing to demonstrate that you have met the listed district criteria or qualifications.* It is appropriate to ask a trusted colleague or mentor to review your material to determine whether you have communicated your qualifications in a manner that will interest the board. Take full advantage of the application process to sell yourself.

2. *Stating "see resume" when asked to complete information on an application form.* This conveys either arrogance or laziness on your part. This is the district's application process. Meet their expectations as stated.

3. *Listing your work address, e-mail, phone number, or cell phone number as your primary contacts instead of your private, home information.* It is not appropriate to use district resources for your private purposes. Using district resources risks a breakdown in confidentiality. If you do not have a home e-mail address, obtain one prior to starting the application process. Use this for all application communications.

4. *Submitting a photocopied letter where it is evident you simply inserted the name of the district.* Again, this conveys laziness or arrogance.

5. *Using district letterhead or stationary from your current position.* This is using district resources for your own private purposes.

6. *Providing insufficient or sketchy responses to open-ended questions.* These questions provide you the opportunity to market your achievements, skills, and character. Use the opportunity wisely, as other candidates certainly will do so.

7. *Completing applications at the last minute.* A well-prepared and thought out application requires a substantial commitment of time and effort to complete. Work on your application over a period of several days. This permits a full review of all requirements and questions with ample time for editing and proofreading.

8. *Submitting a poorly prepared letter of application.* Online applications do not usually require a letter of application, but traditional, paper applications do. An application letter is an opportunity to introduce yourself to the board and demonstrate how you and your skills fit the district's needs. The letter must be well-written and interesting to read. Use a conversational but professional tone. Letters may be two or three pages single spaced. You want the board to know your success and experience in the areas of required expertise.

9. *Failing to proofread for grammar, spelling, and punctuation.* While spell check and grammar check may be helpful word-processing tools, you are responsible for all errors. You are an educator and expected to model good writing skills. An application with many errors is not likely to reach the board.

Earlier in her career, a search consultant was a high school English teacher. She uses a red pencil to identify spelling, grammar, and word-use errors. Applications with many red pencil marks rarely reach the board.

10. *Failing to properly address issues or problems from your past that could influence the board's decision to hire you.* In this day of instant communications, there is no such thing as privacy. Prior to submitting your name to the board for consideration, the search consultants will search the Internet for your name to learn as much as possible about you. Board members will Google you as soon as the search consultant recommends your application. If you are hired, your entire school community will do so as well.

    In addition to their informal "sleuthing," boards retain private companies to conduct formal due diligence background checks on the final candidate prior to having that person sign the contract. These reports verify what is on the finalist's application. Every degree, honor, award, job, or membership you list on your resume is verified. This is an appropriate safeguard for the community as far too many candidates are not truthful about their education, certification, and previous positions.

    If there is negative information about you in the public domain or if other problems are likely to become known at some future date, contact the search consultant and seek advice as to the best way to communicate this information to the board. Examples may include a substance abuse problem, a less than honorable discharge from the armed forces, a DUI, a misdemeanor, an outstanding lawsuit, or a dismissal or forced resignation from a previous position. Boards vary in their response to these issues, depending on the severity of the problem, how recently it occurred, how the problem was resolved, and local values, tradition, and culture. An issue that is a "deal breaker" in one district may not be of much concern in another. It is always best to address these concerns as early as possible in the process and demonstrate your honesty and integrity to the search consultant and the board.

11. *Failing to explain obvious gaps in your work history or background.* If your background is idiosyncratic, it is important to communicate why in the application. A prime example of this is a gap in your work history. A search consultant will want to know what happened to you or what you were doing for any unaccounted-for periods. Or, if you were enrolled in a doctoral program but did not complete it, explain why.

12. *Failing to stay in any one position for more than one or two years.* Districts do not want to go through an extensive search process to hire a superintendent only to repeat the process twelve to

eighteen months later. If you have had a number of positions in quick succession due to a spouses or partner's job relocation or working for armed services schools abroad, state as much. Also explain how this will not be an issue in the future.

13. *Failing to meet all deadlines.* Search consultants expect candidates to possess sufficient discipline to meet all expectations of the search process. If there is some unavoidable reason why you cannot meet a deadline, contact the search consultant and make an alternative arrangement. Consultants want to find the best candidates and are willing to work with candidates to meet their needs in unexpected or unavoidable situations.

All materials you submit with an application and the manner in which you submit them should paint a clear picture of you as a professional and a person. To ensure your application does this, have a trusted colleague review your application materials. Taking the time to do it right pays off in the long run.

Some search firms include a preliminary screening interview with one or two consultants as part of the application process. As many as twelve top candidates may be invited to a thirty-minute conversation. While these interviews may appear informal they are an integral component of the search process. These interviews provide an opportunity to demonstrate your interest and knowledge of the district as well as your ability to ask good questions and listen. These interviews give the search consultants an opportunity to assess your personality and style against your written application materials before deciding which candidates should precede to the next level.

INTERVIEWS

The next step in becoming a superintendent is your first interview. While many capable and experienced people may apply for a superintendent position, not everyone will be asked to interview. The application and screening process is designed to *screen out*, not *screen in*, candidates. Your job as a candidate is to have the background, skills, and application materials that will screen you *in*. The search consultant's job is to review the applications, letters of introduction, resumes, and reference letters and personally contact some references. The consultant then identifies the candidates most qualified and most likely to match the district's and the board's needs and expectations. These fortunate individuals are then invited to interview.

1. Preparation

As with any step in the application process, planning is essential for success. Know what to expect and prepare in advance. When you are informed that you have been selected for an interview, learn as much as you can about the process from the search consultant.

Questions to Ask About the Interview Process

- What are the steps in the interview process?
- What is the membership of the committees?
- What are the dates for the next steps in the process? If you cannot meet any of these dates, inform the search consultant immediately.
- Where will the interviews take place?
- How long are the interviews?
- How many candidates will be interviewed?

Most search processes include two or more interviews. In a closed search, the candidates meet only with the consultants and the board. In an open search, there also will be community interviews.

Appearance. Search consultants, committee members, and school board members pay close attention to a candidate's appearance. First impressions are powerful indicators of success. Be appropriately dressed for all interview events, even those that may be deemed business casual. Boards and committee members expect you to look professional.

Planning is essential. Do not leave matters of appearance to the last minute. This is not the time to experiment with a new hairstyle or new makeup. Dress as you would for a board meeting. Appearing at your interview with no tie, a baggy out-of-style ill-fitting suit, a gauzy skirt, tennis shoes, a plunging neckline, a tie with stains, or a wrinkled blouse is not the way to make a good impression.

As an experienced professional, prepare your interview wardrobe well in advance of submitting your first application. You need several outfits that look good on you and are appropriate for interviews. If you are unsure how to dress, most major department stores have personal shoppers who will assist you with this at no cost. Err on the side of conservative dress. It is better to be more formally dressed than less formally dressed.

Example

A candidate from the deep South showed up to an interview in the Pacific Northwest in a white suit in the middle of January. When it came time to discuss the candidates, all the board remembered of this candidate was his "ice cream" suit. Needless to say he did not receive the position. Another candidate wore short, bright-colored argyle socks to his interview—everyone remembered him as the "guy with the funny socks."

Practicing. Interviewing is a skill. It can improve with practice. Practicing is particularly important if you have been in your current position for a long time and your last interview is a distant memory. While every committee assumes that a candidate will be a little nervous, first impressions are extremely important. Successful candidates master their nervousness and interview anxieties long before the first interview takes place.

One way to practice for the interview is to stand in front of a mirror and ask yourself challenging questions. Another is to ask a trusted colleague to conduct a mock interview with you. Use a superintendent's job description as the basis for the questions. Turn each duty into a question and respond to it. The purpose of these practices sessions is not to develop pat answers. Rather it is to practice responding to questions in a thoughtful and professional manner. As you practice, do not be afraid to use a little humor.

We all sound brilliant when talking to ourselves, but speaking out loud is more of a challenge. The more you prepare by practicing out loud, the stronger your responses at the actual interviews.

The first interview with the board or selection committee is usually formal, with the same questions asked of each candidate. These questions are based on information the search consultants received from the board and the community during the information-gathering process. The questions will reflect the issues and characteristics identified in the brochure or position posting. Be prepared to address the following.

- Your Professional Background
- Why You Are Interested in Becoming Superintendent
- Your Strengths and Weaknesses
- How You Use Your Strengths and Address Your Weaknesses
- Your Knowledge of the District and Its Issues

Other important questions will focus on teaching and learning; curriculum and program development; instructional practice, assessment strategies, and accountability; professional development; and use of technology or strategies for closing the achievement gap. Other areas of focus may include finance, facilities, communications, community relationships, and collective bargaining.

In some searches the consultants sit in on every interview. In others, the consultants prepare the board or committees for the interviews, assist in developing questions, and debrief with them after the interviews are over. This approach is designed to increase the responsibility of the board for independent decision making and to not distract either the candidates or the board members. In most states, candidate interviews are conducted in confidential sessions with the public excluded.

2. First Interview

All of your preparation up to this point will serve you in good stead as you interview. Your success in your current position, the time you spent learning about the position, the additional courses and workshops, the network of leaders who assisted you, the research you did on the district, the application you submitted, and the practice interviews now come into play.

Prepare psychologically for the interview process. Think of an interview as an opportunity to demonstrate one of the most important skills a superintendent needs, the ability to respond to questions and provide information in a pressured situation. An interview is no different than a board meeting at which an animated public "wants answers." Present yourself as the confident, grounded, and mature professional you are.

Frequently, superintendent interviews are scheduled in locations in the community that ensure candidate confidentiality. This means that one candidate can leave the building while the next candidate enters from another direction. Pay close attention to the instructions given by the district. Scout the interview location prior to the interview to make certain you know exactly where you are going. Getting lost on the way to your interview and arriving late is not a successful interview strategy.

Stay calm as you approach the interview. Take a deep breath, leave your car, and head on in to the interview. Usually someone will meet you as you enter. It may be the consultant or the superintendent's assistant. This person will take you to a holding area and offer to get you water or coffee. Be warm and gracious. At the end of all the interviews, board members may ask whomever greeted the candidates for an opinion of them.

The board chair or consultant will come out to meet you when it is time to start the interview. Before the start of the interview, the chair will let you know the number of questions that will be asked and how much time you have for the interview. First interviews can range from ninety minutes to two hours with as many as fifteen questions asked.

After entering the interview room, approach each person, look at them directly, and introduce yourself with a firm handshake and a warm smile. If you have very sweaty hands, dry them off before entering the room. If there are too many people in the room for a personal introduction, provide a warm hello and look around the room to engage as many people as possible. Take your seat and make yourself comfortable. Normally, water is provided, as well as a pen and paper.

Be gracious and considerate throughout the interview. When leaving the interview, even if you believe you did poorly or discovered you were no longer interested in the position, thank everyone for the time spent with you. If appropriate, again shake hands. It is good manners and you never know when you may see these people again.

Maintain a confident and professional demeanor during the interview. You want the board or committee members to see you as thoughtful, attentive, and responsive.

Helpful Interview Dos and Don'ts

- Do look people in the eye when addressing questions. Do move your head around to include everyone in the room. Don't address every answer to the board president or search consultant, if the consultant is in the room.
- Do ask the person asking the question to repeat the full question or part of the question if you did not hear or understand it. Don't ask that every question be repeated.
- Do listen carefully to the question and answer it completely. Don't be long-winded or lecture the committee.
- Don't respond to a question you feel is legally impermissible. For example, if asked, "Are you planning on having a family?" respond by saying, "I consider all my students my family."
- Do be mindful of your time. Do spend less time on the next question if you spent too long answering the previous question.
- Don't look at your watch. Do look at a wall clock if easily visible from your seat. Or take your watch off at the start of the interview and place it where you can occasionally glance at the time.
- Do take brief notes if a question has a number of parts. Don't write down the entire question. It indicates you have difficulty remembering questions and thinking on your feet, skills superintendents need.
- If any of the interviews involve a meal, do use your best table manners. Don't drink alcohol even if others do, and don't offer to pick up the check.

Example

A candidate was invited to a dinner with the board prior to his second interview. Nervous, he drank four large glasses of wine, greatly impressing the board. He was not offered the position.

After the interviews are over, the board or the committee will meet with the search advisor for a debriefing process. Consultants vary as to how they go about debriefing the committee. However, the outcome is the same, to determine the finalists who will move on to the second interview. Usually there are two or three finalists.

Once the decision is made, the consultant contacts the successful candidates and provides information about the next steps in the interview process. The consultants continue checking references between the first and second interviews, focusing in on areas of concern identified during the debriefing process.

After the first interview, take time to reflect on what you have learned about this position. In some instances candidates realize they are not ready or no longer interested in the position. If you decide to withdraw from the search, inform the consultant as soon as possible. Do not wait until the consultant contacts you. It is best to withdraw after the first interview rather than to wait until after the second as you are taking up the spot of another potential candidate. If you do withdraw, provide a clear and understandable explanation, as you want the board and the consultant to respect you and your decision. Send the board a note thanking them for the opportunity to interview.

The Concept of "Fit." If you are invited to the final interview, congratulate yourself on a job well-done. Reaching the "finals" means that you have credible credentials, interview well, and are considered exceptional by the board. It means that in this board's opinion you have the background, skills, and talent to serve as its superintendent. All that stands in the way of reaching your goal is something called *fit.*

Fit is the elusive chemistry between the board and the final candidate. Fit is the board's determination that you are the person, out of the two or three equally competent and accomplished final candidates, who will best meet the district's needs over the next five or more years. It is very difficult for finalists or even search consultants to fully know or anticipate what a board will decide in the final debriefing. Simply be prepared and be yourself.

Fit works both ways. At the end of the final interview you may decide you do not fit with this board or the needs of this district. Trust your instincts. Do not allow your desire be a superintendent to override your common sense. If the fit is right you will feel comfortable and excited about working with this board.

3. Second Interview

Prepare for the second or final interview by carefully assessing what happened at the first interview. Reflect on the questions asked and the suitability of your responses. Make a list of points you wished you had made and what you want to do better. You now have a better understanding of the issues facing the district. If you believe you failed to adequately respond to some questions in the first interview, bolster your knowledge in these areas before the second. As with all aspects of the search process, preparation is essential.

Second interviews are usually conducted with the board in closed session. They are far less formal, with questions developed with the assistance of the search consultant. Questions may differ for each candidate. They probe areas where your first interview responses were not clear or sufficient. They also cover areas of particular interest to the board. Pay close attention to nuances, as they provide insight into the board's real priorities.

Example

In one district, one of the main criteria listed in the vacancy brochure was improving student achievement. However, all finalists were asked a set of questions about the building of a high school gymnasium. These questions stemmed from the recent passing of a bond. What none of the finalists, nor the search consultant, knew was that three of the five board members wanted a high school gym built as quickly as possible. The person selected was the candidate with the most knowledge about building them. The board rejected the finalist with a proven track record in improving minority student achievement and bond management.

Some second interview processes will include a tour of the district with two board members; others include a dinner with the board. Your spouse or partner may or may not be invited on the tour or to the dinner. These events require a set of skills different from an interview. You must be professional at all times, yet warm, approachable, and engaging company.

Some districts also schedule a final meeting with the board president and a second board member the day after the final interview. This is a time to discuss contract and compensation needs or other issues that may have arisen during the previous interviews. In other districts, this final step is done with the whole board. In these situations the search consultant will brief you on the board's expectations.

4. After the Final Interview

The next step is for the search consultant to meet with the board to debrief the interviews and determine the final, preferred candidate. When the board is in agreement, the board chair or the consultant will contact the preferred candidate and offer the position. The consultant may then contact the unsuccessful candidates or wait until it is clear that the district does have a new superintendent. While this may seem cold and unfriendly, there are good reasons for this approach.

Sometimes during a search, a board does not appreciate a candidate until it comes to the very end of the process. It then realizes the best candidate was eliminated earlier. Or, a preferred candidate turns down the position once it is offered and the board wants to look again at all the candidates. As a result you may be called back for another interview. Boards need to keep all options open. So be patient.

If you are applying for more than one position and the final interviews are overlapping, inform the search consultants. Ask when the board is likely to make a decision. Do not use this as an opportunity to play one district against another. You might get two job offers or you may get none. Throughout, you want to be viewed as a professional who respects the process in each district. Unprofessional behavior may come back to haunt you.

It is to your advantage to know why the board wants to hire you. It may not be for the reasons you think. For example, a powerful board accustomed to micromanaging may hire an inexperienced superintendent so it can continue to micromanage. Other times a board will hire a strong superintendent to "clean up" the district or move it forward. Boards want the superintendent they choose to be successful, as it is a reflection on their judgment. The clearer you are on why you were selected the better you will be at working with the board.

If you are offered the position but have concerns about the district or the board, you should request an additional meeting with the board. The board may request the same if they have similar concerns about you. These additional meetings are important as neither party wants to make an error in judgment.

If you are not selected to move forward in the process, be gracious and express your appreciation for the opportunity to interview. While you may not have been successful in this district, you want the consultant and the board to think highly of you so you will be considered for future and perhaps more suitable openings. Send the board and the search consultant a note of appreciation. Write *personal and confidential* on the envelope so the note does not become public information. Take time to reflect back on your experience and identify what you did well and what you may do differently the next time around.

Call the search consultant and ask for feedback. Some search consultants will, if asked, provide nonconfidential information about your reference check and interviews. Others just offer advice about general areas of concern. Use this information to guide your preparation for future applications and interviews. This is also good information for your professional development. Send the consultant a thank-you note.

SITE VISITS

If you are the selected candidate, the final step in the selection process may be a visit to your district by the board. Depending on circumstances, one or all the board members may participate. Only agree to a site visit if the board formally offers you the position. This offer may be verbal over the phone or may involve a brief written agreement. Usually the offer is contingent on working out the final contract language and compensation details, a successful site visit, and a positive due diligence report.

Never agree to a site visit if the board wants to visit the district of a second candidate before making a final decision. This undermines your current position if the board offers the job to the other candidate. If you are asked to do this, politely decline. The board can visit the district of the other candidate. If it is not satisfied, it then can make you a formal offer and schedule a site visit.

Site visits place demands on you and your current district's board, staff, parents, and community members. A site visit means the loss of any confidentiality you may have maintained. Everyone in your current district will hear that you are a finalist for another position. Your superintendent and board will be anxious. They realize they may soon have to address your departure and fill your position.

Some boards do not conduct site visits. They are concerned they may not get an accurate picture in one visit and so rely on extensive reference checking and due diligence. They also may be concerned about cost.

Site visits provide an opportunity for board members to validate their decision and to get to know further their new superintendent. The board can demonstrate to its community that it has done full due diligence. This may be particularly important in closed searches where the public has limited opportunities to participate or questioned the use of an outside consulting firm.

The particulars of the site visit will depend on what board members wish to see and with whom they wish to meet. Work with your new board chair and put together a tentative schedule for this visit. Normally, your new board will want to meet with your superintendent, board members, district and site-level administrators, union leadership, parent and community leaders, and even students.

Arrange for appropriate meeting rooms and tours of your district. Provide a printed itinerary for each member of the visiting team. Have refreshments available. Work to make the visit run smoothly and showcase your ability to organize and meet expressed needs of your new board. If appropriate, start or end the day with the board meeting your spouse or partner. While the visiting board is responsible for its travel and housing expenses, you are personally responsible for any expenditures incurred by your current district for this site visit.

On rare occasions a board will complete the site visit and change its mind about a candidate. This is likely to occur when consultants have not conducted a thorough reference check beyond the three or four names offered by the candidate. Or, board members may become aware of a huge discrepancy between the size, culture, values, and standards of the candidate's current district and their own. They then have doubts that the candidate can make the transition successfully. Should this occur, maintain a professional stance. Thank the board for its interest and focus your energies on your current position and continue your job search. You will impress not only your current employer but also the search firm.

THE FINAL STEP: YOUR CONTRACT

After the board has made you a formal offer of employment, you will begin the last and oftentimes most challenging aspect of the selection process: finalizing your first contract and agreeing on a compensation package. How you negotiate your contract is your first leadership act with your new board. Throughout this process maintain a positive, friendly, and professional demeanor.

Contracts are one of the greatest sources of disagreement between superintendents and boards. Even seasoned superintendents sometimes find themselves at odds with their board over differing interpretations of their contract language. Your contract is a binding agreement in which the actual words prevail, not what you thought or wanted the words to mean. This is why it is critical for you to learn as much as possible about superintendent contracts, including state and local laws governing contracts, before you start applying for positions. It is very difficult to gain that expertise between the time your new board offers you the position and the signing of the contract.

Your first contract with a new district serves as a foundation for future contracts in that district and future ones in which you may be superintendent. Many superintendents believe their first contract with a district is their best with that district. They want a contract in place that is fair to them and the district and that does not need to be revisited annually for major changes. This allows them to concentrate on the work of the district and reduces public and staff scrutiny of the contract.

You want the contract to meet your needs but you need to be realistic. The board just selected you to be its superintendent. It is likely to make some concessions, just as you should. Few first-time superintendents, or any superintendents, get all they want in their contracts. Avoid holding out for a specific provision or benefit if the board is not interested or willing to provide it unless it is a deal breaker. This should rarely happen as you should have discussed issues like this with the search consultant prior to accepting the position.

Problems between superintendents and boards are more likely to occur when the contract is signed without a real understanding and respect for the compensation package or contract provisions. Or, if either party feels slighted by the other. If you are familiar with contract language, compensation issues, and the recent financial history of your new district, you are more likely to avoid the more common pitfalls of contract negotiations. Never sign a contract without advice or counsel. Mistakes made in negotiating your first contract can be substantial and, in many cases, irreversible.

Do not make the common mistake of signing the contract put in front of you by the district's legal counsel, thinking you will simply change it next year. Circumstances may change during the year. New members may come onto the board, the district may face an unforeseen financial crisis, or union negotiations may prove difficult, all issues that may limit the board's ability or even desire to strengthen your contract. This is why the first contract is so important.

Also, do not make the mistake of feeling that negotiating a contract with your new board is unseemly or unprofessional. First-time superintendents rarely have contract negotiations experience and feel awkward asking for things. If you feel this way, use a consultant or attorney to represent your interests. Even if you are comfortable negotiating your contract, it is well worth the cost to have an attorney review it.

Attorneys understand complex language and know that no provisions are "harmless" in any contract. Every provision is important and *of consequence* to you. Competent education attorneys also know what compensation will and will not apply to your retirement or be taxable. State administrators' associations have lists of attorneys qualified to do superintendents' contracts. Do not ask the search consultant to assist you with your contract. The consultant works for the board, not for you.

1. Contract Provisions

Your new board will ask its attorney to prepare a draft of a contract for you to review. Occasionally the search consultant may assist in this process. Usually the first version of the contract is written to protect and promote the interests of the district. It will not be written to protect you. Once you receive the district's contract, carefully review it with a personal consultant or attorney familiar with your state's contract laws. Your proposed contract will have many standard provisions, including some particular to your district.

Common Contract Provisions

- Superintendent's Role and Responsibilities
- Annual Evaluation Process
- Term
- Vacation Days
- Sick Days
- Salary
- Benefits
- Expense Reimbursement
- Professional Development
- Contract Renewal Procedures
- Termination

These are all important and should be considered carefully. For example, you will need to determine whether you want a traditional work-year calendar or a positive work-year calendar. Each provides the same number of workdays, but in the traditional model you start with more workdays and subtract vacation and holidays from them. In the positive work year model, you simply work a specified number of days with all others viewed as nonworkdays. There are no vacation days or holidays; those come out of your nonworkdays. There are pros and cons to each model and both have retirement and compensation implications. You need to be aware of these as you work with your board, as well as to be aware of the traditions that exist in the district.

Particular provisions you may wish to focus on as a new superintendent are the delineation of your roles and responsibilities, and those of the board, along with your annual performance evaluation. The evaluation process should be based on your job description, the district's mission, and the setting of annual performance goals. If the district has a strategic plan, the implementation of that plan should be included in your goals.

If your district has no superintendent job description or evaluation process, insist that a provision be included in your contract. This provision would state that within sixty to ninety days of your signing the contract, you and the board would mutually agree on a job description and annual evaluation process. Having a clear set of performance expectations and a clearly defined evaluation process provides you a much higher level of support and will guard against arbitrary termination.

Another common provision may be the requirement to schedule yearly physicals, with a follow-up written statement from the doctor that you are healthy enough to perform your duties. Work closely with your counsel or advisor before including such a provision in your contract. These can involve complicated legal issues, particularly if you have a chronic health issue.

Another key provision in the contract is the delineation of your total compensation. As discussed earlier, total compensation is not the same as your salary. Salary refers to how much you will be paid annually for your services. Total compensation includes salary and all other forms of remuneration that are discretionary. For example, the board does not have to pay you a yearly tax-sheltered annuity or provide you a life insurance policy, but it may agree to do so as part of your total compensation package.

If possible, have a formula for yearly salary increases built into your contract. This will relieve you of the burden of discussing your compensation every year following your evaluation. Know what you would like to have as an increase each year, as well as what you are willing to accept. As you discuss this, be sensitive to what the district can afford and what other staff receive. It may be necessary or prudent in difficult financial times to reject any pay increase, even if it was built into your contract.

Negotiating your first compensation package is always a challenge. You want the best possible package for yourself, one that will include a significant increase in compensation from your current position. You believe you deserve a raise and have worked hard to obtain your new position. You want to be paid as much as superintendents in comparable districts. You want your new board to view you as decisive and thoughtful, not aggressive or stubborn.

In turn, the board wants to provide what you want, need, and deserve. However, it wants to stay within its predetermined compensation parameters so it can justify your contract with staff and the community. Boards want you to view them as receptive, wise, and determined, not obstinate or resistant. In the end, a satisfactory compromise is almost always reached, balancing the needs of the new superintendent and the needs of the board and the community.

Contracts also include the length of service and provisions for adding to this. Typically initial contracts are for three or four years. Some have *evergreen* provisions that permit the contract to roll over an additional year each year based on performance. Some states do not allow for any extensions beyond the initial length of time. New contracts are needed to add additional years. Know your state law and the wording that is acceptable for extending contracts.

Once all provisions have been reviewed, return the contract with your recommended changes. It is important to take whatever time is needed to reach agreement on contract terms and language. Do not let the board rush you because of self-imposed district deadlines. You may need to go back and forth several times with the district until a mutual agreement is reached.

2. Contract Addenda

Addenda are side agreements that address specific issues related to your becoming superintendent in the district. For example, there should be an addendum for your transition period specifying the number of days you will work between signing the contract and officially starting as superintendent. It outlines the work to be done, expected outcomes, and how you are to be compensated. The transition itself is covered in detail in Chapter 2.

Other examples of the need for addenda include moving costs, temporary housing costs, and home loans. Of these, perhaps housing allowances and home loans are the most common and controversial. If you cannot afford to move to your new district or within a reasonable commute, you may seek housing support during your contract negotiations with the board. This support may include a housing stipend above and beyond your salary or a long-term loan to help with your down payment. Boards in high cost of living areas use these incentives to hire outstanding superintendents. Less affluent communities may perceive this support as unusual or inappropriate.

Financial support for housing can become a political issue for you or the board, especially as a first-year superintendent. Unions often view this as "padding" the new superintendent's salary. You will hear from unions that, "Our members are paid far less than you and receive no assistance with their housing."

A housing allowance is considered compensation by the IRS. It is taxable but may not count toward the base for your retirement pension. For this reason many superintendents prefer to have the allowance rolled into their compensation. It is best to do this when first hired. When granted later it appears as though you are receiving a huge pay increase. This can have political consequences for you and your board.

Long-term loans to help finance your mortgage have downsides. They too are perceived as padding. The community may not appreciate the board taking funds from reserves for this purpose, especially in difficult financial times. An advantage to the district is that your home serves as collateral for the loan. Districts structure these loans so they have little risk of a loss of capital. These loans are taxable. You need to work with your tax accountant to determine exact liability. They do not count toward retirement.

Loan agreements are complicated. The loan agreement may be mentioned in your contract but due to its complexity a separate addendum, spelling out the provisions of the home loan, is necessary. Before entering into a loan agreement, consult with an attorney who has substantial experience in these matters. The agreement should address all eventualities. For example, what happens if your home depreciates during your tenure or you decide to leave the district before the end of your employment contract?

Example

One superintendent in an affluent district received a substantial home loan from the district. Within eighteen months the local housing market dropped by 10 percent. This superintendent then owed more to the district than the home was worth.

The language in these addenda is as important as your contract language. They actually are part of your contract. It is recommended you have counsel assist you with these.

3. Ratification

Ratification of your contract takes place in either closed or open session, depending on the laws in your state. In most states the superintendent's contract is a public document. Soon the provisions of your contract will be described in detail in the local newspaper or online editions of the news.

Often your total compensation is higher than the previous superintendent's. Do not be surprised if some staff or community members criticize what you are receiving. This is common. It is up to the board to respond in an open and positive manner to inquiries about your compensation.

This public review and scrutiny is one reason why it is important to negotiate a sound, well-thought-out contract when you are first hired and to include provisions for evaluation and future compensation increases. You want to avoid having your contract become an annual conversation in the community. You also want to avoid having a unique contract provision or unreasonably high compensation become the focus of the public's view of you and your work.

Example

One superintendent sends his contract to the union leaders and local media every time it is revised by the board. He does this to guarantee transparency. It has also earned him good will.

Boards carefully orchestrate the final public ratification of the superintendent's contract and the introduction of the new superintendent to the public. The board sends out announcements to the press, staff, and the public providing the date, time, and location of the special board meeting to announce the hiring of the new district superintendent. Everyone, including the press, is invited. The board will ask you for information to prepare a detailed press release.

The night of the announcement, most boards meet in closed session for a final review of your contract. Some boards also schedule a brief meeting for you to meet with key district office administrators while in the closed session.

Afterward, the board moves to public session to approve your contract. It then formally introduces you to the community. In most districts the vote will be unanimous. Even with a unanimous vote, some board members may have preferred another candidate. Frequently boards provide a unanimous vote to demonstrate solidarity for the community. Substantial time may pass before you become aware of the board's differences in perception and preferences. This issue is covered in Chapter 6.

At the board meeting you will be called on to make a few, brief comments. Express appreciation for your selection and how much you are looking forward to working in the district. These comments should be presented without notes or script. If appropriate, have your spouse and family or partner present to be introduced. An informal reception usually follows, providing the opportunity for you to meet and greet the people in the audience.

In the days immediately following your contract ratification, some boards want you to meet with selected staff, parents, community members, or school groups. At these so-called meet-and-greets, be brief, continually express your delight in being selected, as well as your desire to get to know the community. Above all, listen. Also be prepared to speak with the press. Avoid discussing or voicing your opinion on controversial issues. Be mindful you are not yet the superintendent.

Officially you become the superintendent on the start date agreed upon in your contract. You now enter your transition period, which is discussed in depth in the following chapter. Enjoy this special time. You have been successful in obtaining a position as superintendent of schools. This is a new opportunity to work with a board, staff, and community to continually improve the quality of education for the young people in your district.

SUMMARY

This chapter focused on how to become a school superintendent. Following are the major points covered. They are posed in terms of work you need to complete in order to be a successful candidate.

- Reflect on why you want to become a superintendent. Make sure this is the job where your interests, knowledge, and talents can best be put to use.
- Learn about the roles and responsibilities of the superintendent. Take time to talk with superintendents and board members in different types of districts.
- Use a variety of methods to develop the skills and knowledge you need to be a superintendent.
- Develop a professional network of colleagues who can assist you in learning more about being a superintendent, as well as in finding suitable openings.
- Maintain the highest level of performance in your current position.
- Learn how to effectively complete applications so you can be selected as a finalist.
- Learn the role of search consultants.
- Know what must be included in each application.
- Prepare for interviews.
- Understand the importance of the site visit to the board.
- Prepare yourself to be thoroughly screened.
- Understand the process for finalizing a contract.
- Know what is involved in the contract ratification process.

The above points and the material in the chapter provide a framework and a process for you to use in your search to become a superintendent. Following this process requires discipline, knowledge, time, and commitment. As mentioned earlier, "Finding a job is a job." We cannot emphasize enough: only do this if it is the right career path for you and the way for you to make the most positive difference for students.

Transitioning to Your New District

The time between when you were hired and your official starting date is your transition period. Transition times vary depending on when you were hired. Ideally you have one or two months for the transition. Make effective use of whatever time is available. Plan your transition as carefully as you planned for your application and interviews.

During this transition period, learn about the challenges in your new district and meet more staff. Do not be surprised if the issues are different than those described by the board and community during the search process. The differences are in the urgency and nuances surrounding them. Learning more about the strengths and needs of the district prior to your first day on the job is helpful. It allows time to map out your work for the coming year.

As discussed in Chapter 1, once people learn you are the new superintendent, they use Google and other search engines to learn more about you. For example, new union leaders contact your current union leaders to find out how you work with unions and staff. Your local paper will be read online to determine how it is treating your departure. People want to know if the stories or editorials are written from a perspective of "what a great loss" or "it was time to move on."

Recognize that during this transition you are judged by everything you do and everything you fail to do, whom you choose to meet and whom you do not. Judgments regarding your leadership style and "fit" for the district are made. Do not be surprised if everyone is not equally pleased over your appointment. If you were an outside candidate, there will be those who preferred an inside candidate; the contrary also is true. This is the reality of leadership positions.

The information that follows guides your transition. It is based on the ideal of a spring hire with one to two months transition time. Make adjustments depending on the amount of time you have before your official start. If you were promoted from within, use this time to define your identity apart from your current role. The latter half of the chapter covers personal issues that you may need to address as you assume this new role. The job of superintendent affects your personal life differently from the jobs you previously held.

MANAGING YOUR TRANSITION

During contract negotiations you discussed your needs and expectations for the transition. Board members also shared their expectations. Based on this you developed a transition schedule including the number of days you will spend in the district prior to the start of your contract. These five to ten days are compensated by your new district at a per diem rate agreed upon in your contract addenda. Deduct these days from your vacation or workdays in your current district.

Frequently, school boards assume the new and current superintendent need one or two weeks of overlapping workdays to complete the transition. This is rarely the case. At best you need only five to ten hours of focused meeting time with the current superintendent to review the short- and long-term issues facing the district. The rest of your time is better spent as outlined below. Spending too much time with the current superintendent also can signal insecurity or lack of independence.

Share with the board chair and, if appropriate, the current superintendent your intended activities during these visitation days. Include a list of the individuals with whom you are meeting. They can ensure you have not inadvertently left someone or some important group off the list. Err on the side of meeting with more, not fewer groups and individuals.

1. Leaving Your District

Be considerate of your current employer. Share your transition schedule with your district superintendent or board chair. Finalize arrangements for use of vacation days for your absence from the district. If you have no vacation time left in your old district, then take the transition days as unpaid leave. Your new district should compensate you for them.

During the transition period, successfully complete all assignments and responsibilities of your current position. Make certain to identify exactly what projects you are expected to complete before your departure. How you leave an organization can and will have an impact on your reputation and how you are perceived in your new district. Thanks to the Internet—texting and Twittering—what you do in your old district may soon be common knowledge in your new district.

Be prepared to respond to people in your current district who want you to "fix things" before you leave. People will ask for letters of recommendation. If you made a substantial contribution in your current position, be prepared for parties and the need to make speeches. Also, be prepared for some personal sadness and emotional letdown.

Once you are settled in your new job, you may want to maintain connections with your old district. But, it is time to move forward. Communications from your successor and others you thought were close friends and colleagues occur less frequently than expected. This is normal.

2. Planning a Vacation

If possible arrange to take a vacation between the end of your current assignment and the start of your new job. Being rested both mentally and physically helps you face the challenges of your new position. Taking time with family, friends, or even by yourself is important.

The best time to take vacation is in late June or early July as most district administrators other than the chief business official (CBO) take their vacations then. Some new superintendents prefer to work the first ten days in July. They then return to work a few days prior to the return of the full management team. Normally this is some time in early August. However you plan your vacation time, review your schedule with the board president. If you are a mid-year hire taking vacation is more problematic, but find a way to fit in some time.

The vacation days you use come from your new district. Be aware of the total number of days you are responsible for working. This is important whether you have a *positive work year* contract that calls for a set number of days for you to work or a *traditional work year* that includes all workdays less set holidays and a designated number of vacation days.

Most superintendent contracts identify a specific number of days of vacation you may carry over from year to year. These are vacation days you could not take because of ongoing district issues or emergencies that called you back to work from vacation. In both situations your board approves the extra days.

Some new superintendents start work on July 1 and work through the summer without taking a vacation. They take only a few vacation days during school holidays and discover they worked their full number of contracted workdays by the end of May. Unless their contract specifies they may carry over these days, they have created a conflict with the board. They worked more than their contract year but not due to an emergency or crisis. If you report such days to the board, the board has two choices: pay for the extra days or allow the extra days to be carried over to the following year. Even though they might want to do so, they will not ask you to work the days for no compensation or stay home.

Compensating the superintendent for working days beyond the contract is perceived as padding the superintendent's total compensation. Padding is not appreciated by unions, the public, and other administrators. Working beyond the contract year also demonstrates a lack of planning by the superintendent. Avoid this dilemma by carefully planning your work year.

One way to avoid this is to start your first contract year with vacation time. Then plan your calendar with days off during nonteacher workdays. If your contract allows for carryover of unused vacation, keep within your limits. If circumstances arise that require you to work beyond your contract days, notify the board well in advance and discuss the various options with them. This is another aspect of managing your contract.

The contracted workdays considered here do not reflect all the hours and days you will work. Superintendents work more hours and days than their contracts specify. You are a highly compensated employee contracted to do an important job. Do not watch the clock. You will work the occasional eighty-hour week and, at minimum, fifty-hour workweeks. You will attend night meetings and weekend events and may put in extra days on weekends to catch up on your work. Do not count these days toward your work year unless you specifically work this out with your board in advance.

3. Making the Most of Your Transition Days

A district has only one superintendent at a time. Work with the current superintendent and participate only in those decisions that will have a substantial impact on your work. These issues include hiring key district office staff and principals, the selection of key consultants, or planning for a bond or special tax election. Until the current superintendent leaves and your contract starts, you do not have the authority to provide day-to-day leadership. Be sensitive to the needs of the current superintendent. One day you will leave this position and will want similar respect.

Working out your relationship with the current superintendent is challenging if you were an inside candidate. Meet with the superintendent to develop protocols for your relationship, and that with the board, during the transition.

At all costs avoid getting trapped into making quick decisions regarding matters about which you have little information or those championed by your predecessor—or worse, one or two board members. Ask the superintendent to delay less urgent decisions until you become superintendent and have more information on which to base a decision. Some decisions are best made once you have a deeper understanding of the culture and values of the district. Sometimes, holding off on potentially controversial decisions is the best way to demonstrate your leadership abilities.

No matter what you think of the current superintendent, this person has valuable insights to share and may help you avoid pitfalls. Most departing superintendents want to pass on the lessons they learned, information about the workings of the board, or thumbnail assessments of key district personnel. Learn all you can about the educational, legal, and political decisions facing your new district.

Staff Memo. After your appointment as superintendent, send a communication to staff. Review the timing of this memo with the current superintendent. Use the district's normal communication channels. These may include e-mail or a print copy for those employees without access to a computer. In your message, let everyone know how pleased and honored you are to be their new superintendent. Include your transition schedule, first day of work and an invitation to stop by and visit. Be brief, enthusiastic, and factual. Do not lay out your plans for the next five years, as most staff members have not even met you.

Meetings. Use the meeting schedule you developed and shared with the board. Leave time for additional meetings with people or groups you may have overlooked. If you have few transition days, use the phone to talk with some individuals. Then ask your administrative assistant to set up a face-to-face meeting for after you arrive.

Meet separately with your district office administrative team. Schedule separate meetings with your deputy, assistant or associate superintendents, and business manager or CBO. Use these meetings to learn about the district's instructional program and finances.

If you are in a small district with few administrators, meet with those individuals who do provide support to you. They may be teacher-leaders, parent volunteers, or support staff. Even the smallest district usually has a business manager with specialized training in school finance. Your county office also may provide support to the district. If so, meet its staff.

Hold individual or group meetings with other district office staff. Meet with union representatives for each and every union found in the district. Meet with the presidents of parent organizations, school site councils, and any local school or district foundations. Attend community events as time permits.

Visit with principals. Ask the executive assistant to set up a visitation schedule. Your first visit with a principal should be at the school. The length of your visit depends on the number of schools in the district. If you have limited time, just meet with the principal, visit a few classes, and schedule a follow-up visit for after you begin your tenure.

At the end of this visit, meet with the principal and validate what you observed. Do not provide critical feedback. Inform the board of your visit and what you observed. Hold off on making critical judgments. Principals and staff talk with their peers, so be mindful of first impressions. Use these visits to listen and learn. Do not express your opinion or make judgments about controversial issues.

How many schools or work sites you can visit and how many community events you can attend depends on the size of the district, the length of your transition, and whether school is in session. It also depends on the current superintendent and what events or visits are appropriate for now and which should be scheduled for when you officially begin work.

Meet with individual board members. This is a good opportunity to ask why you were hired and why they see you as a good fit for the district. Ask what their top three priorities are for your first six months and first year. Ask why they ran for the board and what they have learned from their experiences.

These initial one-on-one meetings are an important step in building a strong relationship with each trustee. When meeting with the board chair, it is appropriate to ask if there were any inside candidates and if your hiring is likely to cause any internal problems or challenges. Depending on the situation you may want to meet with this person. At the very least you need to be aware of the situation.

Example

One new superintendent assisted the inside candidate in finding a superintendent position in another district. This inside candidate was unhappy with the manner in which he perceived the board had treated him. It was good for both him and the district when he found a new job. He was successful in his new district.

Find time, either by phone or in person, to meet with the district's legal counsel. At this meeting focus on the perceptions counsel has about the district and board. Ask about recent or pending litigation and collective bargaining challenges. Counsel works for the board but can provide invaluable insights about the district.

Meet the local newspaper editors. You never know when you may need them and, at the present time, you are "the story." If you have time during your transition days also meet with the following.

- ✓ The Mayor
- ✓ City Manager
- ✓ Police Chief
- ✓ County Superintendent
- ✓ State and County Legislative Representatives
- ✓ Local College or University Presidents
- ✓ Superintendents of Local Districts, Especially if These Districts Feed Students Into Your New District (or Yours Into Theirs)
- ✓ Heads of Local Community Groups Such as Rotary and Chamber of Commerce
- ✓ Heads of Local Church Councils

Whenever possible, meet each of these individuals or groups in their offices or at their work sites. This demonstrates respect for their time and provides you an opportunity to see them in their own work environment. You learn from seeing how these individuals greet you, treat their staff, and have their office or school arranged.

Questions to Ask During Meetings

- What are the strengths of the district?
- What long-term challenges face the district?
- What issues need immediate attention?
- How can the district improve student programs?
- Do you have any advice for me?

First impressions are informative. Listen carefully and take notes. Do not assume anything. Do not respond to negative information about the previous superintendent or the board. Do not say negative things about the current administration, no matter how poor a job you believe the previous superintendent did. You gain nothing from being negative. In fact, you may offend people with this approach and have a difficult time regaining their confidence and trust.

Hold off giving your opinion on issues. You lack the full picture of the district and may inadvertently create a negative impression. A big mistake new superintendents make is to assume they know something about the district, a person, or a program and not bother to listen and find out what people are really thinking and know. This is your opportunity to gather information.

Avoid talking about your successes in your current district and your desire to bring these programs or practices to your new district. No one wants to hear how much better someone else's work is. If possible, do not mention the name of the district you came from unless asked. More new superintendents offend people by saying "We did this better in my old district and I hope we can do this here." Do not impress people with anything other than your listening skills. Everyone is aware you have the expertise to do the job or you would not have been hired.

You are still an outsider and can view issues in a different light. This is one reason keeping notes is helpful. It allows you to retain the insights you are gaining about the district and staff. Plan to review your notes six months or a year into the job to see if your perceptions changed.

Many people want to meet with you. During your transition period and your first summer, make every effort to meet with anyone who asks to meet with you. This is a great way to connect to your community.

Example

One very successful superintendent offered to meet with anyone in the community for fifteen minutes. Hundreds took her up on this offer. She set aside several hours each day, kept to the fifteen-minute rule, and made sure everyone had an allotted time. She said it was the most valuable thing she did. It also bought her goodwill when the district was forced to make deep budget cuts.

Thank each person or group you meet with, preferably with a hand-written note or letter, but at least with an e-mail. It is amazing what this small gesture can do for the staff morale and parent and community perceptions. Before long everyone in the district will know that the new superintendent is "classy."

In some instances, as part of the search process consultants meet with stakeholders and prepare a written report about the district and stakeholder perceptions. Ask the board for a copy of this report or any other search materials that are public documents. You will benefit from having the broadest possible view of the district.

4. Using What You Learn

At the end of your transition, review your notes and any materials you gathered. List the district's and staff's strengths. Include what you learned about the history, culture, and mores of the district. Determine if there are issues of concern to you. Since you have a newcomer's perspective you may see things others learned to "live with."

Examples of What You May Learn

- Student achievement in language arts at the elementary grades improved substantially over the past three years.
- There has been a significant reduction in expulsions in the middle schools over the past year.
- There is substantial support for a districtwide facilities bond.
- Teachers respond positively to the new standards-based professional development program.
- Parents are not attending parent conferences because schools schedule conferences in the mornings when many parents are unable to take time away from their jobs.
- The new math text is difficult for parents to understand so they do not help their children with homework.
- Parents claim the K–8 program is great but the high school does not have challenging curriculum.
- The parent club president sits in on cabinet meetings.
- Some board members are not respected by staff.
- Among the staff there exists a pervasive negative attitude toward change.
- You have talented individuals on your staff who are not used to capacity and others about whom you have strong misgivings concerning their performance.

This list has several purposes. One is to provide a list of initial impressions you can refer to during the year. These impressions may prove to be right or wrong. A second purpose is to assist you in recommending to the board your performance goals for the first year. Goal setting is addressed in detail in Chapter 4.

A third purpose for this list is to compile a brief board report. It can be shared in a board meeting or in a Friday letter (Friday letters are discussed in Chapter 6) shortly after you begin your tenure. Present your findings as challenges, not criticisms of the district. Include the strengths you see, as these perceptions may be new to the board. If your findings include personnel-related concerns, communicate these in a closed session. What you share and how you share depends on the size and complexity of your district and the receptivity of the board and district to the information you wish to provide.

Example

One superintendent developed such a report and shared it at his first board meeting. He used the information to both praise the district and to reinforce the district goals for that year.

Once you begin your job, you may wish to share your findings with your management team. This could occur at the start of a school management retreat. It reinforces that you listened during your meetings with them. No one expects you to have answers to every problem. But, they do want to be involved in the problem-solving process. They want to know that you have perspective and will not treat each issue with the same degree of intensity.

During your transition, staff and community members formed an impression of you. They shared this with friends, colleagues, and your board. Do not be surprised if your board president schedules a meeting with you to provide some feedback. The feedback should be positive, especially if you have been a good listener. But be prepared for some negatives. You will not please everyone.

5. Your Executive Assistant

Your transition provides an opportunity to develop your relationship with your administrative or executive assistant. Superintendents' secretaries usually have titles reflecting their status and substantial responsibility in the organization. Their position is unique—they often serve as both your assistant and the board's secretary. Other than the board, no one is more central to your success than your administrative or executive assistant. Always treat your assistant with respect.

Most executive assistants worked their way up the support staff position ladder, serving at multiple sites in the district. They have history in the district. Superintendent assistants often have strong relationships with both current and past board members, district office administrators, parents, community, union leadership, and site administration. In larger districts they have their own support staff.

Administrative assistants know how things are done in the district and how to get things done. They are your face to the staff and community.

They serve as gatekeeper, giving others access to you, as well as keeping people from you. Through their connections, they also can gain access for you to others.

Superintendent assistants do not get these positions unless they are bright, competent, and capable, with well-developed political skills. Despite this, recognize that your assistant works for you and asking for support during the transition period is appropriate. However, the assistant also works for the current superintendent and board. Be sensitive to the assistant's workload and monitor your requests accordingly.

Before your first meeting, obtain a copy of the assistant's job description and review it. Speak to the board president and even the current superintendent about the role and responsibilities of the assistant. Then set up a meeting and begin the process of getting to know each other. Both of you are probably nervous at meeting one another. Listen to the advice and recommendations your assistant gives.

Occasionally, a new superintendent will find that the executive assistant lacks the skills needed to meet the expectations of the position or has a negative reputation among board members. In this situation, do as you would with any other employee. Review the last evaluation and meet to review the expectations of the job description. The problem may not be performance capabilities, but rather problems stemming from a lack of clarity of expectation from the previous superintendent or board members. This assistant may respond favorably to your style of leadership and fully meet your expectations. If not, you may need to take steps to remove or demote your assistant. Do not move aggressively on this without reviewing this decision with your board. While your assistant may not meet your needs, your assistant may meet the needs of some board members.

Work with your assistant to review office practices and listen carefully to how and why things are done the way they are. Go slow in recommending changes to office procedures. Just because you did things a certain way in your former district does not mean that the new district staff will see the wisdom in making the change. Initiate change carefully and thoughtfully. Be respectful of traditions and the experience and skill of your assistant.

Ask your assistant to arrange for temporary office space for you during your transition. You need a phone, keys, alarm codes, appropriate stationary and business cards, and a district e-mail address. Some districts save considerable cost by not printing personalized stationary. They use only district or school letterhead with the appropriate name and title in the signature block, or each office does customized letterhead using their computers. Do not change what your district does. Teachers and other staff will watch how you manage this, especially if they are constantly short on supplies.

Technology issues are important to address prior to your official start. Have your assistant schedule a meeting with the district's technology director to review your needs and expectations and the details of the district's computer, e-mail, Internet, and phone systems. In smaller districts this may be a teacher with a release period or a support staff person. If you need a new computer or upgrade, determine if funds have been budgeted for this purpose and notify your board chair. If you expect a new laptop for your use at home and at work, this expectation should be included in your employment contract.

Ask your assistant for materials that you can take home and review. They should include the following.

- ✓ Recently Approved, Revised, or Proposed Board Policies
- ✓ District Organization Chart With Names
- ✓ List of Management Team Members, Including Phone Numbers
- ✓ Board Telephone Numbers and Addresses
- ✓ District Calendar
- ✓ Board Meeting Calendar
- ✓ Routine Board Meeting Agenda Items Scheduled for This and Next Year
- ✓ Key Board or Staff Reports From the Prior Year
- ✓ Student Achievement Data by District, Grade, and School
- ✓ Parcel Tax or Bond Information, if Applicable
- ✓ Job Descriptions and Employment Contracts for District Office Administration
- ✓ List of Key District Consultants With Work They Do
- ✓ The Board-Adopted Budget, Along With Interim Budget Reports
- ✓ List of Organizations Whose Meetings the Superintendent Routinely Attends
- ✓ District Public Relations Information or Publications
- ✓ District's Strategic Plan or Yearly Goals and Value Statements
- ✓ Meeting Schedules of Schools or District Office Departments, Including, if Applicable, Superintendent's Cabinet Meetings

Review how you will maintain your meeting calendar and how appointments are made and changed. Establish protocols for interruptions during meetings—when and under what circumstances. Also review protocols for the opening, distribution, and response to paper mail and e-mail. Give your assistant permission to let you know, quietly, and unobtrusively, when you are about to do or say something you will regret.

A helpful strategy is to establish file sharing between you and your assistant so draft documents or memos can be easily reviewed and finalized. An administrative assistant cannot function to capacity if not informed. Your assistant needs access to the majority of your documents and communications. This is particularly true for board meeting materials. Most, if not all, executive assistants are trusted with highly confidential material and information and can provide insightful advice and counsel.

Your Executive Assistant Can Help You

☐ Learn the "nuts and bolts" of your new office.

- How does my phone work?
- Do I answer my own phone?
- Who do I call if my computer shuts down?
- Where are the supplies?
- What bathroom should I use?

☐ Learn about the culture of your district office.

- What district office or districtwide events must I attend?
- Does the district office staff have lunch together?
- Where do I eat?
- How are birthdays celebrated?
- Where is the coffee, who makes it, and how is it purchased?
- Who cleans up the staff lounge? Do I take a turn?
- Does everyone have a reserved parking space or just me?
- Is Friday a "dress down" day?
- How are holidays observed in the office? Is there an annual holiday party?

Asking about these practices lets staff know you are interested in learning about the district's traditions. It does not mean that you may not change these over time or even add to them. But asking now shows a sensitivity to the culture of your new district. Ironically this makes it easier if and when you do make changes.

6. Your New Office

A challenge for new superintendents is how to set up their offices. Usually, this does not occur until you officially start. While seemingly an innocent task, preparing your office can be a minefield if not approached with care and common sense. Your goal is an inviting professional office that allows you to work comfortably and meet with others. A secondary goal is to move into your office without doing something controversial.

Every superintendent is entitled to an efficient, attractive, and fully operational office. But you put yourself at risk if you create an office that exceeds the standards for other district office administrators. Avoid expensive and extensive remodeling when everyone else is making do with what is available. All the effort you make during your transition to set the right tone for when you officially begin is undone in an instant by demanding what no one else has.

If a remodel or a new desk and chair for you are included in the district's budget, be certain your administrative assistant's needs are addressed also. Stay within the set budget limitations. Do not remodel your office if no funds are included in the budget or if no other high-level district office administrator's office has been remodeled in years.

Example

One superintendent started off her year tenure in the district by asking maintenance to fully paint her office during their busiest time of the summer, and then, not liking the color, asking them to repaint with a different color. Needless to say, the entire district knew about this by the first day of school in August.

When decorating your office, there are some dos and don'ts that make for a more comfortable work environment. Avoid having a "bragging wall" with diplomas and awards on display. It is far better to display student art, photos, or other artifacts that reflect your work as an educator. Keep in mind your office represents your district. This is where you meet with board members, teachers, administrators, parents, attorneys, union representatives, mayors, and other visitors. What you have in your office says a lot about what you value as a superintendent.

It is good practice to have your desk face the door so you can see your assistant when someone comes into the office. So too, with where you sit at your work table. Face the door so you have instant visual communication with your assistant and can see who is waiting outside.

Your office needs a clock within easy view of wherever you are sitting. You do not want to show the person with whom you are meeting that you are impatient with the time expended. This may mean you need more than one clock in your office.

Also have window coverings that ensure privacy, especially if your office is on the ground floor or your windows face a hallway. You need privacy. You do not want everyone passing by your office to know with whom you are meeting. Work out protocols with your administrative assistant for when your door will be closed and how to ensure confidentiality.

Some superintendents have whiteboards or electronic bulletin boards installed in their offices. They use these to list goals, to-do lists, and other work products. Where this may appear to be a useful tool, it can cause problems as well.

Example

One superintendent left a list of proposed support staff reductions on a whiteboard. These reductions had not been reviewed by the cabinet or the board. The night custodian read the board. The following morning union leadership demanded a meeting.

Your office needs sufficient chairs for visitors and small meetings. Ideally these chairs should not be across from your desk. Your position carries with it significant power. Forcing people to talk across a desk only emphasizes the imbalance between you and those you meet.

If your office is large enough, have a conference table. This enables you to hold small meetings, including ones with your cabinet, board, and visitors. It also doubles as added workspace for you. If you lack room for a table, set up a small area where three or four chairs can be placed for small meetings. Find out what larger meeting area is available for you to use on a routine basis.

ADDRESSING PERSONAL ISSUES

During your transition you meet a wide array of individuals, groups, and organizations. You learn how many people want part of your time because you are the community's new educational leader. You also learn that because you are paid with public dollars many people believe they have the right to talk to you whether you are at work, home, or out for an evening with family or friends.

The community observes, judges, and comments on your every behavior and action. When you begin your official tenure, you may experience a profound loss of privacy. This is a challenge. It forces you to examine the balance between personal and professional life. It also underscores how intertwined these are once you are a superintendent.

As you transition, be aware of a number of issues affecting both your personal and professional life. Each has ramifications, and how you address them may have unintended consequences. These issues also may influence how staff and community perceive you. More importantly, they impact your effectiveness on the job—for good or bad. Take time to think through your decisions regarding these. What works for one superintendent may not work for another.

1. Where to Live

One of your first decisions is deciding where to live. Many school boards prefer, or even expect, their new superintendent to live within school district boundaries. They want you to be part of the community. They assume if you do so, you are likely to make connections and will remain in the district longer.

Living and working in the same district is a wonderful experience. It deepens your understanding of the community. You experience the same challenges faced by everyone in the community, giving you greater legitimacy. They see you as one of them and not an outsider. Participation in community events generates friendships and contacts that support your work. For example, if in the course of your tenure you ask the community to support a bond to upgrade facilities, citizens know you will be paying the tax increase as well.

Living near your office allows you to go home before board meetings or other evening events. If you have a family you can have dinner with them on a more regular basis. Or, on occasion, you may even go home for lunch. You can make quick trips to the office on the weekend to get work done or pick up papers. A short commute saves time and money.

The down side of living in your district is a loss of privacy for you and your family. With the advent of cell phones, texting, and Twitter, you may unknowingly be recorded or written about while running errands or attending a private party. As a public official, people are interested and curious about you and how you live. Unfortunately, some will gossip. Your neighbors may overhear you fighting with your spouse or scolding your child. Your spouse may be accosted at the grocery store by a well-meaning but nosey neighbor who attempts to get the scoop on who will be the next high school principal. It is difficult to know if people in the community are befriending you because you are the superintendent or if they actually like you.

If you are single, neighbors observe who you entertain. They may watch guests entering and leaving your home. They are interested in who your friends are and what you do in your private life.

Example

One superintendent reported that she couldn't garden in her front yard, a favorite hobby, without neighbors coming by to discuss school issues with her. One even made a critical comment about her roses.

Reasons Superintendents Elect Not to Move to Their Districts

- Moving is stressful and costly.
- Their current home is equidistant to the district and the job of their spouse or partner.
- They are reluctant or unable to sell their home.
- They are unwilling to sever their involvement or connection to their current community.
- They desire to retain their privacy.
- Their children are reluctant to move or it would not be beneficial to them.

Most boards understand these issues and support superintendents who live nearby and do not move to the district. However, even if supportive your board will not limit its expectations. It expects you to attend school and community evening and weekend events. This is an essential aspect of your role. Superintendents with ninety-minute commutes each way may have difficulty in their new positions. They may be exhausted at work or fail to make important community connections.

Housing costs frequently determine where you decide to live. It is financially draining to move from a low-cost to a high-cost housing area. As indicated in Chapter 1, take this into consideration before you submit your application. During contract negotiations, resolve any district financial contributions toward your housing. Most superintendents are responsible for their own housing.

You may decide to rent before purchasing a home. This provides an opportunity to get to know the community before deciding where to live. If renting, find a real estate agent to assist you in locating in a neighborhood where you will be comfortable. Sometimes board members want to assist you in finding an agent. However, it is best to find this real estate agent on your own as it keeps your personal and professional life separated.

One superintendent's board chair was a Realtor. He wanted to represent the superintendent in finding a home or a rental. This would have required the superintendent to disclose personal financial information to the board chair. Instead this superintendent found an agent through family friends. In the short term it was uncomfortable. In the long term it allowed for a better working relationship between them.

Another variation on renting is maintaining your current residence while renting a small apartment to use during the week. This involves commuting back and forth on weekends and even some evenings. This is stressful. It can become a major family issue if the living arrangement lasts more than a year. Your new community may perceive you as a carpetbagger and assume you are not planning on staying long. This can undermine your support in the district.

A compromise is to buy or rent a home in a community near your district. This provides privacy, opportunity for lower costs, and a short commute. Many superintendents do this to their advantage.

Whatever you decide about your residence will affect your personal life and your community's perception of you. Carefully examine each option. Then make the best decision for you and your family.

2. Where Children Attend School

Where your children attend school is a major consideration in determining whether you move. This is an important issue to you and your community. The decision becomes more complicated if your new district is less affluent or lower achieving than your current one.

Most boards assume you will send your children to the local public schools. Enrolling your children demonstrates to the community confidence in the quality of education provided students. It also communicates confidence in your ability to maintain and strengthen the schools.

This decision is challenging if you have a special needs child. Work with the special education staff of your new district to review your child's Individualized Education Program (IEP) and determine if the district has a program to meet your child's needs. You have the same rights and privileges of any special needs parent, including the right to private school education if appropriate.

During the selection process, inform the board of your child's needs. Most boards understand the need for you to make a decision in the best interests of the child. But if your child attends a private school, some district parents may use this as an excuse to criticize the district's special education programs.

The transition to a new district is usually difficult for high school students, especially those in their junior or senior year. These students have strong peer groups, participate in a number of activities, including sports, and worry about getting into their college of choice. Some superintendents do not apply for new positions during this time or do not move their families until their children graduate from high school.

The transition is less difficult for younger students. They often are more flexible and may even view the move as an adventure. But they too will miss their old school and friends. How your children react depends on their personalities and needs, as well as how you as a family plan and execute the move.

Though issues may arise if you decide to move your children to your new district and send them to the local schools, none are insurmountable. For example, some teachers are threatened by having the superintendent's child in their class. Newer, less-experienced teachers are more likely threatened than more experienced teachers. They may treat your child differently than they treat other students. This treatment can be for better or worse.

Your child should be treated the same as all other children. This means not having higher or lower academic or discipline standards or any special privileges. Of course, you need to inform your child that the teacher will treat him or her the same as all other students. Make it clear to your child not to seek or expect special privileges.

News media may be critical of some of your decisions and run front page stories that your children may read. Neighbors or community members may criticize some of your actions in front of your children. Actions such as these are disconcerting to children especially if they are unprepared for them and are not used to having a parent in the spotlight.

During contentious union negotiations, it is not uncommon for some teachers to make negative comments about the superintendent and how negotiations are going. Some purposefully do this in front of, or directly to, the superintendent's children. In addition, many high school students are aware of the district's political issues and decisions. They often take sides or even attend board meetings to state their case. Often student newspapers run editorials critical of the superintendent and decisions that adversely impact their school. Some superintendent's children find these disturbing.

You do not lose your rights as a parent because you are the superintendent. If boundaries are crossed, do not hesitate to say something. However, it may be best for your spouse to handle most day-to-day interactions with teachers and the school. This is particularly true if your child has an occasional discipline problem or is a special needs student. Single parents do not have this luxury.

No matter who handles day-to-day interactions, attend school functions such as Back to School Night, open house, and parent conferences. You are the parent. Your child's teacher and principal expect to see you at these events. Nothing is more humbling as superintendent than to jam yourself into a tiny kindergarten chair and listen to your child's teacher give an assessment of your "bright star's" low reading readiness level and then recommend you spend more time reading to your child at home.

You have every right to seek redress if you believe a teacher is behaving unprofessionally toward your child. In these situations do what you expect any parent to do: follow the school's complaint procedure. Make an appointment with the teacher and address your concerns. If this does not work, seek assistance from the principal.

Most principals are thrilled to have the superintendent's children at their school. They see this as an opportunity to get to know you on a more personal level and to demonstrate their competence. Most principals will "keep an eye out" for the children of superintendents and even board members, just to make certain all is going well. Some principals even handpick teachers or show some other form of favoritism. While this is not appropriate behavior and should not be encouraged, it happens.

Why do you not want special treatment and handpicked classes for your child? You need to know firsthand what parents in your children's schools are experiencing. If your child has a weak teacher, it is a reminder that children of less influential parents also suffer with that teacher. This will motivate you to initiate stronger supervision, evaluation, and staff development programs.

3. Evening and Weekend Events

The number of events you attend outside the workday varies from district to district. In some districts you are the public face of the district and attend a broad array of meetings and events. You may find yourself out four to five nights a week, including at least one weekend event. In other districts the board prefers the superintendent to focus on day-to-day district leadership. Board members assume the public face of the district, joining community clubs or representing the district at events.

During the application, interview, and transition process, learn the board's expectations in this regard. Not all boards fully understand the effect attending these events may have on your personal and professional life. Reach agreement with the board on the level of outside activities in which you will be involved.

Every district has must-attend events for the superintendent. These include foundation fund-raisers, award dinners, school plays, or other annual community events. They are activities superintendents have always attended in the past. Your administrative assistant and board chair can assist in identifying these events. Include these in both your school and private calendars.

Most experienced superintendents attempt to limit evening meetings to no more than three each week, with a few weekend events. As a new superintendent you will exceed that number as you become acquainted with your district and community. You also will exceed it if your board expects you to be the public face of the district.

Avoid creating the expectation that you are always available and will attend every event or meeting to which you are invited. You do not need to accept every invitation for events involving students, staff, or parents. You do not need to accept every invitation from every community group. Be strategic in the invitations you do and do not accept. Put school and district events first.

If you accept every invitation during your first year, this expectation follows you into your second year. When you then turn down invitations you may hear that you are slighting groups or even slowing down. Better to attend different events, especially community events, each year. When asked, you can say, "I cannot attend this year due to a schedule conflict but would enjoy doing so next year." Exercise good judgment and avoid extremes by establishing a level of participation that fits your needs and board and community expectations.

Strategies to Help You Find a Balance

- Do not attend every meeting or event from beginning to end. If you have competing events on the same evening, notify the event chairs you will arrive late or leave early due to the conflict. Ask them to inform the audience why you are not there for the entire meeting.
- Schedule one or two events on the same evening rather than one event per evening.
- If you are asked to speak at an event, request to be scheduled at the start of the meeting so you can leave early to attend another event.
- Treat schools and organizations in the same way. Do not consistently stay for all of one parent-teacher organization meeting and leave early for the others. The only exception is the parent organization meeting at your child's school.
- If you have restrictions on the number of weekend events you can attend due to religious or family issues, inform the board before you sign your contract.

Your district staff needs to know your personal limits. While there may be situations in which an assistant superintendent could fill in for you, people expect to see the superintendent. This is especially true in small districts where you are the only district administrator. Also recognize that district administrators have personal lives. They will resent you if you consistently ask them to fill in for you.

Work with your executive assistant to monitor your workweek and calendar. Schedule no early morning meetings after night meetings, no more than two to three weekly evening engagements, and no more than three weekend engagements per month. This takes discipline. Flexibility is also important—you will need to add events. Remind your staff that only you and your assistant can change your calendar.

During your first year it is helpful to have your spouse attend some events. As discussed in Chapter 1, address spousal issues before you apply for a superintendent position, not after you start your new job. Some spouses enjoy attending football games and district events, while others do not for personal or professional reasons.

The same holds true if you are in a nontraditional relationship. Your partner may or may not want to attend events with you. This is your joint decision, not the board's or the community's. If you are in such a relationship, you are under no obligation to inform the board prior to completing the hiring process. Direct inquiries by the board may violate either state or federal law. However, boards do not like surprises. It may be best you inform them before they learn from other sources.

Single superintendents face different challenges. Often boards or community members assume you have no personal life. They think you want to attend everything to meet "that special someone" and try to fix you up with another single community member. Gently but firmly let your limits be known. Do not be afraid to say no. You do not have to attend every event because you are single.

Extracurricular events present a special challenge. While you want to limit your evenings and weekends away from home, it is difficult not to attend events that highlight the talents of your students. Attending student athletic, art, music, and drama performances demonstrates your commitment to the students, district, and community. These events also provide an opportunity to involve your family in your work. They can be fun and good stress reducers. In addition, you meet the school community in a more informal setting. If you attend few if any events, your absence will be noted. Understand your community and make sure to attend the events that are central to it.

You are entitled to a private life. However, you are a public figure and expectations for superintendents are different than expectations for other staff members. Know this in advance of submitting your first application. Find a district that is compatible with your personal needs.

4. School and Community Donations

As superintendent you are asked to donate money to school, district, and community fund-raising activities. Often people believe that since you are part of the community, and paid with public dollars, you should contribute generously. However, few realize how frequently you are asked for contributions. Over a school year, the amount you donate can be substantial, often running into several thousand dollars. Many superintendents include provisions in their contracts for an expense allowance to cover some of these extra costs, such as attendance at community fund-raisers.

Guidelines to Manage Your Contributions

- Make small contributions when directly solicited. The exception is the school your child attends; give generously to it.
- Treat all like entities the same. If you donate $25 to one parent club, donate $25 to all parent clubs. If you give to students at one high school do the same at all high schools.
- Support district-wide efforts to raise funds for the schools. These can be through a foundation or a joint parent club effort. Make donations appropriate for your income level.
- If you have the resources and want to make large donations, consider doing so anonymously. Do not make a grandiose contribution as it may raise questions about your motivation. It may even spur rumors that you are paid too much.

Whatever contributions you make, do not attempt to influence other staff to do the same. This can be perceived as harassment. Nobody wants to be pressured to "give until it hurts" by an immediate supervisor. However, if district policies permit, it is appropriate to let school organizations send solicitations to staff. How individual staff members respond is a private matter.

5. A Healthy Lifestyle

Being a superintendent is no easy task. At times you will work seven days a week. You may have a late night meeting followed by an early morning breakfast meeting, or an early morning breakfast meeting and a late evening meeting on the same day.

No matter how hard you work, take care of your physical and emotional self. This is easier said than done. You are in a new position where everyone expects you to perform at the highest levels. But if you are emotionally spent, grouchy, hyperactive, out ill on a regular basis, or always feeling tired, you will not perform well. Worse, you will make errors in judgment and even some irreversible mistakes.

The board expects superintendent candidates to be healthy enough to perform the duties of the position. Boards do not want to hire a superintendent only to have that person constantly out due to illness. Work to maintain your health so you can perform.

A healthy diet, regular sleep and exercise, time with friends and family, and routine physicals are important. Walk or bicycle to work on days you do not need a car (but arrange access to one in case of a school emergency). You also may want to join a gym. Avoid sitting for hours in front of your computer—get up and stretch. Instead of calling or e-mailing people in your district office, go to see them.

Most successful superintendents work between fifty and seventy hours a week, depending on the issues at hand. However, keep in mind that success is not measured by the number of hours you work but by your productivity and the quality of your work. If you work excessively long hours on a consistent basis, assess what you are doing and how you are doing it. With rare exceptions, over time a seventy-hour workweek decreases productivity and quality.

Find a way to decompress at the end of the day. For some superintendents this means returning e-mails and catching up on staff reports before going home. This enables them to prepare for the next day and relax once they leave the office, even after a long board meeting. But if you do this, do not expect staff to do the same and do not expect return e-mails until the following workday. Respect your staffs' needs at the end of the workday. You want them healthy and rested.

Make every effort to avoid grazing or eating junk food at work. Every district office has a staff lounge or gathering place. These inevitably have a selection of fattening food for everyone to eat. Often staff members bring this food from home as a way of keeping it from their families. Parents, vendors, board members, and school staff drop off treats as a way of saying thank you to staff. It takes great discipline not to eat at this wonderful smorgasbord of fattening food. A great strategy for dealing with this is to always keep on hand healthy snacks and drinks. Many superintendents purchase a small refrigerator for their offices for this purpose.

Take your allotted vacation days. This is important for maintaining your health and well-being. You could work every day of the year and still not accomplish all you want and need to do. Schedule at least one two-week vacation each year and several three-day to five-day vacations that include long weekends.

Vacation is time away from the stresses and strains of the job. It should not include days when you are on your cell phone, checking your e-mail, making "one more call," or texting staff. It is a time to relax and recharge. However, as superintendent you do need to be reachable in case of emergency. Leave numbers for this purpose.

6. Friendships

Friendship issues are a challenge for many new superintendents. Whatever your previous job, it is likely you had a peer group. It might have been another assistant superintendent, one or two district office directors, a group of principals, or even a combination of these. These were people who provided fellowship and camaraderie at work and were often part of your social life. Some even become lifelong friends.

You depended on them for guidance, validation, and encouragement. These were people with whom you shared some discreet, risk-free criticism of the superintendent or the board, "Can you believe how long public comment took at last night's board meeting? Wish there was a way to streamline that."

Now things are different. You are the superintendent. You soon discover how lonely the position is. You have no peer group in the organization and there is no one with whom you can share confidences. You may have heard about this before you became the superintendent but did not truly understand it.

The truth is you are different from other staff. You have no peer in the organization. You decide whom to promote and whom to demote. You determine budgets and allocate resources. You make decisions that affect other people's lives.

Friendships at Work. Your position does not preclude having friendly relationships with members of staff. It is important to be supportive and caring. Staff members appreciate this. But district office administrators, even those you hired, are subordinates. Maintain appropriate boundaries.

Be sensitive to staff jockeying for your ear, "sucking up" to curry favor or acceptance of ideas, or perceiving you as having favorites. A personal connection to a particular staff member creates problems with other staff. They will question your ability to make objective decisions involving your friend or "drinking buddy." While a promotion given to one may be well-deserved, others will view it as favoritism.

Your relationships with other administrators, including your cabinet, should be professional. A lunch or dinner during the workweek may be appropriate, but not on a regular basis with the same person. You can attend occasional family events such as a wedding or silver anniversary. But avoid socializing with staff on the weekends unless the event is for all cabinet or administrative staff. These guidelines apply to teachers and support staff as well as board members. Staff members want to see you working closely and professionally with the board while maintaining your independence.

A board member, despite working closely with you and even sharing confidences, is your immediate employer, not your best friend. The board hires you, sets your goals, determines your compensation, evaluates your performance, extends your contract, and, should the time come, lets you know when your services are no longer needed. You may develop caring and collegial relationships with individual board members. But when called upon, your friends on the board are likely to remain true to their oaths and vote not to extend your contract if you fail to perform.

Many superintendents learn this lesson the hard way. A board member should not be your social friend until you leave the district or the board member's term has ended.

Example

A superintendent and board member were close allies during the twelve years she was on the board. During that time they refrained from any social engagements. The first Saturday night after the end of her final term, they and their spouses finally went out to dinner together. They remain fast friends to this day.

In some situations a close working relationship develops into an emotional or even sexual entanglement. This happens when two people work together daily for long hours in a stressful environment. Sometimes superintendents are not aware they are emotionally entangled with a board member or a subordinate. However, others in the organization may be aware of this leading to serious consequences for both parties.

One consequence is that the subordinate may interpret the superintendent's behavior as sexual harassment. Superintendents have positional power. This influences how staff members respond to you. While you feel your warm, close relationship with your beaming subordinate is just fine, your subordinate may perceive your intimacy as unwarranted and undesired. The difference in perception can lead to gross misunderstandings and the unraveling of the superintendent's tenure in the district.

Keep in mind that when you interact with subordinates, you are not "Joe, the plumber," but "Joe, the superintendent." People listen to you and react accordingly. Avoid sarcasm, telling off-color or ethnic jokes, wise-cracks, and impromptu conversations about race, religion, politics, taxes, upcoming elections, and other sensitive topics. You never know, until it is too late, if you offended someone's religious or personal beliefs.

While it is appropriate to give compliments, avoid thoughtless statements about an individual's clothing, new hairstyle or coloring, weight loss, smile, weekend activities, or sexual preferences. You may have innocent intentions, but what you say can be interpreted by some as a criticism or even a directive. You may be perceived as attempting to influence them in matters not related to school or professional business.

Do not assume you are a subordinate's friend or that they like you because they are especially nice to you. Most employees are nice to you as they want you to see them in a positive light. Far too many superintendents fail to adhere to appropriate professional and interpersonal boundaries. Exercise common sense. Your goal is to be respected for the work you do and be perceived as a caring professional who makes good decisions.

Maintaining Your Outside Friendships. Another challenge is maintaining friendships outside of work. How much should you confide in them about your job? Who should you talk with about your anxieties and stress? Again use common sense. Do not share with casual friends who do not know you well. Likewise do not share with friends or relatives who do not understand and are not interested in your leadership position and responsibilities. Be wary of sharing information about your work with friends who live in the school district.

Enjoy your casual friends, talk about their lives, and engage in activities you both enjoy. Just remember they are not your confidants. You may not think of yourself as a celebrity, but they do. If they believe they have the "inside scoop" about the district, they will share it with others. This can be embarrassing for you and even undermine your credibility.

As with other aspects of your personal life, consider carefully who becomes a confidant. It might be a long-time friend, close relative, or a trusted member of your network. Some superintendents talk candidly with clergy. It might even be a combination of these people. Confide in and share with people who are interested in your personal well-being.

Maintaining confidentiality is essential. This is a very small world, made even smaller by e-mail, texting, and Twitter. You need to trust these people explicitly. Nothing can be repeated. A breach in boundaries may cause unforeseen difficulties. For example, a close friend who confides to a mutual acquaintance over a cup of coffee that your board chair is "driving you nuts" should not be surprised if that comment gets back to one of your board members. Talk about these possibilities with your confidants so they understand the issues you face.

Do not give up having friends, just be aware of the boundaries within which you work. Treasure your close friends in whom you can confide and enjoy the casual friendships you have.

7. Effect of the Job on Spouse or Partner

Normally, people share their true feelings with their spouse or partner. Before you start your tenure, talk with your spouse or partner about the challenges you face. Stress the need for confidentiality. Let them know you have heard that the first year can be intense and stressful and how much you appreciate their care and support.

Be aware this is also a time of change for them. Discuss how each of you can "cut some slack" for the other. If your spouse or partner has a similarly challenging position, or if you have young children who need lots of daily attention, realize there is added pressure.

Every experienced superintendent attests to the need to work out family dynamics. Each family has a different way of adjusting. Marriages and relationships succeed when they include open communication, shared feelings, commitment to common goals, and a strong sense of give and take. Keep in mind how becoming superintendent and achieving one of your life goals is a key component of your collective life plan. In turn, show support to your partner and your children.

A challenge for superintendents is how to relax after a demanding day or harder yet, after a long, late night board meeting. It is best to avoid late night, one-sided debriefing conversations with a spouse or partner, particularly if your spouse has to get up early the next morning to take children to school or go to work. Superintendent's confidants also do not appreciate late night or early morning calls to debrief your meeting. If you cannot sleep, try those things that have worked for you in the past. It may be reading a book, catching up on e-mail, having a glass of milk, or meditating.

On some occasions, despite your best intentions, taking on this new position will cause serious relationship problems that affect your ability to perform. Some contributing factors are realizing the job is far more stressful than anticipated, having young children, moving to a new area far from family and friends, commuting a long distance, or living away from home during the week. These are compounded if you are a single parent or if your partner gave up an important position to be with you. Sometimes underlying or unresolved marital or family issues are exacerbated by the new job.

As superintendent you have multiple responsibilities, but your most important responsibility is always to yourself and to your family. If your new job causes family or marital issues, seek professional assistance.

Support can include family counseling, individual therapy, or working with clergy. If you are concerned with community perceptions, find a therapist outside your community. If you improve your home situation, you are more likely to be successful at work.

8. Professional Growth

You are the educational leader of your district. Continuing to learn enhances your knowledge and skills and models the importance of life-long learning for staff. In selecting areas for professional growth, focus on where you may need improvement, such as technology, computer adaptive assessment, or facilities management. Use the feedback you received from the consultant and the board when you were hired. Look at the performance goals the board set for you. Once you have a focus you can select appropriate professional development activities.

Professional Development Activities

- Work with a coach.
- Attend conferences at the state and national levels.
- Enroll in appropriate university programs.
- Review materials from state and national professional organizations.
- Read professional publications.
- Learn from experienced colleagues.
- Take on leadership positions in local, state, or national organizations.
- Participate in accreditation reviews.
- Reflect and remain intellectually curious; read widely.
- Know what is going on in the nation and world.

Limit outside activities during your first year. But keep abreast of the latest research through reading. Also, look for ways to engage in professional development that involve minimum expenses and travel. For example, bring consultants to your county meetings instead of traveling to a conference, or engage in video conferencing.

A word of caution: some superintendents are so enamored with their professional development they attend every conference and outside workshop to which they are invited. Staff members come to believe they are never in their office working, "especially on Fridays!"

Be careful about bringing too many new ideas to your district from the workshops and conferences you attend. When you bring back new ideas for programs, make certain they relate or reinforce the goals of the district. Organize and fund attendance at key workshops so a cross-section of teachers and site and district office administrators can attend. In the long run this approach will have the greatest influence on change in the district.

Example

One superintendent attended several curriculum and instruction workshops each year, always bringing back ideas for the district. He wrote ten- to twenty-page summaries of all he learned, including examples of what work staff could do to implement these ideas. Staff dreaded his attending conferences and receiving these summaries. Finally an assistant superintendent suggested he take others to these conferences. He accepted the advice and the reports stopped. The staff who attended incorporated the new materials into their ongoing work.

Coaching. A coach is like a mentor, someone you bounce ideas off of or ask for advice. A coach helps you plan your first Friday letter to the board, your welcoming e-mail to staff, and your first board meeting or provides advice on challenges you face as superintendent. You also can talk about your insecurities. Retain a coach if you do not have a mentor who can assist you in this way.

Coaching is not therapy. It deepens your understanding and knowledge of your leadership style. Coaches help you work more effectively with board and staff. New superintendents who regularly work with coaches are less likely to make serious, job-threatening mistakes, and an increasing number are using them.

Some enlightened boards are mandating and funding coaching support for new superintendents. These boards recognize the district has a vested interest in the superintendent's success. They just completed a broad and expensive search process, paid top dollar in compensation, and even funded the superintendent's moving costs. The last thing a board wants is for the superintendent to fail and the community to go through another search in a year or two. It is more cost-effective to provide the funds for coaching support.

Even if you pay for it yourself, it is recommended you retain a coach for your first two years. The only exception is if you have access to a mentor willing to step into this role for you. In the long run, the support received is well worth the personal expenditure. If you pay for the coaching, inform your board. You do not want them to learn of this later and feel there was a breach of confidentiality.

Coaches can be found through some search firms or statewide administrator associations. When retaining a coach, be certain to work with someone you trust and who has a successful track record as a superintendent or coach. Check to see if they have had professional training as a coach, and check their references. Coaching usually involves a few hours a month. Some of the work can be done by phone or e-mail between visits.

Many first-year superintendents are reluctant to seek coaching support. They do not want their board or school community to believe they are not fully prepared or capable of taking on this new position and being successful. Unfortunately, this can be a losing strategy. The challenges of the first year are so great that even the most highly prepared superintendents experience difficulties that could be readily addressed with a little help. It is far better to have a very strong first year with a minimum number of mistakes due to coaching than to go it alone and make mistakes that may require years to overcome.

Professional Organizations. Active participation and leadership in your county, state, or national professional organizations is an excellent way to develop professional skills. In many districts, this participation and leadership parallels similar participation by board members in school board organizations.

Most boards expect superintendents to be involved in some professional organizations. These organizations provide opportunities for collegiality and professional development and support. They are often an ongoing source of information about state and national school funding and legislation. Superintendents and board members share the information they receive from their respective state organizations. They then use it to lobby their state and national elected representatives.

Participating in state organizations offers a model for your subordinates. If they see you actively involved in these activities, they are more likely to do so. Avoid taking on major organizational responsibilities during your first two years unless your district expects you to do so. The board, staff, and community expect your full involvement and attention during this challenging period.

As discussed earlier in this chapter, meet with your executive assistant and review the outside meetings and organizations your predecessor attended. Determine which are of importance to you. You also may wish to review your decisions with the board. Oftentimes your predecessor chose to participate in groups you have no interest in or do not need to join.

If you hold a major office in a state, local, or national organization when you are first hired, review these leadership expectations with your board prior to finalizing your contract. It is better the board knows in advance that your position requires you be out of the district for a substantial number of days each year. Some boards view your leadership role as a plus, reflecting positively on their sound judgment for hiring you.

Others support your role but may not want to pay you for the days you are out of the district. Still others might determine having you out of the district for so many days is a deal breaker.

In some districts, the superintendent is expected to take on leadership responsibilities in various county or statewide organizations that benefit the school district. This often happens in larger or better-funded school districts. In these districts there may be district office support to assist you in taking on these additional responsibilities. Even if additional support is not available, you are expected to take on the work.

During your first two years, carefully monitor the time required for these activities. Try to avoid spending too much time away from your work in the district. Your primary focus needs to be the district and student instruction. If these outside organizations become an issue for you, work with your board to find ways to modify the responsibilities. In some districts, board members may well step into these organizations and be able to represent the district.

Who Pays? Your contract should address the issue of reimbursement for professional activities. Most districts reimburse the superintendent for membership in one or two professional organizations, or allocate a dollar amount. Note however that you should not expect boards to pay for any portion of the dues that may be allocated toward partisan political lobbying.

Most superintendent contracts also include a provision stating that the superintendent is either reimbursed or the district pays directly for all work-related expenses. Some districts will have a dollar limit and others may not. Work-related expenses include expenses associated with participation in organizations and activities that are mandatory or essential for the superintendent's work in the district and are not elective. If in doubt, clarify the details with your board.

Whatever your contract permits, adhere to district policies and procedures for reimbursement. Do not overspend your budget for these purposes without communicating with the board. Do not expend taxpayer funds on anything you do not want to see on the first page of your local newspaper. Pay attention to district culture and experience, especially for expenditures that may be viewed critically by staff and the public, such as attending conferences out of the country.

Your commitment to professional development becomes a model for your staff. Pay close attention to the budgeted, or contractually defined funding limit for these activities. If everyone in your cabinet or administrative team is without funds for professional development, seek funding for them from the board, or reduce or eliminate the funds you spend on yourself. If there are no funds for professional development for you or anyone else in the district due to severe budget constraints, use your own funds as an investment in your professional development. But make certain your board and leadership team knows that you are doing this.

Some districts offer superintendents a credit card. Unless your position requires extensive travel, and most do not, use your own credit card for expenses. Seek reimbursement through the normal procedures where you provide receipts for all expenditures. Having a district credit card may seem like a positive new perk. But in too many known cases, inadvertent or careless use of a district credit card for personal expenses has led to a superintendent's dismissal.

Reimbursement for meals is particularly touchy. While taking somebody to lunch at district expense may be appropriate and necessary, doing so on a regular basis is likely to generate criticism and even animosity. Questions such as, "Why don't I ever get taken to lunch?" are raised. It is even more difficult if the district has limited funds. Pay for the lunch yourself if you have any questions about whether it is reimbursable. Further, while you may believe you are honoring a subordinate by taking her or him out to lunch, oftentimes they prefer not to do so but are reluctant to reject your offer.

SUMMARY

Your transition is important to your future success. It allows the board, staff, and community to learn about you and your leadership style. It allows you to assess the strengths of the district and the challenges you face as superintendent. Listen, observe, and read. Should your district be in crisis, listening is even more critical. Remember the Chinese proverb, "A crisis is another word for opportunity."

The following points cover the major issues you face during a transition.

- Plan with equal care your exit from your current position and your transition to your new district.
- Use the transition to learn all you can about the district, while leaving the decisions to the current superintendent. Review your transition plan with your board.
- Plan your work year carefully.

- Know the questions you wish answers to and listen carefully to the responses. Do not make judgments or respond with solutions.
- Develop an ongoing list of all the issues and perspectives you learn. Use these to determine the strengths of the district and the areas that need improvement. Always build on the district's successes.
- Work with your executive assistant to gather needed materials and information. Understand the important role your assistant plays.
- Learn about the personal issues you face and how to address them.
- Commit to lifelong learning. Develop ways to achieve this.

Your transition is when you recognize the realities and complexities of the work. Some nights you may leave the district wondering why you wanted to be a superintendent. At these times remember why you accepted this position: to improve the quality of education for the students of the district. Finally, realize that no matter how hard you prepare for this change, something you did not plan on will happen. This is life. The best advice is to laugh and find humor in the situation. As the old saying goes, when you can do this, you become mature.

Getting Started

Organizing to Lead

You are now the district's leader. Your main responsibility is to improve learning for all students. To do this, build on the knowledge you gained through the transition. Use your first impressions of the district's history, values, culture, strengths, and challenges as a guide while you continue to learn.

Set high standards and expectations for staff and ensure a strong organizational structure is in place. These provide a foundation for leadership. The following overview of systems and strategies represent years of experience and the value of hindsight, "If only I had known this before I started my first superintendent position . . ." It focuses on the basics of running a school district. This is challenging work. You need three to five years to make a sustainable difference.

Adjust these recommendations to reflect the size of your district and the number of administrators and staff. Superintendents in very small districts or districts with little or no staff often feel, as one K–8 superintendent/ principal said, "we meet with ourselves." These superintendents use their leadership skills to organize teachers, support staff, parents, board members, and community volunteers to accomplish what is done by managers and administrators in larger districts.

They succeed by working closely with their boards to identify the essential work and then focus available resources on it. They work in a less formal environment, where roles and responsibilities are less bound by job descriptions and formal expectations, with "everyone pitching in." They also know when to use district resources to retain the services of outside consultants to perform tasks that require expertise not available within the district.

SCHEDULING FOR SUCCESS

1. Meeting Schedules

As superintendent you schedule meetings for others to attend and attend meetings scheduled by others. Some superintendents complain, "All I ever do is attend meetings." This is a reality of the job. The goal is to organize them so they are effective and productive.

During your transition you saw the schedule of meetings you are expected to attend and the purpose of each. These included, among others, meetings with your board, district office administrators, site administrators, parent and community groups, and union leadership. You listened to board members and key staff members discuss the effectiveness of each meeting and which were most important.

As superintendent you can maintain this schedule or make changes to reflect your style or needs. Avoid major changes until you have more experience in the district and can determine what is really needed. Sometimes the benefit of meeting with groups becomes apparent only after considerable time passes. Making changes to meeting groups may have political implications and consequences if the people or group dropped from the meeting feel slighted.

Ask for feedback from those affected by potential meeting changes. Learn when and why the meeting group was formed, its purpose, and possible consequences of meeting less frequently or not at all. Before making modifications, listen to your staff. They will appreciate this even if they disagree with the decision you make. If you do make major changes, inform everyone of your decision and why you made it.

Avoid currying favor by eliminating meetings you may need to reinstate later. Once you give up meeting dates, it is difficult to get them back. Staff will fill these now free dates with other meetings and events. If later you request additional meeting time, you appear disorganized. Staff resent last minute calls from the district office rescheduling meetings previously canceled.

How you spend your time is a reflection of your goals and priorities. Staff members observe you and make judgments. You run the risk of getting a reputation for being "office bound" if you spend more time in staff meetings than in visiting schools and classes and meeting with parents and community.

You may not have an opportunity to change meeting schedules if you start in July. Well-run districts complete meeting schedules in early spring for the following school year. Once approved, these schedules are distributed to the board and the full management team. This allows staff to avoid conflicts with their meeting schedules.

Most school districts have groups that meet on a regular basis without the superintendent. In larger districts there can be a broad array of curriculum, instructional, or administrative groups that schedule meetings. Meeting space is often scarce. Days and times for meetings are limited as teachers usually need to meet after the school day is over. Most districts designate specific days of the week for school staff meetings and district-wide committee meetings. Some districts even have these in their union contracts. It takes considerable expertise and advanced planning to eliminate conflicts and complete the scheduling process.

2. Meeting Groups and Agendas

Superintendents organize meeting groups in different ways, depending on tradition, the needs of the district, and their leadership style. Districts have differing names or titles for these groups. You want an effective, well-planned-out cycle of meetings with various meeting groups. This is crucial for the efficient operation of the district.

The schedule outlined below works well. The key to this schedule is the sequencing of meetings, not the specific weekdays. Make no changes before learning why the current schedule is in place. Build your meeting calendar around the board meeting schedule. Chapter 6 discusses in detail school board meetings, including scheduling and agenda setting.

Executive Assistant. Schedule a standing meeting with your assistant first thing on Monday morning. At this meeting, review the calendar for the week, schedule appointments, review agendas and materials needed for meetings, identify unresolved problems and problem solve, and organize what needs to be done for the board. No formal agenda or minutes are required for this meeting. This meeting helps you both prepare for the week, as well as address issues that arose over the weekend.

Superintendent's Cabinet. This cabinet is a high-level, strategic decision-making group consisting of the district's top administrators. Membership is usually small and includes assistant superintendents or directors representing instruction, student services, human resources, and business. In some smaller districts the superintendent's cabinet includes all principals. When appropriate, other administrators are invited to attend to address specific issues. Start with the cabinet you inherited. Modify membership once you are more familiar with the district.

Schedule cabinet meetings mid-morning or immediately after lunch on Monday. This allows cabinet members time to meet with their secretaries and staff, respond to weekend e-mails and phone messages, and get organized for the week. Cabinet meetings can be lengthy. Require everyone to set aside three hours and be prepared to remain longer if needed. You do not want key team members leaving before the work is complete.

This is *your* meeting with trusted staff, where important decisions affecting the district are made. These meetings are essential for your success. Set the tone. Work with the cabinet to develop group norms, including specific expectations for confidentiality. You want everyone to feel comfortable participating and expressing opinions, even if those opinions differ or conflict with yours. Once you reach a final decision, everyone should fully support the decision, and all of them should know their role in implementing it.

It is best to provide an agenda with set times for each item. Distribute the agenda the previous Friday afternoon or immediately after your Monday morning meeting with your assistant.

Superintendent's Cabinet Meeting Agenda Topics

- Any or All Aspects of Policy-Level Decision Making
- Review of Board Agendas and Requests
- Leadership Team Agendas
- Budget Issues
- School Support and Principal Concerns
- Review of Student Assessment Data
- Personnel Issues and Negotiations
- District Goals

Start the meeting with a review of decisions made at the last meeting. The agenda should include items from other cabinet members and time for them to alert you to emerging issues within their divisions. This is an excellent way to avoid surprises, the bane of all superintendents. Whatever the item, the discussion and decisions should be focused on what is best for students.

In some districts, superintendents distribute brief action minutes of these meetings to the full administrative team so the members know what is discussed at the cabinet level. These minutes usually are taken either by your executive assistant, who sits in on the meetings and provides operational support, or by you. These notes should exclude information about confidential decisions or discussions about topics such as negotiation strategies or personnel decisions. Do not share these minutes with the board, as sharing invites board members to micromanage the superintendent's work. If board members or even the press obtain copies, review confidentiality protocols with your cabinet or others who have access to these minutes.

Once distributed to staff, minutes may be accessible to the public. Do not include information you do not want made public. Board policies and state and federal laws govern the public's right to access information. Know what information can be withheld from the public and what information you must provide if requested. Normally, confidentiality applies to the sale and purchase of property, active and potential litigation, collective bargaining considerations, personnel issues, and some student-related issues. When in doubt, consult with district counsel. Understand and adhere to the applicable policy and law.

Leadership Team. Schedule a leadership team meeting once or twice a month. Participants at these meetings include the cabinet, principals, and other district office administrators you want present. Every district has its own unique name for this group. Change the name if you intend to change the role and function of the group. These are important meetings as the participants make up your team. They are the people you rely on for advice, expertise, day-to-day management of the district and schools, as well as the implementation of district policy. They oversee the primary function of the district: the education of students.

Schedule these meetings the week prior to board meetings to review upcoming board agendas. If the issues raised cannot be resolved in one meeting, identify additional time. Be respectful of the leadership team members' schedules. Additional meetings should occur when it is most convenient for them. This demonstrates respect for team members and their work.

Set the agenda for all leadership team meetings with your cabinet and distribute it in advance so members can prepare. Encourage principals and other leadership team members to submit items for the agenda. Assign someone to take minutes and distribute them as soon as possible to help guide their work and to inform those who were absent.

In smaller districts, assistant principals may attend these meetings on a regular or occasional basis. In larger districts, elementary and secondary principals may meet separately once a month and as a total group once a month. In these districts it is not uncommon for an assistant superintendent to chair the meeting with the superintendent dropping in to lead specific agenda items. Staff members who normally do not attend but have knowledge pertaining to specific items should attend the meeting in which that item is covered.

Make the meetings productive. You want principals to feel that coming to the district office for a meeting is a positive event, a time for meeting with colleagues, problem solving, and committing to the achievement of common goals. It is critical these meetings have a student-centered focus. This is an opportunity to discuss how to improve teaching and learning. Avoid crowding agendas with routine information items that are best addressed at other meetings or through e-mail.

Develop protocols to ensure everyone arrives promptly and is prepared to address the agenda items. Address confidentiality issues. As these meetings can be several hours long, refreshments are essential. In many districts, participants take turns bringing "goodies" for the group.

Leadership Team Meeting Agenda Topics

- Review of Upcoming Board Meeting Agenda Items
- Review of Board Requests From the Previous Board Meeting
- Student Achievement Strategies
- Review of Formative and Summative Student Assessment Data
- Student Issues
- Instructional Issues
- Operational Issues
- Site Problems
- Professional Development Planning
- Problem Solving
- Long-Range Planning

These meetings provide you and cabinet the opportunity to hear from site administrators and mid-level district office administrators about the possible effects of impending decisions or recommendations going to the board. They are also an opportunity to clarify board policy decisions and their impact on schools. This can result in greater site administration commitment to the board's policy decisions as administrators feel more connected to the decision-making process. In addition, you gain insights as to the effects of a proposed board decision. This helps you make recommendations to the board that are more student centered and are supported, or at least understood, by principals. It develops a greater sense of team and commitment to the district's vision.

Avoid devoting most of the meeting to operational issues best resolved by e-mail. Principals need responses to their questions and time to resolve problems involving their schools. Frequently issues are raised that may not be a high priority to you or district office administrators but are of great importance to site administrators. For example, "What process are we using to post class lists when school opens?" "Somebody please explain the new special education guidelines?" This is why meetings should be scheduled to last a substantial time, usually three hours. It is easier to let the meeting out early than to ask everyone to stay late.

Instructional Meetings. Schedule monthly meetings with site administrators devoted entirely to curriculum and instruction issues. Depending on the size of the district, these meetings may include assistant principals. Some larger districts schedule separate meetings for elementary and secondary principals. In districts with three or fewer schools, the superintendent may opt to meet individually with each principal to review specific grade-level issues.

Your scheduled principal or leadership meetings do cover some instructional issues, but usually they lack sufficient time for in-depth discussions and reviews. Instructional meetings fill this important gap.

Instructional Meeting Agenda Topics

- In-Depth Reviews of Assessment Data
- Planning Curriculum, Programmatic Interventions, or Innovations
- Aligning Professional Development Activities With District Goals
- Upcoming Curriculum Adoptions
- Addressing Instructional Technology Issues
- Resolving Common School-Related Problems

These meetings provide a more informal environment for strengthening communications between the district office and schools. They allow principals time to share ideas and experiences with peers, a powerful learning experience. Distribute agendas and minutes of these meetings to the full management team.

Depending on the district's size, these meetings may be led by the superintendent, assistant superintendent for instructional services, or a director of curriculum and instruction. If you do not lead the meeting, review the agenda before the meeting. On occasion stop by the meeting and sit in for a few minutes. Do not hesitate to ask for time on the agenda to present or review important issues. Receive an update after the meeting. This can occur at the next cabinet meeting or through minutes. Let the meeting chair know to contact you immediately if an issue arises that has substantial policy implications.

Like the budget, the instructional program is always your business. While you may delegate key aspects of instructional leadership and site support to an assistant superintendent or director, you are accountable for the district's instructional program and student learning. If you abdicate this responsibility, you risk both your success and tenure in the district.

Management Team. In larger districts, there are management positions other than site administrators and cabinet members who support the work of the district. These individuals report to cabinet members and may be coordinators, teachers on special assignment, or support staff managers. Their expertise may be in technology, special education, assessment, specific subject areas, finance, human resources, school transportation, grounds maintenance, food service, or other areas.

These managers attend principal or cabinet meetings when their specific expertise is needed. It is the responsibility of their supervisors, who regularly attend these meetings, to keep them informed about impending and approved decisions. These managers have valuable insights, and you should ensure their supervisors bring these ideas forward at meetings.

The full array of district administration is usually referred to as the *management team.* Every management position supports the core instructional mission of the district. Team members work directly with principals and teachers. They must understand the district's mission, short-term and long-term goals, and their role in achieving the mission and goals. Use your time with this group to build a strong learning organization.

In addition to the annual August retreat that includes the entire management team, schedule monthly or at least quarterly management team meetings. At these meetings review district goals and progress made to date, highlight board actions, discuss current issues, listen to their ideas, problem solve, and discuss how their work affects student achievement. Management team meetings are also excellent venues for mandatory professional development activities, such as a review of laws pertaining to sexual harassment, special education, and safety.

The way the management team interacts and builds on the strengths of its individual members is an indicator to the board and community of the health of the district. Between meetings, communicate with management team members to reinforce this message. This is discussed in greater depth in Chapter 9.

Meeting Staff at School Sites. Visiting schools is a top priority for all superintendents. It is the only way to observe classroom instruction and learn about what is actually happening in the school. Set up a school visitation calendar at the beginning of the school year. Resist the temptation to cancel or reschedule these meeting because you are "too busy."

Use every opportunity to be in schools. For example, schedule one-on-one meetings with principals at their school sites instead of the district office. This demonstrates respect for their busy schedules and your interest in their school. You learn about issues specific to that site and the work of the principal. While at the school, visit a few classrooms. Parents and staff will note that you are at their school. More about how to conduct a successful site visit is covered in Chapter 9.

Site visits provide an opportunity to interact informally with support staff. Before meeting with the principal, find the custodian and say hello. Drop by food service and greet the cafeteria workers. Spend a few minutes chatting with a library clerk, classroom aid, or school secretary. If a grounds or maintenance crew is working at the site, seek them out as well. Ask what people are doing and how things are going. Stop and listen carefully to what they have to say. Get to know their names. Thank them for their hard work.

District support staff are essential to a well-run district. They can provide important information and insights about the district and what is going on in schools. Most are loyal supporters of the district, frequently parents of children in the schools, and of course voting taxpayers. Treat them with the respect they deserve.

Support staff members are often highly educated, especially in their fields of expertise. You may be surprised that the teacher's aide possesses a teaching certificate but chooses not to teach. Do not underestimate them. They are attuned to leadership and are good barometers of the community as a whole. They are the first person visitors run into as they enter a school or the district office. These individuals are purveyors of information to the community. Demonstrate your respect for them through your communications with them.

Example

A new superintendent visited the district's "lighthouse" elementary school. He spent the morning observing outstanding teachers and wonderful student-centered programs, meeting with a deeply committed and generous parent club and an extraordinarily talented principal. As he walked through the parking lot to his car, he noticed the custodian standing next to the large metal waste bins, muttering to himself. The superintendent walked over and asked if something was wrong. The custodian then treated the superintendent to a twenty-minute lecture about a major rat infestation. These rats were in the classrooms, the play fields, and the waste containers. Were it not for the custodian, the superintendent would have not known of this health hazard.

While scheduling school site visitations, also schedule visits to auxiliary sites such as those devoted to food service, maintenance, or transportation. In some districts, superintendents rarely visit these sites. This is a mistake. Auxiliary services affect the daily lives of students. You want to see firsthand how they are managed. For example, many principals will tell you that how students are treated on the bus in the morning affects their behavior the entire day.

Other Meeting Groups. Many other meetings will appear on your schedule on a regular basis. These may include meetings with the following.

- Parent Club Presidents
- Teacher and Support Staff Union Leaders
- Management Team Representatives
- Superintendent Groups
- School Site Councils
- Community Service Groups
- Foundation Leaders
- District Committees and Councils
- Parent Groups With Particular Issues
- Special Education Parents
- City Leaders
- Groups Particular to Your District

In addition, there are meetings with parents or community members who have complaints or concerns about the schools, meetings with teachers, administrators, or support staff with particular problems, and meetings with board members.

Work with your administrative assistant to efficiently use your time. Schedule back-to-back appointments to avoid gaps in your schedule and keep to set times for individual appointments. Have your assistant inform you through prearranged signals when the time is almost over. For example, "Dr. Jones, your next appointment has arrived." Leave blocks of open time for site visits and focused work time. Schedule open time in the days immediately before and after completing board packets.

3. Annual Management Team Meetings

Management Retreat. The annual retreat is usually scheduled in mid-August after all management staff returns from summer break and before teachers report. This is one of the busiest times of the school year. Site administrators are opening schools. They are under considerable pressure checking enrollments, and finalizing class lists and teacher assignments. They also are hiring last-minute replacement teachers and support staff. Each day is important to them, so provide a meaningful retreat experience.

If your work year began in July, it is likely the retreat was planned by the previous superintendent. Ideally you reviewed these plans during your transition. However, it is possible your predecessor did not plan the retreat before leaving.

Meet with your cabinet to review or set plans for the retreat. Learn the past history and purpose of retreats in the district.

Questions to Ask in Planning Management Team Annual Retreat

- Who attends? Does it include board members?
- What is the superintendent's role?
- What is the role of district office administrators?
- Does the district use consultants? Why or why not?
- Where is the retreat held?
- Who pays for it?
- Have recent retreats been successful? Why or why not?

Your first retreat is important for you and for your management team. Everyone has high expectations and a little anxiety. For some, this is the first time they meet you. For others, this is an opportunity to impress you. People are curious about your leadership style. They want to know your expectations. What will change? What stays the same? Should they worry about their jobs or their status?

Normally, retreat dates are set in advance as part of the previous year's management team meeting schedule. If not, or as a reminder, inform your team of the retreat dates and your expectation that attendance is mandatory. Participants are responsible for arranging schedules and vacations around these dates. Avoid exceptions, unless there is an emergency or the administrator's approved work year includes an August vacation. It is more difficult to get off to a great start if key members of your team are missing.

Depending on the district and available resources, the retreat may be two or three days in length and may or may not include an overnight stay. Some districts schedule retreats in the district to save funds. If possible, and if funds have been budgeted, out-of-district or overnight retreats can be an advantage. That makes it more difficult for individuals to be pulled from the meeting, and everyone gets to know each other better in a more informal setting.

Another important consideration in planning a retreat is whether to use an outside consultant to lead or support the retreat. A consultant makes it possible for the superintendent and all team members to participate fully. A skillful consultant assists in planning a successful retreat and helps avoid pitfalls. Trained consultants debrief you and the cabinet after the retreat. They process evaluation feedback and plan appropriate follow-up activities for the school year. Only use consultants in whom you have confidence and who have experience in working with similar groups. If you have little experience with consultants, interview the one you are considering. Set the parameters.

If you are uncomfortable using a consultant or the cost is too high, conduct the retreat in house. Do not use a consultant if the district is in cost-cutting mode. Instead use this opportunity to demonstrate your leadership and professional development skills. Use other cabinet members to assist in facilitating the retreat. This sends a message to the team that you value the staff you inherited. A well-planned, minimal-cost retreat at the district office or a local business can be a smash success while a poorly planned, high-cost overnight effort with an inexperienced consultant can be a miserable failure.

Set aside sufficient time prior to the retreat to determine the proposed outcomes and activities with your cabinet and retreat planning team. Identify a theme linking the retreat activities to the district's mission and goals for the coming year. This develops support for the agenda and endorsement of the consultant or process you use. Once plans are finalized, provide your board an outline of the events and the expected outcomes of the retreat.

Use the retreat to accomplish the following.

✓ Set the tone for the year.

✓ Get to know each team member better.

✓ Lay out expectations.

✓ Conduct professional development activities.

✓ Develop management team norms.

✓ Engage in team-building activities.

✓ Problem solve.

✓ Recognize and validate the previous year's accomplishments.

✓ Provide opportunities for staff to demonstrate their leadership skills.

✓ Demonstrate your listening skills.

✓ Validate the values, interests, and concerns of the team.

✓ Revisit the district's philosophy, mission, and goals.

✓ Brainstorm ways to meet the district's annual and long-term goals.

While the retreat should be relaxing and enjoyable, the overall purpose is to further the work of the district. Retreat time is too valuable to schedule mundane administrative work or low-level staff development activities. Use it to explore big picture issues and strategic goal implementation. Focus on student achievement. Ensure that the outcomes of the retreat are defined, the selected activities support these outcomes, and everyone's assignments are clearly stated. This is easier to do if you started in mid-year and the planning is entirely under your watch.

Your first management retreat can provide you enormous benefits. It can set a positive tone for the year and unify the team under your leadership. It also can buy goodwill needed when there are bumps in the road. But if not done well, the retreat can have negative consequences, with everyone thinking "What a waste of time! I needed to be at my school." Or, "Why did the board hire this person?"

The retreat sets the stage for the monthly or quarterly management team meetings. Use it to generate clear expectations for the work of the management team and an understanding how that work ties into the effective implementation of the district goals and student achievement.

In some districts, the board joins the management team at the end of the retreat for a lunch, dinner, or some other informal social get-together. If district funds are tight, pay for this event yourself. Or seek sponsorship from parent clubs or a local business.

This can be a wonderful opportunity for the board to validate the work of the management team and get to know administrators better in an informal setting. If this is not an established practice in your district, hold off initiating it until you discuss the idea with the cabinet and leadership team. If a lack of trust exists between the board and the management team, proceed carefully. Look for other opportunities to bring the two groups together.

At the least, especially if you do not have an overnight stay, host a social at the end of the retreat for the entire management team. This can be done at the retreat site or your home. Hosting a simple event for your management team demonstrates that you value them.

Provide a brief report on what was accomplished at the retreat at the next public board meeting. Board members will have heard from team members about the retreat. Your overview validates what they heard and permits you to reinforce the work planned to carry out the district goals. This report further informs your community about your leadership skills. It helps them understand the importance of the retreat and the value of expending district funds for it.

Other Before-School Management Meetings. Schedule additional management team meetings after the retreat to review any unresolved issues raised at the retreat and to address the operational needs of the district and schools prior to opening day. Place on the agenda "nuts-and-bolts" topics not suitable for a retreat.

These are important meetings, mandatory for your full team. Allocate enough time to cover all issues, including any problems or concerns raised by site administrators. These meetings set the stage for a school year that focuses on student instruction. Inform your board of these meetings and provide an overview of what was covered.

Before-School Management Team Meeting Agenda Topics

- Finalizing Plans for the Opening Days of School for Staff and Students
- New Teacher Staff Development Activities
- Changes in Curriculum and Instructional Expectations
- Fall Calendar
- Transportation or Food Services' Concerns
- Facilities Issues, Including Summer Cleaning and Maintenance
- Changes in State Law or Board Policies
- Review of Sexual Harassment Policies and Other Mandated Training
- Changes in Union Contracts
- Changes in District Budget Due to Higher or Lower Funding
- Enrollment Review
- Filling of Current Staffing Vacancies
- Review of Operational Procedures
- Review of the District's Emergency Preparedness Plan
- Clarification of District Protocols

Clarification of protocols is important to a smooth-running organization. These include confidentiality, management team attendance at board meetings, board-administrator communications, emergency response, and work year expectations. Depending on the district, and whether administrators are represented by a formal association, there may be more. Each year these need to be reviewed and, if necessary, revised. They also should be shared with the board, so it knows your expectations.

The board needs to agree to protocols for management attendance at board meetings and board-administrator communications. While they are discussed as well in Chapter 6, these two protocols are of particular importance to you. Having management team members, especially principals, sit through long board meetings in which the discussion is only tangential to schools is a poor use of their time. If mandatory attendance for all administrators is currently in place, work to modify this. Have administrators, with the exception of the cabinet and perhaps a principal representative, present only if an item directly pertains to them. Administrators will thank you and feel respected.

Expectations for board-administrator communications are more challenging. Your administrators expect you to serve as a buffer between them and the board. They need clear direction on how to respond in differing situations. Work with the board to establish a communications protocol and share it with the team. Whatever the protocol, emphasize your need to be kept informed of communications with board members. Do not attempt to limit casual conversation between board members and staff, board participation on district committees or councils, or board attendance at events or scheduled school visits. This is normal and occurs in every district. This protocol may need to be revisited as board members and administrators change.

Protocols surrounding emergency response are discussed in Chapter 9. Review these carefully with management so everyone is aware of their mandated responsibilities and how you will communicate in an emergency. This is especially important for new administrators.

4. School Year Events

New Teacher Orientation. Most districts schedule meetings before the start of the school year for new teachers. These meetings provide an orientation to the district, including the instructional expectations. You are expected to welcome new staff, and board and cabinet members are introduced. It is a wonderful opportunity to meet new teachers and underscore the importance of their work. Following your welcome, training is usually provided under the direction of a principal or district office administrator.

Opening Day for Staff. This is an important event for a new superintendent. District staff is welcomed back for the start of the new school year.

With proper planning, opening day is one of the most enjoyable days of the school year. In many districts this is the only time during the year when all staff members are in one room. Like the management team retreat, a well-planned and orchestrated opening day staff meeting is essential for your success.

Meet with your cabinet to learn the history and traditions of opening day, as well as what is expected and appreciated by staff. Avoid changes that might offend the traditionalists in the audience. You want everyone to leave excited about you and the new school year, not complaining about the loss of a cherished tradition.

Send a welcome back e-mail or letter to everyone invited to attend. Include the entire staff, not just teachers. This requires giving specific directions to support staff and their supervisors. Remind your maintenance director that you want all maintenance, grounds, and custodial workers to attend. Do not forget to invite your school board. Depending on your district's traditions, you also may include the mayor or heads of local philanthropic groups.

Review the contractual implications of inviting all staff to this event. In many districts the work year for some support staff starts the first day of school for students. You may have to negotiate a change in their work year with their union. Or, it may require additional compensation for their time. Most unions are pleased to be invited to participate and will work to make this cost neutral.

Where funds permit, provide an inexpensive continental breakfast. In many districts, parent clubs provide the refreshments. At the least have coffee, tea, water, and juice available. Ask a middle or high school music teacher to bring a student group to sing or play while the staff assembles.

In some districts, superintendents serve as the master of ceremonies, or emcee. This provides an opportunity to demonstrate your sense of humor, personality, and style. You can engage in some light banter with the different people invited to speak to the group. In other districts the superintendent is not the emcee, permitting other administrators to showcase their talents. Either way, staff members watch what you do throughout the event.

The meeting usually includes brief welcoming remarks from the president of the school board and those of the teacher and support staff unions. Introduce board members and new staff. Some districts introduce staff who just earned tenure. Some acknowledge staff earning their twenty-, twenty-five-, or thirty-year service pins.

The superintendent's speech is the highlight of the opening day ceremony. This is your opportunity to introduce yourself to staff and let everyone know what you believe and value. This is when you validate the accomplishments of the previous year, highlight key individuals and events, and focus the attention of the staff on the goals and expectations for the current year.

Draw a thread of continuity through the speech. Start by building on the accomplishments of the past. Make students and improving their learning the focus of your words. Include an inspirational story or poem that ties into teaching and learning. This is not a lecture. You want your audience to like and respect what you say and leave the room feeling good about the upcoming school year, the state of the district, and their chosen profession.

Because your speech is critical, prepare in advance. This is not the time for casual, off-the-cuff comments. You will be nervous when introduced and you face your new board and staff. This is not the time to stutter or stammer. Be prepared!

Example

One superintendent whose opening day speeches were respected and appreciated started preparing in March of each year for the following August. Another successful superintendent presented a PowerPoint show of photos of teachers and students along with his inspiring words of wisdom.

Every superintendent has a different strategy to prepare for a major speech. Every superintendent differs in public speaking skills and confidence. Some superintendents use an outline, others read from a text, skillfully looking up at the audience, while others speak extemporaneously from memorized notes.

Plan in advance what you want to say. Then practice, practice, and practice more. The less you depend on notes the more you connect with the audience. This makes for a better speech. If you must use notes, learn the speech well enough that you only look down occasionally. Limit your comments to fifteen minutes. You want everyone to remember what you said, not how long it took you to say it.

Some districts invite distinguished outside people to speak to the staff. If this was planned in your district, do not cancel the invitation. Set aside time to speak after the guest speaker is done. Do not pass up this opportunity to introduce yourself and set the tone for the school year. If well-done, this event helps affirm the board did well in selecting you as superintendent.

Other Staff Events. There may be other events during the school year to which teachers and staff are invited. These may include end-of-year retirement parties, holiday gatherings, or high school student award ceremonies. In one district the board hosts an end-of-the-school-year barbeque for all support staff. The board cooks the hot dogs and burgers and serves everyone personally. In another district the superintendent hosts three after-school support staff meetings each year. The superintendent provides an overview of the district and then takes questions. Learn your district's traditions. If these events do not exist, work with your board and staff to create them. They build a sense of community.

OTHER RESPONSIBILITIES

1. Extracurricular School Activities

As you organize the district, include a review of its extracurricular activities and learn their role in the overall culture of the district. Most parents and educators believe extracurricular programs are essential components of a well-rounded education. These may include athletics, choir, band, dance, student publications, art, robotics, and other programs that involve students in after-school activities. The number and type of activities depend on the size of the district, its grade configuration, and available funding. Extracurricular activities and, in particular, student athletics may be of more concern to smaller districts or districts with long histories of athletic rivalries.

The level of support for different activities varies, depending on the district's history, culture, and resources. In more affluent communities, entire programs may be funded by parents through contributions to parent clubs or school or district foundations. In other communities, local community groups, including business federations, municipal agencies, or service clubs fund or sponsor programs or activities.

During times of financial distress, funding for extracurricular programs comes under fire. Parents, staff, and students who support these programs fight fiercely for them and work to obtain funds and grants to preserve them. Fund-raisers are held to support whatever programs are in jeopardy. It is not uncommon to have an audience of parents, staff, and students at a board budget meeting intensely stating their case for continued district financial support for their particular program.

Work with your chief business official (CBO) to learn the total cost of the extracurricular activities in your district. These include not only the cost for teachers, coaches, and support staff, but also the cost for equipment and supplies, upkeep of practice rooms and fields, and travel expenses. In addition, most extracurricular activities have revenues stemming from ticket sales, parent clubs, and even foundations. Some of these contributions are intertwined with the district's revenues and costs.

Example

One K–12 district pays for an elementary arts teacher for six elementary schools. The local community pays for six artists, who do not have teaching credentials, to work daily in the schools. The district teacher supervises these artists and works with them on the skills and techniques being taught. The district is known for its exceptional art program. Superintendents in that district are aware that in tough economic times reducing the one teacher would in effect wipe out the entire elementary art program.

Understanding the true cost of extracurricular activities helps you work more effectively with program advocates. You do not want to be seen as favoring one activity over another. Therefore, exercise caution before adding resources to one extracurricular activity and not another.

Also be aware of any safety issues that arise as a result of students' involvement in extracurricular activities. Most people think of athletics when the topic of safety is raised. But safety is involved in activities like journalism, where students work late at night in classrooms to complete the school paper, or in robotic competitions, where students work evenings and weekends with a teacher and interested parents to complete the construction of a project. Understand the liabilities involved. Have appropriate parent permissions, know the district's insurance coverage, and be sure that campuses are secure. Be particularly watchful of student safety when you have middle or junior high students involved in extracurricular school activities.

Superintendents who fail to understand the importance of extracurricular activities will find themselves at odds with staff, students, and community members who passionately support them. Extracurricular activities often involve teaching and support staff positions. This is particularly true at the high school level, where students are required take elective classes for graduation. In turn, these elective classes form the foundation for extracurricular activities. For example, students enrolled in band and drama classes during the school day are the same students who participate in after-school band or plays. The extracurricular activities are dependent on the classes.

The most important reason to support extracurricular activities is the link between them and student performance. For many students, their passion for the arts, robotics, journalism, or athletics is what keeps them coming to school and doing well academically. It ignites their love of learning and helps them develop good interpersonal skills with peers and adults.

Strong extracurricular programs support the instructional program and reinforce acceptable student behavior. Many students would not graduate without the support of teachers, music directors, athletic or robotics coaches, and teammates. Learn the extracurricular activities that are of importance to your community. Support these through your attendance at events. Your presence will be noted. You also will learn a lot about your community and your students by observing their work and behavior.

Student Athletics. While there are many extracurricular activities, often people think only of athletics when this topic is raised. This is especially true for districts with high schools. Superintendents whose districts include a high school often voice the opinion that their communities care more about sports than classroom instruction. While this may be an exaggeration, if your district has a high school you need to know about how to manage the athletic program.

Sports are often an important part of the culture and tradition of a school community. In some districts, especially smaller suburban ones, Friday night football or basketball games draw huge crowds. They may even be covered by radio, TV, and the print press. A strong athletic program can be a source of pride for everyone. Superintendents with high schools are expected to demonstrate support for high school athletics, including attending sporting events.

In elementary and middle schools, games are usually held after school or on a Saturday morning. Often weekend games are organized by parents or the city and do not involve the school. While these do not require your attendance, parents appreciate your acknowledgement of these programs. You can do this by attending a few events and recognizing these programs when you attend parent organization meetings.

For many community members, their connection to the sports program is their only connection to the high school or even your district. They are a vocal and committed constituency. They often provide substantial financial support to your high school's athletic program and students, as well as supporting districtwide measures. Successful superintendents learn to respect this well-organized, well-funded, and cohesive group.

Managing a high school athletic program requires close cooperation and communication between district and site administration. The major issues principals, assistant principals, and athletic directors face include safety, hiring coaches, enforcing student eligibility, resolving parent and community complaints, and participating in county or state athletic governance bodies.

Either you, as superintendent, or a designated district office administrator need to work with school staff on these issues. Whether you work directly with the program or not, keep informed about it. Be aware that board members may be involved in student athletics at the school, district, or county level. Some districts even have board-appointed athletic councils to advise the board on athletic issues.

Well-managed athletic programs engender parent and community support for the district. If not managed well, considerable time, effort, and political capital are spent responding to complaints and negative media coverage. Determine if the district athletic program works well and is governed by up-to-date board-approved policies and procedures.

Ensure that administrators and staff follow board-approved procedures as well as athletic conference standards. The procedures and standards include eligibility provisions, requirements for the training of coaches, and safety requirements. Prioritize concerns about how the procedures and standards are followed. Discuss problems and solutions with major athletic program stakeholders, including the board. If needed, develop an improvement plan.

Attending athletic events gives you an opportunity to observe firsthand if safety standards and expectations are enforced. You do not want to see a story about how badly students behaved spread across the front page of your local newspaper, with follow-up stories and critical editorials. More importantly, you do not want anyone injured. Insist on excellent preparation for each event, including good prevention strategies.

Even with these standards in place, problems may occur. You may have to make unpopular decisions involving student participation in athletic events. Even the best student athletes may do something that removes their eligibility to participate in sports. This can include a loss of academic eligibility, a suspension for disciplinary violations, or even a residence issue. In these situations, there may be tremendous pressure to make an exception so the student can participate. Sometimes parents bring their case to you or the board. While your immediate school community may resent your actions, your outside public will respect that you uphold the rules.

Example

A number of students on a top-ranked football team were caught drinking beer on the bus returning from a hard-fought game. The district suspended nine of the best players. This made them ineligible for the final league championship game. Parents and students were outraged by the district's actions and appealed the principal's decision to the board and superintendent. The district refused and the team lost its next game. Three weeks later, the district's facility bond was overwhelmingly approved by voters. Many community members said they had not planned on voting for it but were so impressed by the integrity of the board and superintendent they changed their minds.

Some schools have different sports that are their special area of strength. Learn about these for your district. Mark the important games, such as homecoming or regional championships, in your calendar and make every effort to attend. If you have multiple high schools, attend games in which your own teams are playing each other. As superintendent you probably will receive a free admission pass to all athletic events. If your athletic program is in need of additional funds, you may want to pay in spite of having this pass.

Other Extracurricular Programs. In addition to athletics, districts often have other exceptional extracurricular activities. Students participate in juried art shows, science fairs, robotics competitions, plays, choir, orchestra, speech, journalism, debate, and other events. Some of these are part of regional, state, or national events. Others may involve overseas travel to perform at invitational competitions. These events are valued and well-attended by parents and community, and they are as important to them as any athletic event. Parents and students often form clubs and sponsor events to raise funds.

Your attendance at these events and at some of the state and national competitions is crucial. Identify district programs that involve extracurricular activities. These may be at the elementary, middle, or high school level. Ask principals to inform you about class or school plays, band concerts, science fairs, school art shows, or other similar events. Send announcements to board members in the Friday packet (which is discussed in Chapter 6). Note these events in your calendar just as you do for athletic events. Attend as many as you can, especially those that are of particular pride to the community.

Visit classrooms where the training for these programs occurs. The parents of these students feel as strongly about these programs as do the parents of student athletes. Many support both programs with equal enthusiasm. These parents expect their superintendent and board members to support these programs.

Student journalism and media are also extracurricular activities. Experienced superintendents with high schools know free speech issues arise from student publications or student-produced news shows. Many states afford these publications and shows, including yearbooks, the same rights afforded public media. Other states are far more restrictive, or delegate responsibility for determining limitations to local school boards. Many new superintendents, especially those with little exposure to high school student publications, often err in adjudicating student publication or production issues as they lack an understanding of federal and state law. These mistakes can be expensive, and even embarrassing, especially when outside legal advocates take up the case and successfully challenge the district in court.

Review your state laws and district policies governing student publications and news shows. Most state and federal laws permit substantial editorial latitude for high school newspapers or shows, especially if associated with a journalism class. This means that students can take editorial positions critical of school and district administration and policies. Criticisms may cover principals, teachers, superintendents, and boards without risk of adverse consequences.

Ensure the principal and the teacher-advisor for student publications annually review the state guidelines and district policies. Work with legal counsel to make certain they are up to date. Pay attention to articles about student publications included in communications from law firms.

Finally, work with your principals to monitor the progress of all extracurricular activities. Ensure adequate funding, safety for students, and the viability of the program. In particular ensure that these programs are a complement to the instructional program.

2. Working With Consultants

The work of a school district is broad and complicated. It requires specific levels of expertise. Your challenge is to know the level of expertise of your staff and when and for what purpose you may require outside help. In using consultants, remember the following.

- ❏ Asking for assistance is not a sign of weakness.
- ❏ In some situations, not using a consultant demonstrates poor judgment.
- ❏ A consultant should be maintained or dismissed based on performance.
- ❏ The cost-benefit of using a consultant should be tracked over time.

Many people view consultant expenditures as unnecessary. Newspapers frequently carry articles or letters to the editor from irate parents, staff members, or community members complaining about the high cost of consultants for school districts and other municipal agencies. Your challenge is to demonstrate how the careful and deliberate use of a consultant assists your district and saves money. Address this by providing a clear explanation of the cost-benefit of using a consultant and the effect on the district and taxpayers if the consultant is not used. If you cannot provide a persuasive argument for the use of the consultant, then perhaps going in-house for assistance may be the better solution.

Legal Counsel. A district's most important outside consultant is its legal counsel. Many superintendents have learned that in the long run it is best to call the lawyer first rather than to make a costly error in judgment about a complex issue. Calling on outside legal expertise is a wise use of district resources. Districts are governed by state education codes, government codes, federal law, case law, and local union contracts. It is too easy to unintentionally violate the law or contracts. Districts that reduce the use of counsel to save money often find truth in the old adage, "penny wise and pound foolish." It is well worth the time and cost to seek legal assistance if a district has issues that could result in litigation.

A guiding rule for good practice is: it is far easier and less costly to do something right the first time around than to go back and fix something already done wrong.

Example

A new California superintendent was required to send layoff notices to several teachers. He assigned this role to a trusted office clerk. He assumed all that was necessary was to have the notices delivered, with the employee signing off that it was received. Just as the clerk was about to depart for this mission, she innocently asked, "Does it make a difference that I'm not an American citizen? I'm Canadian, you know." Of course, the superintendent did not know and quickly called his attorney to check. Sure enough, in California only a U.S. citizen can properly deliver a layoff notice. Had the notices been delivered by the clerk, the essential layoff action would have been invalid. This would have jeopardized the superintendent's relationship with his board and perhaps his tenure in the district.

Having counsel you trust is as important as knowing when to call for assistance. You want competent counsel that works for the district's best interests. Counsel should provide clearly reasoned and factually correct answers to both simple and complex questions. The counsel should know enough about school district operations to provide you and the board sound opinions and recommendations. If you have concerns about counsel's advice, it is appropriate to seek a second opinion.

While legal counsel is employed by and works for the board, it is usually the superintendent who recommends the continuation of the counsel's contract or recommends new counsel. Counsel cannot be retained without board approval. Some districts routinely put all legal counsel contracts to bid every two to three years. Other districts prefer the continuity of legal counsel, especially if the current legal counsel also assists with negotiations. Know the practices of your district before recommending changes.

In some districts the board has a long-standing relationship with a specific attorney or law firm. Exercise caution before challenging this relationship. Give counsel an opportunity to demonstrate competence. If you find you do not like or trust the attorney or the firm, then recommend a change. Make certain you explain your reasons to the board. Do not recommend a change just because you liked the firm your previous district used.

It is normal for districts to retain different law firms based on needed areas of expertise. The most common areas where legal counsel is used include negotiations, special education, facilities bonds, land-use issues liability suits, second opinions, and difficult personnel actions. Work with your CBO to review the district's legal contracts and the firm's specific area of expertise. Determine if any changes are needed and bring your recommendation to the board.

Keep the board informed of legal issues or challenges facing the district and the status of them. This is best accomplished during closed sessions and through confidential correspondence. In some instances, legal counsel should be present. The board makes the final decision in these issues, so make certain sufficient time is allocated for a full discussion. Check with district counsel and ensure these meetings are posted according to state law.

Do not delegate your responsibility to legal counsel to advise and make recommendations to the board on issues of importance to the district. Use counsel to help you make wise, legally correct recommendations on what is in the best interests of the district and its students. The opinions provided by counsel are just that, opinions. Ask counsel for the pros and cons of each opinion and recommendation that is made. Ask for the legal citations used to support any opinion.

While you should trust the advice of counsel, recognize they are fallible and may err on either being to conservative or too broad in their interpretation of the law. Mistakes are made. Or, counsel may not understand the political impact of a recommendation. In the end, you must determine if the recommendation makes sense. Do not allow yourself to be intimidated. If not satisfied with a recommendation, ask for a second opinion, either within the firm or with another attorney. Let your board know why you are doing this.

Occasionally legal counsel will recommend spending money to save money. This occurs in situations in which counsel believes it is in the best interest of the district to agree to a settlement rather than expend substantial human and fiscal resources to win the case. These situations include workers compensation claims, liability lawsuits, or the occasional nuisance suit. As superintendent, your first instinct is to defend the district, especially if you believe the district will and should prevail.

However, you will learn that compromise is often in the best interest of the district. In these cases follow legal counsel's advice and recommend a settlement to the board.

An important aspect of your professional development is becoming familiar with your state education code and keeping abreast of changes in state and federal case law that affect school districts. State education codes can be lengthy and a challenge to read and to understand. Fortunately, many of these codes are now available online for easier access. Review the information provided by law firms and state and national associations. All of these groups publish bulletins, often online, to keep members informed of pertinent changes in the law. Also, law firms have catalogues of past legal opinions that are available to superintendents online.

Do not fool yourself into believing that because you read the bulletins you are now a legal expert. This information simply assists you in asking better questions, weighing options, and making decisions regarding recommendations. Do not hesitate to call counsel, especially in the first few years of your tenure.

A helpful practice is to maintain a log of questions you ask counsel and the advice received so you do not have to call repeatedly on the same question. Some superintendents keep a binder of case law materials from different law firms and publications to assist in making decisions. It also helps to use sticky notes to reference key provisions in your state education code reference book.

Many superintendents give specific administrators the authority to contact counsel directly. Only key administrative staff should have this authority. This controls legal costs and ensures you know about problems that occur. In larger districts the head of human resources makes the majority of calls to legal counsel regarding personnel issues, the CBO for financial or construction issues, and the curriculum and instruction head for student issues. Principals may be authorized to contact counsel in emergencies if no cabinet member is available. Let administrators know you expect them to notify you if they contact counsel.

Many of the calls to legal counsel are on routine matters concerning contract interpretations or employment law. They require only a quick verbal or e-mail response. However, if the issue is potentially one that requires board action, request a written opinion with legal citations. In these situations, legal counsel often attends the closed session when the issue is discussed and answers board members' questions.

You are responsible for monitoring legal costs. Attorney fees are based on an hourly rate. Fees may vary for different attorneys within the firm. For example, the fee for a senior partner is higher than the fee for a junior partner. Written opinions and attendance at board meetings are far more costly than phone communications.

If your district uses legal counsel on a regular basis, ask for a defined contract that allows for a set number of legal counsel hours with additional time billed at an hourly rate. This can save the district money. Review this with your CBO. Legal counsel also can assist you and your key administrative staff on when and whom to call. Good law firms want to be cost-effective and are aware of what items usually result in problems for a district.

Without clear guidelines, legal costs can soar and rapidly exceed budgeted allocations. Conduct regular reviews of your district's legal expenditures with your cabinet and define boundaries where needed. However, sometimes the district is faced with circumstances requiring substantial expenditures for legal fees. In these circumstances, regularly provide fee information to your board.

District legal counsel is not your private counsel. Retain private counsel if you have more than just a routine question regarding your contract or other personal issues. Likewise, if the school board meets in closed session without you and the posted agenda topic is "Superintendent's Employment" you may need to retain your own legal counsel. The majority of state administrative associations and the American Association of School Administrators include access to legal counsel as part of their membership packages.

Other Consultants. Sometimes a district needs to use outside consultants to manage district construction projects, plan and implement major technology upgrades or new communications systems, conduct a strategic plan process, assess public receptivity to a tax election, oversee a district facilities bond election, develop a communications plan, negotiate health care benefits for employees, provide assistance with textbook selection, conduct staff training, or review a district's emergency preparedness. These consultants have specific expertise that can be used to address a need. Some save districts substantial amounts of money.

Example

A medium-sized district hired an outside consultant to review a district's employee health care coverage. The district saved $8 million dollars in health care costs over a six-year period by a careful review of its costs and minor modifications to plans. Insurance broker fees were renegotiated. Case review and liability insurance coverage was changed. These savings were realized through a $30,000 yearly consultant contract with a consultant trusted by both unions and management.

If you are looking for a consultant to oversee a major project such as school construction, seek recommendations from staff or other superintendents. Develop a list of firms and send out a *request for proposal* (RFP). If appropriate, create a small committee or task force to help screen candidates or firms. Ensure a thorough reference check is conducted prior to bringing a recommendation to the board. Your CBO should ensure that all state bid requirements are followed.

Review consultants currently in your district, the tasks they are performing, and the source of the funding for their contracts. Make certain these consultants are not used in lieu of paid staff but rather are used for specific, time-designated projects.

Labor union contracts and state and federal laws govern the use of consultants. For example, it is appropriate to hire a consultant to review your district's safety procedures to ensure they meet current local, state, and federal guidelines. However, if the consultant has an office at a school and works full-time for six months or more, the district's auditor may claim that the person is serving as a district employee and is subject to all state and federal employment taxes, as well as to employee benefits.

To ensure you are not hiring contractors in place of regular employees, have your CBO determine that the contract templates used by the district meet state and federal guidelines. They should specify the work to be done, the time frame for the work, and the level of compensation. Legal counsel can assist in developing these templates and keep your district from violating laws or contracts.

Some school districts retain retired employees to serve as consultants. They are given set retainers for doing work in their areas of expertise. Teachers serve as substitute teachers, curriculum writers, or staff development presenters. Administrators serve as mentors to principals, write reports for the district, or head a one-time committee for the district. In most situations their knowledge and expertise are great assistance to a district. In other instances these retainers were an incentive for early retirement or a means of padding a teacher's retirement pay. If so, the benefit to the district is minimal.

Public funds pay for these retirees. Annually review the work being done. You may conclude that this work is no longer needed or the funds could be used for a more important purpose. Review your concerns with your cabinet before making changes. You do not want to unilaterally abrogate an agreement made with a retiree before your arrival.

If the agreement was verbal, check with your board as it might have participated in this understanding. Honor all district obligations. In some situations, approach the retiree and offer to negotiate a change in the arrangement. It is important to treat retirees with respect. They served the district long and well and often have strong ties to the community, board members, and your staff.

SUMMARY

Organizing a district to lead effectively is no easy task. You need to learn how to work productively with the staff, board, and consultants. It is far too easy to get caught up in meetings and day-to-day work and lose sight of what you are trying to accomplish.

The following points will assist you in organizing the district. Realize that your organization reflects your leadership style and the work you value. Work to have that reflection be one that values student learning above all else.

- Understand the importance of developing effective meeting schedules and agendas for the various individuals and groups with whom you work.
- Plan carefully an annual management staff retreat. Use this retreat to set a tone for the district and develop group values, norms, and protocols.
- Schedule major before-school meetings and events in addition to the management retreat. How you approach these meetings and what you say can help you establish high expectations and good rapport.
- Develop a school site visitation schedule. Visits allow you to see teaching and learning in practice.
- Meet with support staff and understand the role they play in a smooth running district.
- Schedule school board meetings and develop effective agendas for them.
- Develop an appreciation of the importance of extracurricular activities in your district.
- Learn how to use consultants to assist you in areas where you or the district do not have a particular expertise.

As you organize the district, be sensitive to its traditions and culture. Only make changes you believe will have a positive influence on the work you are doing.

Moving the District Forward

4

You now have your organization in place. Effectively using it requires decision making and goal-driven accountability systems. These systems allow you to build on the strengths of the district while minimizing its weaknesses. What follows will assist you in developing and putting into practice appropriate systems and processes. Use these to move the district forward.

DECISION MAKING

Making good decisions for the district requires an understanding of how they are currently made. Start by reviewing the job descriptions of key district office administrators. Familiarize yourself with the formal and informal lines of authority and responsibility. Review the roles of key decision-making groups such as the cabinet and leadership team. In smaller districts, be sensitive to differing patterns of leadership, role differentiation, and decision making. Ask your assistant to describe how a recent decision was made and whether the process used was typical. Conduct similar conversations with board members, assistant superintendents, and principals.

Avoid making arbitrary changes in decision-making procedures that work well. Change procedures identified as slow and cumbersome, or that result in poorly accepted or implemented decisions. Determine who to involve at each stage of the process and who is ultimately responsible. Clearly delineate how you will gather information and data, how decisions will be made, and with whom and how they will be disseminated. Be aware of unintended consequences when changing long-standing procedures.

Whether or not you make changes, you are responsible for everything that happens in the district. Do not blame others for poor decisions. Accept responsibility, work to correct the problem, and move forward. While you may not have the luxury of time, you definitely do not have the luxury of making decisions without knowledge. "Deliberate with haste" when needed and whenever possible "move slowly and with deliberation."

Involve Others. Bring major initiatives to the cabinet for comment, feedback, and discussion before submitting them to the leadership team and the board.

Invite feedback from staff before making important decisions in response to problems or issues. Every decision has unintended consequences, often disagreeable. In anticipation, listen carefully to your staff's ideas and suggestions. Encourage staff, especially senior staff, to offer an adverse opinion. You want the best from each and every staff member. You are not well-served without a dialogue that includes other options and disagreement.

Incorporating subordinate staff suggestions may improve the initiative and further ensure their support. You gain by listening to the advice and wisdom of others. If you must exercise your veto authority, subordinates are more likely to support your decision if they were heard.

Serving as superintendent can be lonely; not everyone will like or even respect you. However, you will achieve greater success for students by hiring strong people and encouraging them to present their best ideas as you make decisions.

Build on the Positive Accomplishments of Those Who Preceded You. The district did not start with your arrival. Even if you follow an unappreciated or less-than-competent superintendent, do not delude yourself that nothing of value was accomplished. Often a lingering emotional attachment to prior leaders—even unpopular ones—may present challenges when moving a new initiative forward. Even the most reviled superintendents leave a legacy of accomplishment in some area. Overturning decisions made by your predecessor may revive a problem that previously had been resolved. This undermines perceptions of your judgment.

Using the power of your position to get your way may be expedient but is counterproductive in the long run. The more you use positional authority instead of processed logic and persuasion to reach a decision, the less effective your leadership will be. Use your positional power judiciously, especially when it comes to major changes.

Another negative effect of overturning decisions without careful thought is how it affects the problem-solving capabilities of staff. When you reject what is in place, staff are more likely to ask you to make their decisions or solve their problems. This may cause you to micromanage and lose sight of the big picture. This will not improve staff decision-making skills. You want them to solve problems that arise in their departments or schools, consult you as needed, and keep you apprised of their progress.

MASTERING THE BUDGET

Mastering the budget development process and understanding the details of the district budget are essential to your success as a superintendent and the fiscal health of your district. This is particularly important during fiscally challenging times. More superintendents lose their positions over fiscal mismanagement than over low test scores.

Human and financial resources are needed to achieve district goals and provide an outstanding education for your students. How your district allocates scarce resources is a reflection of your priorities. If you are committed to improving student learning, your budget needs to reflect this. In times of severe financial crisis, your district expects you to provide wise leadership and informed decisions.

A fiscal crisis may arise at any time, even after the board approves the budget and the school year starts. Provide strong leadership throughout this crisis. To do this requires a firm understanding of district finances and the ability to speak with calm assurance to the board, staff, and community about complex fiscal and financial management issues.

The budget should be readily understandable and reflect district priorities. A budget that clearly does this helps the community understand the district's values. It also helps recruit organizations to partner with the district to fill budget gaps.

Learn how the district budget is affected by local property taxes and assessments, and by the state's budget. Your board and community expect you to advocate at the local, state, and even national level about your district's financial positions and needs. Advocacy is covered in greater detail in Chapter 9.

The Chief Business Official (CBO). The CBO can be a director, manager, county employee, or assistant superintendent. This person is central to the fiscal solvency of a district and to your success. It is essential that trust and respect mark this relationship. You and your CBO are responsible for managing the district's resources and adhering to state and federal requirements. Some people believe the CBO is the direct representative of the taxpayers and responsible for ensuring the wise use of district resources. However, when a fiscal crisis is caused by the CBO, the board and community hold the superintendent responsible, not the CBO.

Many board members lack a real understanding of school finance and budgeting, and they seek advice and support from the CBO. Some are concerned they are not receiving all the pertinent financial information they need. Others attempt to influence how the CBO presents information and recommendations to the board.

Insist that your CBO meet with board members, as it is essential the board understands the budget. Have your CBO inform you of these meetings and any questions that might arise from them. This helps you understand board member concerns and issues.

While boards frequently ask CBOs direct questions in board meetings, you are responsible for communicating fiscal and budgetary recommendations. You must understand the financial issues and what needs to be done.

Some community members, union leaders, or parent club presidents ask to meet with the CBO to "review the books." These meetings may consume considerable time. Most CBOs recognize the political complexity of their role and develop a sophisticated set of survival skills.

CBOs understand how to communicate complex financial information to the superintendent, board, and community. They act responsibly to maintain the district's financial health. As a group they tend to be conservative, reporting the least favorable news regarding revenue and expenditures. They are prone to underestimating revenues and overestimating expenditures. Take this pattern into consideration when making recommendations to your board.

Encourage your CBO to speak frankly when decisions under consideration have substantial fiscal impact on the district. In turn, involve your CBO in the decision-making process. This is particularly true when the district is in the midst of union negotiations or a financial crisis.

Establish a clear understanding that whenever there is a serious concern about any aspect of the district's financial operation or long-term fiscal status, this concern should be brought directly to you. This is true even if it means calling you out of a closed session with the board to speak privately or calling you at home at 4:30 a.m. It is your responsibility, not the CBO's, to determine if the issue is sufficiently serious to warrant board involvement.

You must support and monitor the work of even the most talented and trusted CBO. It is irresponsible and potentially fatal to your tenure to delegate all fiscal management to your CBO with no oversight. Everyone makes mistakes and CBOs are no exception. However, your CBO needs the authority to manage the district budget without your day-to-day involvement. Do not micromanage.

Meet Regularly With the CBO and Deepen Your Knowledge of the District's Budget. Schedule regular meetings to review finances. Many aspects of the budget need study and attention. Review the district's general fund, including both restricted and unrestricted allocations. Restricted funds are used for specific local, state, or federally determined purposes, while unrestricted funds are used for any board-approved legal purpose.

Include in Your Budget Review

- Revenue Sources
- Planned Expenditures
- Projected Ending Balances
- Source and Purpose of Transfers, Both in and out of the Budget
- Reserves and Their Stated Purposes
- Multiyear Projections
- Audits and Audit Exceptions
- History of Unrestricted Net Ending Balance Projections
- Audited Unrestricted Net Ending Balances

Ask as many questions as needed. Your CBO should provide sufficient detail so you understand each line item. In subsequent meetings ask follow-up questions and ask to see the data to back up the answers.

1. *Review the error rate in determining the number of certificated full-time equivalent (FTE) positions generated each year.* Is your district budgeting for more teaching FTE than actually needed? If so, you are overstaffing and "hiding" funds that could be allocated for other purposes.

   A pattern of overstaffing is a cause for concern. It leads to a lack of trust between the district and employee unions. The opposite is also true. If your district consistently underestimates the number of teaching positions needed, you are likely to operate at a deficit, using scarce reserves. This undermines your credibility and the credibility of your district's budget process.

2. *Review the proportion of the general fund budget allocated to staffing costs, usually 85 percent to 95 percent.* Staffing is the largest item in any school district budget and one of the most transparent. A low percentage means more discretionary funds available to meet district goals.

3. *Review the relationship between human resources (HR) and the business office.* These two departments should work together to manage the FTE staffing numbers and expenditures, or *position control.*

Inadequate position control frequently causes districts to lose control of their budget. If the district cannot manage the number, FTE, location, compensation rate, and health benefit costs of the staff throughout the year, it is likely to greatly overspend the budget and end up in a serious budget deficit. This frequently occurs when the business office and the human resources (HR) department fail to communicate, the offices are understaffed or undertrained, technology systems are inadequate, or position control is not seen as a priority.

Ask how the district budget is modified after the board approves personnel decisions. For example, if a teacher goes on maternity leave for several months and a substitute teacher is hired to replace her, there is a resulting complicated set of budget reductions and increases.

In most districts, many such actions are approved by the board each month for both teaching and nonteaching employees. These changes must be carefully tracked. If HR fails to communicate with finance, changes are not recorded. Over time, the budget becomes less and less accurate. This loss of position control may cause a huge accounting error by the end of the fiscal year.

Work with your CBO to assess whether your district's position control meets all appropriate standards. Review the backup information for various staff-related line items in the budget. For example, if the budget shows an expenditure of $1 million for teachers, ask the CBO to justify the amount by presenting a detailed breakdown for all teaching positions showing FTE and compensation totals. The CBO should have backup data by category and even by school. Be concerned if the CBO is using rough estimates or placeholders and says the district has "always done it this way."

If important decisions are based on inaccurate financial information, the district may soon have a financial crisis. Or, the crisis may be political if the district believes it lacks sufficient resources for an employee salary increase and discovers after the annual audit that the district actually generated a large operating surplus.

4. *Review the history and purpose of all district funds other than the general fund.* Over the years your district may have established a variety of funds for differing purposes. These may include food service, facilities, deferred maintenance, technology, adult education, and

developer fees. Districts with high schools are likely to have more funds than elementary districts. Some funds are required by state law while others are established by the board for various purposes. Some funds have a specific revenue source while others are funded by transfers from the general fund.

Each fund has its own budget, including reserves. Some of these funds may have greater reserves than the general fund. Sometimes monies from one fund may be transferred to another. Normally only the board has the authority to transfer monies between funds. Learn the laws in your state governing these transfers.

Occasionally a district establishes a fund for a particular purpose and transfers monies from the general fund reserve to that fund. Years pass, board members come and go, as do superintendents and CBOs. Soon everyone in the district forgets about the fund and why it was established. Examine each fund and learn its history and purpose. Let the board know the fund is no longer needed.

Failure to manage all district resources can be catastrophic for a superintendent, especially if employee contract negotiations are challenging and the district is found to have "extra" money "hidden" in an obsolete fund reserve. This has occurred in numerous districts with superintendents losing their positions because of it.

5. *Review other revenue sources.* These include parcel taxes, bond revenues, categorical funding, foundation donations, nonprofit grants, parent club funds, local city or regional partnerships, and state and federal grants. Each of these may come with its own restrictions, including required reporting and board action.

6. *Review categorical program funds.* These are funds provided by the state or federal government for specific programs. These funds have very specific guidelines on how the funds are to be spent. States monitor district expenditures and adherence to the guidelines. This may limit district flexibility.

Some states have few categorical programs. Others have many but let districts group the programs into blocks for greater flexibility. It is critical to learn how categorical funding is allocated in your state and how it can be used.

The cost of operating categorical programs may exceed their revenues, causing a program deficit. When the general fund absorbs the deficit this is called *encroaching on the general fund.* Carefully track and monitor these funds. The board should approve each encroachment as part of the annual budget development process.

As a new superintendent, insist on a careful accounting and identification of all these encroachments.

Special education is the largest categorical program in most school districts. Special education students make up approximately 10 percent to 12 percent of the student population. These students face challenges ranging from mild to severe. School districts have a federally mandated responsibility to meet the needs of these students from preschool through age twenty-two. The cost of providing for a special education student can range from a few hundred dollars per year to more than $100,000.

These costs are partially covered by special education funding from the federal government and the state. The district's general fund makes up the difference. The amount of the local contribution to the general fund differs from school district to school district. The amount is usually substantial due to the lack of full funding by the federal government. Most districts contribute about 80 percent of the funds needed to support the program. Many districts enter into cost-sharing agreements with neighboring districts or their county. However special education is structured in your district, you need to be familiar with the programs and how they are funded.

The district administrator charged with the responsibility for the special education program must work collaboratively with principals, special education parents, and the CBO to provide a cost-effective educational program. Whatever the costs, the needs of these students must be met.

In some districts this creates a rift between the parents of special education students and those of regular education students. Some regular education parents feel their children receive a less-than-adequate education due to the proportionately higher expenditure of district resources for special education children. In turn, some parents of special education students claim that their district fails to meet the standards outlined in federal statutes. Recognize that these competing priorities and interest groups represent a political minefield.

Avoid conveying an impression that the special education program or students are a burden to the district. In some districts, the general fund contribution to support special education services is referred to as an encroachment rather than a contribution. *Encroachment* means "taking away from" while *contribution* denotes "giving to," a positive act. You want your community to take responsibility for the education of all students, not just the students who are high-performing or relatively less expensive to educate.

If you become superintendent in a district with a less-than-outstanding special education program, or where negative attitudes prevail, address this issue and provide the leadership needed to turn things around. This is true for all programs addressing the needs of a specific group of students, such as gifted and talented or English language learners.

Mandated Budget Deadlines and Reports. Every state has mandated budget deadlines and reports. Learn what reports and deadlines are required by your state and district. As an example, in California the following reports routinely appear on the board agenda calendar.

❐ Adoption of the Coming Year's Budget (June 30)

❐ End-of-Year Review of the Current Budget (June 30)

❐ Review of Unaudited Actuals for the Prior Year (September 30)

❐ Review of First Interim or Current Year Receipts and Expenditures (December)

❐ Adoption of Audit Report for the Previous School Year Budget, Along With Any Needed Recommendations (December or January)

❐ Review of Second Interim Budget Report (February)

❐ Preliminary Budget Discussions for the Coming Year (March)

The cycle of reports then begins anew. These reports are provided for all district funds, and the board receives monthly budget updates in their official board meeting materials packets. Chapter 6 discusses the contents of board packets in detail.

Schedule special meetings with your CBO to review each report before it is submitted to the board. Use these meetings to monitor revenues from local voter-approved tax levies and bond expenditures, donations or unexpected one-time expenditures, and substantial increases or decreases in general fund expenditures. Use these meetings to solidify your understanding and mastery of the budget process and fiscal condition of your district.

New superintendents often find the budget process daunting. Even experienced superintendents are frustrated by budget issues. It is important that you attend fiscal workshops and other budget-related professional development activities. Every state has organizations dedicated to helping district administrators and board members better understand the complexities of school finance. These organizations retain experts to review fiscal issues and prepare daily bulletins for superintendents and CBOs. They are helpful if you are having a particular problem with your budget or with your CBO.

Example

One new superintendent was in difficult negotiations and could not convince the CBO to support a pay increase of 3 percent even though the district had a 12 percent reserve and revenues to fund the raise. The board was reluctant to accept the superintendent's recommendation for the raise. The district faced an impasse and a possible strike over this issue.

The superintendent scheduled a meeting with the CBO and the director of a state finance association. The director reviewed all the district's budget documents and identified additional unallocated funds. He then informed the CBO that without this raise the district would likely end up in arbitration and be forced to give 6 percent.

As a result of this meeting, the board made funds available for negotiations, contracts were settled, and the new superintendent earned the respect of the board and unions. The new superintendent also learned how to better read the district budget.

Make certain board members are well-informed about fiscal and budgetary matters. Encourage them to attend fiscal workshops, especially new board members. Whenever possible, you or your CBO should attend with them to respond to questions that arise about your district's budget and fiscal circumstances.

Budgets are finite no matter how well-managed. Often superintendents have programs they believe make a significant difference in meeting the district's goals but for which there is no funding. They turn to their CBOs and ask them to "find" the money. One CBO famously responded to such requests by saying "the money is not lost, it just isn't there."

Knowledge of projected revenues and expenditures allows you to look critically at current expenses to determine if funds can be reallocated to programs you believe are more essential to meeting the district's goals. It takes time to learn, but without this knowledge you cannot even begin this process. You are responsible for knowing the limitations of the budget and the flexibility within it. With this knowledge you can better serve the needs of the students.

IMPROVING TEACHING AND LEARNING

Your primary responsibility as superintendent is to improve teaching and learning. Learn as much as possible about your district's instructional program. Schedule meetings with the cabinet members responsible for curriculum, instruction, and assessment. In smaller districts, principals and teachers assume these roles. Larger districts may have an assistant superintendent for curriculum and instruction and an assessment director.

Include principals in these discussions. They are central to what occurs in the classrooms.

Questions to Ask Regarding Teaching and Learning

- How is the curriculum developed and selected?
- How is instruction monitored and improved?
- Do the current district and school goals focus on students attaining high levels of achievement? If not, why not?
- What student assessment data is used? Is it disaggregated by student, grade level, subject, and classroom?
- Is student assessment data used to make decisions about instruction and teacher professional development?
- How are teachers and administrators being held accountable for student achievement? Is teacher and principal evaluation based on student performance growth?
- Are teachers and principals trained to use data, build on student strengths, and differentiate instruction?
- Is instructional time at the schools respected and interruptions kept to a minimum?
- How are resources allocated at the school and district level to support teaching and learning? Does the budget reflect student learning as the district's priority?
- Does the curriculum foster critical thinking and creativity?
- Do students enjoy learning? Do teachers build on student interests?
- Are teachers and principals trained on how to use technology to support student learning? Do they understand how students gather, analyze, and share information?
- Is the curriculum based on state standards? Are instructional materials standards driven?
- Are principals expected to visit classrooms and observe and assess the delivery of instruction?
- Are professional development programs linked to student performance?
- Do board policies support teaching and learning?

Use the information from these discussions to determine areas of strength as well as areas of needed attention and improvement. Work with your leadership team to identify priorities for change. Use these priorities to determine district goals. These discussions send a clear message that teaching, learning, and high levels of achievement for all students are your priorities.

1. Using Assessment Data

During your transition you reviewed student assessment data. Now, working with your instructional leadership team, examine that data in greater depth. Include the following in your examination.

- ❒ The Performance of Each Class on Assessments by Grade and Subject Level

- ❒ The Performance of Students Disaggregated by Ethnicity and Socioeconomic Status

- ❒ The Performance of Cohorts Over the Past Three Years

- ❒ The Number of Transfers or Dropouts Within These Classes of Students

- ❒ Subtest Data to Determine the Strengths and Weaknesses of Students in Particular Areas

- ❒ Any Trends That the Data Yields

Work with the available data. Identify what is missing and plan to obtain it. If needed, ask your local county office or state department of education for assistance. These agencies may, for a nominal fee, disaggregate the data for you and chart any trends.

Some districts hire outside consultants to assist in managing, analyzing, and interpreting instructional data. Larger districts employ a director of assessment. This support is especially important if your district uses an instructional data management software program. Other districts train principals and teacher-leaders for this purpose. The goal is to have people on staff who can help teachers and principals use assessment data to inform instruction at individual student, classroom, and school levels.

Test publishers offer a variety of standard formats for presenting assessment reports. They provide additional reports for a fee by grade level, school, and individual teacher. Only order what you need. Start with reports that principals and teachers are comfortable using. Purchase additional reports when staff members become more competent and knowledgeable in the use of data. While these additional reports may cost the district more, they are an invaluable resource to you and the instructional team.

Work with your principals to review how they and their teachers are using student performance data. Ideally the previous year's teachers use end-of-year assessments as summative data while current year teachers use the assessments as formative data. The data should inform decisions on how to improve instruction for individual students, classes, grades, or subjects. This presupposes that the data is received prior to the start of the school year or shortly after opening. It also assumes you can manipulate the data to identify returning students.

Example

One high school principal took the data from each year's assessments and divided it by subject area, flagging returning students. Department chairs were given data pertaining to the subject areas tested. Decisions were then made on how to build on the strengths of the current year students and improve instruction. Departments also reviewed end-of-year teacher tests. Where no state assessment data was available, the departments met prior to the start of school to discuss the performance of the students.

The above is an excellent example of data-based instructional decision-making practices. Work with your instructional leadership team, principals, and teachers to spread these good practices throughout the school district. During your discussions, use the following questions as guides. These questions build off of the earlier examination of the data, looking at it from a different perspective.

Questions Regarding Student Data

- Do we have enough data, by student, classroom, and grade level, to make assumptions about student performance and needed instructional changes?
- What other data do we need?
- If the data shows discrepancies between gender, ethnic, socioeconomic, or other subgroups, what factors may contribute to this? Are there classrooms where subgroups flourish?
- What do the students at each grade level seem to do well? How do we build on this information to improve instructional practice?
- How do we present this data to teachers and to parents?
- What are the implications of this data for teacher training and accountability?
- Do we have a cadre of teachers within each school that can develop instructional models around this data?
- Does the district have the necessary technology infrastructure to support this process? If yes, do teachers and principals understand how to use the technology?

Some districts administer assessments beyond those required by the state. They either develop their own or use assessments from organizations like the Educational Records Bureau (ERB). The advantage of using outside assessments is that you can benchmark your students against students in similar districts across the country. Further, many of these tests inform instruction. Parents in high-performing districts often demand this additional type of testing and benchmarking. This additional data better informs your district's instructional decisions.

Example

One high-performing district determined that their upper elementary grade students were underperforming on writing assessments. Middle school teachers complained that incoming students were not prepared for rigorous writing. The district began using ERB's writing assessment program (WrAP) that asks students to write essays in response to prompts. The writing is then examined on six separate traits. The assessment showed the need for deeper work in word choice and sentence structure. Elementary teachers focused on these areas and used writing practice programs available from ERB. As a result, elementary and middle school writing performance improved considerably, with few complaints. And the district now had benchmarked data for teacher and parent use.

Some districts are exploring computer adaptive testing, in which students are directed to specific types of questions based on their performance on a small set of introductory questions. While this type of testing is new and used primarily in math, it is being perfected and likely will be used widely in a few short years. It will provide teachers with a good snapshot of each student's needs for individualizing instruction. The challenge will then be individualizing the instruction for that student.

Keep abreast of this and other cutting-edge work. Districts throughout the country are employing new and innovative strategies to use data to inform instructional decision making and accountability. Race to the Top is working toward regional and national testing that will assist with this. The goal is to empower teachers to improve the performance of students at every level of instruction, with a particular emphasis on lower performing subgroups.

2. Driving Student Success

You are the instructional leader, responsible for making certain that all children in your district learn at the highest possible levels. You have assessed the strengths and weaknesses of the instructional program and are preparing to use this information to set improvement goals for yourself, your staff, and the district. This is a crucial task, one that requires high levels of competence, information, training, and perseverance.

Once these goals are set, you must drive the change process, working with your board, leadership team, and staff to implement the changes needed to strengthen teaching and learning. While you can delegate many aspects of instructional leadership, you may not delegate the ultimate responsibility for driving student success.

You must model instructional leadership with your staff. If you focus on instructional issues at cabinet and leadership team meetings, your principals will do the same at their staff meetings. If you schedule one-to-one meetings with your principals to discuss student performance data, they are likely to do the same with teachers, teacher-leaders, and department chairs. If you visit classes to observe instructional strategies, your principals are likely to do so as well.

To be an effective instructional leader, keep abreast of what is happening in the field. While you cannot be expected to be an expert in every area, you should know the right questions to ask, how to best expend resources, and how to hire the very best people. Read, attend conferences, and discuss these issues with your board and leadership team and fellow superintendents.

For example, the current literature on modes of student learning is rapidly expanding. Researchers recognize that many new factors influence learning. Much of this is due to students learning and socializing in ways unfamiliar to most adults. Technology has irrevocably altered how young people interact with their environment. We must change how instruction is delivered if we expect students to pay attention or learn. For example, the book *Disrupting Class: How Disruptive Innovation Will Change the Way the World Learns* (McGraw-Hill, 2008) can lead to discussions that challenge assumptions about teaching and learning.

Online classes are another avenue to explore. Current estimates indicate that over a million students are enrolled in them. This number is expected to jump upward of ten million students within ten years. Work with teachers and principals who use this technology to provide courses for students who would otherwise not have the opportunity to take them, due to rural isolation or low enrollments.

GOAL SETTING AND EVALUATION

Goal setting and evaluation are additional factors essential to moving the district forward. Goal setting allows the district to focus its work on the core mission of educating students and to effectively and efficiently direct resources to those needs. It allows the board and superintendent to say yes to demands and expectations that support district goals and no to those that do not.

During your transition, you reviewed background materials to fully understand the district's goals and how they were developed. These materials included district policies defining the goal-setting process; district mission, philosophy, and belief statements; the board-approved strategic plan, if available; and board-approved district goals. Now you must use these important systems to move the district's work forward.

1. Strategic Planning and Long-Term Goals

Most districts engaging in a strategic planning process use a broad-based community involvement model. Normally, strategic plans cover a five- to seven-year period, with an annual review for mid-course revisions. A strategic planning process usually includes a review of the district's philosophy and mission statement. These statements reflect the district's values and drive its work. Today, most mission statements define expectations for teaching and learning.

Strategic planning provides a unique opportunity for a district to look at its performance and the long-range needs of its students and direct its resources to meeting these needs. It is a time to envision new directions. The global issues facing this generation of learners demand new ways of interacting, working, and living. Our finances, environment, academic priorities, and communications are all intertwined. Schools must prepare students for this future and examine not only what is taught but how.

At the end of the strategic planning process, the board adopts long-term district goals. Student success should be the cornerstone of whatever goals are adopted. Each long-range goal may have several subgoals. These goals drive the work of the district. Depending on issues facing the district, long-range goals may areas address the following.

- ❏ Instruction
- ❏ Student Achievement
- ❏ Student Services
- ❏ Staff Relations
- ❏ Finance
- ❏ Facilities

❏ Professional Development

❏ Technology

❏ Governance

District long-term goals should have wide distribution and visibility. Some districts include them in their policy manual or archive them with board agenda materials. Other districts print the goals on all board agendas, frame the goals and hang them on the walls of the board room, or post the goals in each classroom.

Most boards expect a new superintendent to engage in a strategic planning process. This occurs even if long-range goals are in place. It allows you and the board to work together to redefine the long-term goals. This sets the foundation for accountability and high expectations, two key ingredients for student success.

Boards expect superintendents to use their leadership skills to forward the district's mission. They want high standards for teaching and learning for all students—regardless of race, ethnicity, or socioeconomic status. To achieve this, many boards adopt "nonnegotiable" goals with clearly delineated standards for student achievement and include teacher and principal accountability measures. The strategic planning is the framework for this forward movement.

A thorough strategic planning or long-range goal-setting process takes about eighteen months. The board is involved in all steps of this process.

Steps in the Strategic Planning Process

☐ Planning for the Process
☐ Determining Constituencies and Their Representatives
☐ Assessing District Needs and Emerging Issues
☐ Engaging in the Approved Process
☐ Adopting the Goals
☐ Developing Action Plans
☐ Providing Resources Through the Budget Process
☐ Agreeing on Assessment Procedures, Including Indicators of Success

---

Due to the importance and complexity of developing clearly defined and attainable goals, most districts employ outside consultants to support the strategic planning. In some districts, experienced consultants from private industry donate their time or provide assistance at reduced rates. Other districts seek foundation grants to support the process. Venues for holding the needed events may be donated along with supplies.

There is a plethora of information on how to complete a strategic plan from both state and national administrative and board associations. Use this information, as well as contacting other trusted superintendents for the names of consultants who did a great job for their districts.

2. Annual District Goal Setting and Evaluation

Goal setting and evaluation are interconnected. The district has long-term board-approved goals. Your annual performance goals are based on the district's goals. You are evaluated on how well you achieve your goals and meet the expectations of your job description. Your performance goals include achieving the board-approved district goals identified above and achieving personal performance goals.

In turn, you evaluate administrators on their annual performance goals and how well they meet the expectations of their job descriptions. Their annual goals reflect the expectations of the district's goals and the particular needs and expectations of their areas of responsibility. This is reviewed in greater depth later in this chapter.

Depending on the board and district practice, each goal statement should include the following.

- ❏ A Statement of the Goal
- ❏ Standards to Measure Achievement
- ❏ Resources Needed to Achieve These Standards
- ❏ An Outline of Implementation Activities
- ❏ A Timeline
- ❏ An Assessment Process, Including Specific Measures of Success
- ❏ A Determination of Who Is Responsible for Achieving the Goal

These expectations apply to both district goals and performance goals for you and your management team.

Eighteen-Month Planning Process. Goal setting and evaluation are key components of what we refer to as the *eighteen-month planning process.* When followed, the process moves the work of the district forward and can ensure good planning and validation of work performance.

Learn the normal sequencing of this process and make certain the steps are followed within reasonable periods. You may need to modify this sequence in your first year. The normal sequence follows.

Charting the Eighteen-Month Planning Process

When	Who	Task
January	Board	Reviews the district's mission, philosophy, strategic plan, and long-term goals and affirms or initiates changes.
February	Superintendent	Recommends next year's district goals.
February	Board	Adopts preliminary next year district goals.
Spring	Superintendent	Reviews preliminary next year district goals with management team.
Spring	Admin Team	Develops action plans with budget support for next year's goals.
By June 30	Board	Completes superintendent evaluation based on current year district goals and superintendent performance goals.
June 30	Board	Reviews preliminary recommendations for your next year's performance goals.
June 30	Board	Approves next year's district goals with action plans.
June 30	Board	Approves next year's budget with resources to support district goals.
July 31	Board	Finalizes superintendent's evaluation goals.
August	Superintendent	Meets with cabinet members to finalize their performance goals.
August	Superintendent	Conveys overall direction of district to district staff at annual back-to-school meeting.
September	Superintendent	Completes performance goal-setting process for all subordinate administrators.
Ongoing	Superintendent	Provides ongoing support to staff for goal implementation.
January	Superintendent	Conducts mid-year performance review with all administrators.
January	Superintendent	Reports to board on progress to date on meeting district goals; recommends changes as needed.
January	Superintendent	Meets with board for mid-year performance review.
Jan./Feb.	Superintendent/ Board	Initiates process anew for following school year while completing process for current year.

Your cabinet should participate in preparing and presenting the reports noted above. While the reports are submitted under your name, the information provided reflects the work of the entire staff. Always identify the support staff responsible for major aspects of the work and acknowledge them in the reports. This is an excellent growth opportunity for them. It also demonstrates how you delegate responsibility.

The eighteen-month planning process provides for sequential planning. It also provides staff an opportunity to plan for the coming year by developing action plans and directing resources to meet these goals.

3. Superintendent Evaluation

Performance Goals. It is essential that you and the board agree on what the board expects you to accomplish, especially during your first year. The first step is to review your job description to make certain you and the board agree on all provisions. If not, work with the board to change it. Do this as soon as possible.

The next step is to set your performance goals. Performance goals are established each year as part of your evaluation process. They are confidential and approved in closed session. They include meeting district long-range and annual goals. They also may address confidential topics such as collective bargaining, personal professional development, resolution of management team issues, targeted administrative supervision, board-superintendent relations, and staff evaluation issues. These goals may reflect concerns raised during the interview and the transition process, as well as issues the district faces currently.

Goals can be confusing. Long-range district goals are broad visionary directions usually included in the district's strategic plan. District goals are set by the board as part of the eighteen-month planning process and serve as direction or targets for the district for the year. Superintendent performance evaluation goals are confidential goals identified by the board and superintendent.

Plan Your First Year's Goals. During your transition, you reviewed district goals and action plans prepared by the previous superintendent. If they were approved by the board, you may decide to recommend modifications to these goals based on your transition report and feedback from your cabinet or leadership team. Or, you may accept them as approved. Either way, use these goals as the basis for developing your performance goals for the year. Meet with the board as soon as possible to review them.

If no district goals were approved during the spring, as is frequently true when superintendents leave a district, work with the cabinet to identify district goals for the year. Then meet with the board and present your recommendations. These will be based in part on the goals from the prior year and your assessment of district needs based on your transition report. Review your recommendations with the cabinet before submitting them to the board. Once the board approves district goals for the year, present recommendations for your personal performance goals.

In both scenarios the board can accept, reject, or modify your recommended performance goals. These changes may be based on their assessment of your strengths during the hiring process, your performance during the transition, or new information or concerns raised by the community during the hiring and transition process.

Not all boards are comfortable with superintendents recommending their performance goals. In many districts the board dictates the superintendent's performance goals. Explore this during your transition before submitting your performance goals. Irrespective of who proposes the goals, the board has the final word. Boards usually provide greater autonomy for goal setting over time.

What to Include. Some performance goals lay the groundwork for future success. Work closely with your board before finalizing these. Following are some examples.

- *Increased Student Achievement.* Recommend a thorough review of student assessment data to find areas of underperformance. Develop a plan to identify the causes and how to systematically reverse them.
- *Collective Bargaining.* Identify goals for improving relationships with your employee groups. Address unresolved problem issues from past negotiations, such as the need for nonadversarial bargaining or revising the teacher evaluation system.
- *Administrative Supervision and Evaluation.* Identify any administrators about whom the board has concerns. Commit to a focused assessment of their performance, intensive supervision, and a timeline for recommending changes.
- *Personal Professional Development.* Provide strategies to address issues or concerns raised by the board about you and your background during your interviews and transition. Review expectations and the purpose of conferences or coaching.
- *Governance.* Provide strategies to work with the board to address issues raised during the interview or transition, such as the need to shorten board meetings or increase communication between the board and the staff.

Some Words of Caution

1. Err on the side of having fewer rather than more performance goals. Do not set yourself up for frustration and possibly failure by committing to more goals than you can reasonably achieve.

2. Work with your board to establish priorities and, if necessary, move less essential performance goals to the following year. This permits adding a new goal or two during the school year to address any new challenge that might arise, such as an unanticipated fiscal crisis.

3. If the board wants the majority of your performance goals to focus on your management style instead of achieving the district goals, you may need to work with the board to delineate your respective roles. This is an important issue.

   Example. One well-known and respected superintendent's contract stated that he was solely responsible for staffing decisions. Yet the board continuously criticized how he made staffing decisions and wanted to set goals concerning how he staffed. They parted company within eighteen months.

4. If you have difficulty coming to an agreement on your performance goals, consider that your board may have some doubts about your performance, or the board lacks cohesion in its vision for the district. If this occurs, suggest to the board that you bring in a consultant to assist in this process.

Once your performance goals are approved, you can move forward with confidence as you and the board are in agreement as to what you should accomplish during your first year.

Mid-Year Evaluation. Your evaluation process should include a mid-year evaluation. This is particularly helpful if your relationship with the board starts to unravel or new board members join the board. The mid-year evaluation can be informal, but should include a written report with recommendations for improvement if the board deems any aspect of your performance as less than satisfactory.

Provide the board a confidential progress report delineating your accomplishments to date in implementing your performance goals. Indicate what remains to be done for each goal. This provides you and the board an opportunity to discuss any issues and challenges that may have arisen or new challenges you are facing. Set aside substantial time during a closed session to fully discuss your performance.

Some boards schedule more frequent meetings to discuss the superintendent's performance. This may be due to a number of reasons, such as a desire to discuss controversial issues in closed session, a need to closely monitor the performance of the new superintendent because of an unsatisfactory experience with the previous superintendent, or concerns with the new superintendent's performance.

Monthly or quarterly closed sessions to evaluate the superintendent raise questions for staff and community. If this occurs during your first year, you may wish to seek outside assistance to resolve problems with your board. Chapter 6 discusses superintendent-board relationships at greater length.

End-of-Year Evaluation. As with most aspects of the superintendent's job, your final evaluation requires advanced planning. Review the expectations of the evaluation process with the full board in February and March and set evaluation dates for May or June. Most final evaluations require at least one closed session, or in some instances up to three separate ones for the board to meet to deliberate, write the evaluation, and meet with you to discuss the evaluation.

In some districts, board members travel extensively for business or personal reasons, making it difficult to identify dates in May and June when all board members are available. Insist that the board adhere to all steps in the process and all board members attend every evaluation meeting. You want the voice of each member heard so you can best meet the needs of each board member and the board as a whole.

Example

A board member failed to participate in a superintendent's evaluation process because of a family reunion. She returned in time to discuss his contract extension. The board member raised doubts about the extension due to concerns she had about how the superintendent addressed his goals. The superintendent was not even aware she had concerns.

Review the process with your board chair. Two weeks in advance, send the board the materials needed for the evaluation. Answer any questions individual board members have about the process. This is especially important for new board members.

Depending on your agreed-to evaluation process, the board completes the final evaluation of your performance by the end of June. Most superintendents provide the board a detailed written report outlining, goal by goal, what was achieved during the year. The more detail you provide, the more information the board has to make an informed judgment. Some superintendents provide the board a spreadsheet so members can assess their performance on each provision of the job description.

Schedule a closed session with sufficient time for the board to review board member perceptions and determine what the full board wants to communicate. Normally, the board chair writes the evaluation, reviews it with the other board members, and gives you the final version. Your executive assistant prepares the report.

Review the evaluation and meet with the full board to discuss it. This is important as you benefit greatly from hearing directly from board members. In some districts the final written evaluation is completed after you meet with the board. This is preferable as it is difficult to change an evaluation once it is finalized. It also allows for more dialogue. A copy of the evaluation is signed by you and the board chair and then placed in your personnel file. You have the right to attach a written response to the evaluation.

Let the board know you appreciate its work in preparing the evaluation and value their validations, comments, and recommendations for improved performance. Pay close attention to what the board communicates in the written evaluation and says in the follow-up meeting. Use their comments and feedback as guides to your continued professional growth and development.

Base next year's personal professional development goal on the recommendations made by the board.

Do not attempt to second guess the board to determine if recommendations represent the opinion of all board members or only one or two. Treat each recommendation as though it received the endorsement of all members. Remember, a majority of the board had to agree on the evaluation and its recommendations.

Unsatisfactory Evaluation. If your evaluation includes areas of less-than-satisfactory performance, develop an improvement plan outlining the specific steps you will take to bring your performance to a satisfactory level. In these situations it is appropriate and beneficial to schedule more frequent meetings with the board to review your growth and performance.

If you receive an unsatisfactory evaluation, contact a private attorney or a representative from your state superintendent organization and seek guidance on how best to respond. Do not hide. Do not write a response. Take no action. There may be substantial consequences to you and your career. You need support and independent advice on how to proceed. Chapter 10 provides more detail on how to address negative evaluations.

4. Administrator Evaluation

Administrators are evaluated on meeting the expectations of their job description and their own personal performance goals. The administrative evaluation process is a powerful tool for recognizing excellent work, motivating higher performance, and moving the work of the district forward.

Evaluations are a powerful accountability tool. You can use the evaluation process to identify weak performance and motivate improvement. You also can use evaluation materials to support promotions, dismissals, or reassignments.

As with district goals, administrators should develop actions plans for each approved goal. These action plans illustrate how the goal will be achieved and measured. They also provide a road map for how the district will achieve its goals.

Review Evaluation Procedures. As a new superintendent, review the district's administrative evaluation process to learn how it works. Review the previous year's performance goals and evaluation reports for all members of your management team. These reports provide valuable insights on how the goal setting and evaluation process was conducted by your predecessor. Confer with trusted cabinet members to determine how your predecessor used the evaluation process.

As noted earlier, the district goals and your performance goals serve as the basis for the performance goals for members of your cabinet and management team. Goals for district and site administrators reflect the applicability of these goals to their particular responsibilities.

Focus Areas for Administrator's Goals

- Student Performance Goals Linked to Assessment Data
- Program Development Goals Linked to District Goals
- Site and Department Goals Linked to District Goals
- Personal Professional Development Goals
- Personal Professional Development Goals Based on the Prior Year's Evaluation
- Supervision Goals
- State Standards
- Budget and Fiscal Management

In some instances, cabinet members bear full responsibility for the implementation of a particular goal. Meet with them and set their goals based on this work, as well as your expectations for their position, their areas of strength, and areas needing improvement identified in their most recent evaluation. Use this same process with principals.

Be aware that principals and cabinet members may have started implementing action plans and expending resources based on decisions made by the board and the previous superintendent before you arrived. Take this into account as you set their goals and action plans.

Try to limit the number of goals to no more than five. In some instances, goals can be multiyear. Student performance, professional development, and supervision goals should be annual goals. Keep a copy of the performance goals of all administrators in a work file in your office. Each administrator and supervisor should maintain a copy as well. Unless required by agreement, policy, or state law, these statements do not require placement in the administrator's personnel file.

Cabinet members and principals should use this same process with administrators they supervise. This allows for clarity and continuity of purpose throughout the district as everyone moves together to meet the established board direction.

The best time to set the performance goals for key members of your cabinet is in late June, July, or early August prior to the August management retreat. This gives them time to plan for their work for the following year before the principals and teachers return to work.

Principal performance goals are best finalized after the August retreat and the start of school, usually by late September. This gives principals time to review last year's student assessment data. However, after your first year, preliminary goal setting can take place in May or June during your annual evaluation meetings. You can finalize the performance goals in September, after the opening of school.

The evaluation process includes formal meetings during the course of the year to review the progress made in meeting the performance goals.

- Set goals in August or September.
- Conduct a mid-year review in January or February.
- Conduct the formal evaluation in June.

The June summative evaluation is signed by both the superintendent and the administrator. This document is filed in the person's confidential personnel file maintained in the HR office.

Avoid delegating the total responsibility for evaluating principals to a subordinate. In larger districts, provide performance feedback to the administrator charged with the evaluations. It is helpful to gather data for the evaluation from the key district office administrators. For example, ask the CBO to comment on how principals manage their budgets.

Schedule one to three regular meetings with each principal at his or her site. Use those meetings to review the principal's goals and the needs of the school. The focus should be on what the principal is doing to improve teaching and learning at the school. If you determine the school is not meeting student needs, follow up with clear suggestions and needed support. Carefully monitor the progress of the principal and students. Validate improvement.

Visit classes and ask questions about what you observe. Schedule time to meet with teachers, parents, and support staff. Observe how the principal interacts with students. Examine the principal's office.

Example

A superintendent learned there was a deep gulf between a principal and staff by observing the layout of the principal's office. It faced the playground and classrooms, with many windows for viewing. However, the principal's desk faced away from the windows and the blinds were always closed. The principal resigned after one year. Staff and parents expressed concern that the principal seemed indifferent to the students, parents, and staff.

In June, read and review each evaluation, including those of mid-level managers, coordinators, and assistant principals. You need to know how members of your management team are performing and how well they supervise their direct reports. Your board will want to know who is performing well and who is not.

Do not change an evaluation written by a supervising administrator. If you have concerns about someone's performance, meet with the supervisor to review your concerns before that person meets with the administrator. You do not want to undermine the supervisor's authority.

If your work year began after the administrative goal setting for the year, meet with each of your direct reports to review performance goals. If needed, recommend changes to meet your expectations. If there are no performance goals, meet with each administrator. Ask them to identify what they are working on for the year. Use their self-identified goals, along with their job description, as the basis for evaluating their work. Do not skip an evaluation cycle unless you began work after April.

If No Process Is in Place. Establish evaluation procedures if none are in place. Determine if administrative evaluation is addressed in board policy or administrative regulation. Review pertinent state law as well. Determine the past history and practice of your district's evaluation process.

Unless restricted by state law, board policy, or prior agreement with a district-recognized administrator group, you may have the legal authority to implement a process unilaterally. However, it is better to work with your administrators, listen carefully to their needs and expectations, and develop a process that works for all parties. Whatever the circumstance, developing and implementing an evaluation process must be a high priority.

Many superintendents require administrators submit a portfolio as part of their evaluation. This provides evidence of the work done to meet the performance goals and action plans. Proceed with care if you intend to introduce this new practice. Your team must understand why you believe this is important and what needs to be included in the portfolio. This can be threatening to administrators and principals, so they will need your support and encouragement before fully embracing this idea.

Other superintendents and boards insist on a data-driven evaluation process, with standardized tests and other assessments used to measure achievement goals. Some principals find this intimidating. You must demonstrate how the effective use of data drives sound instructional decision making, rewards excellence in teaching, and motivates students to higher levels of achievement. Work with your board, teachers, and principals to address concerns about performance-based accountability. The current Race to the Top program includes similar provisions.

Ideally, every administrator should have an annual review. However, in many districts and in some states, evaluations are only required every other year, except for first and second year administrators. If given the choice, opt for annual evaluations as most administrators serve at the discretion of the board and benefit from close communication and feedback on their performance.

An important issue regarding administrator evaluations is whether you should share the results of the evaluations with the board. Review board policy, any agreements with the management team, applicable state law, and prior district practice before sharing. If you have questions about what is permissible, check with legal counsel.

The board expects you to keep them informed about administrative performance. Keep the board apprised of the status of the evaluation process throughout the school year. Bring issues of less-than-satisfactory performance to the board. These discussions must be in closed session and properly noticed.

Inform the board how you provide support to administrators identified as performing at a less-than-satisfactory level. Boards fully expect all staff to be treated well. The more informed the board is of your concerns and what you are doing to support the administrator, the more likely it is that the board eventually will support your recommendation to dismiss or reassign the administrator. No board likes to be surprised at the last minute with a recommendation to remove an administrator. Last minute recommendations are the ones that are most frequently rejected by boards.

In some districts, bonuses are given for excellent performance when the administrator has been in the current position for three years or more. In other districts, movement on the administrator salary schedule is governed by the evaluation. This can mean not receiving a step increase until performance reaches a satisfactory level or having the board approve a double step for exceptional performance. Make certain you are aware of these practices as you begin the evaluation process.

Whatever process you use for administrators' evaluations, you may determine administrative changes are needed. The information you have gathered will assist you in documenting why the change needs to occur. It can help individuals improve their performance as well. Administrators can be mentored and their talents used to improve the education of students. Changes in administration are discussed in greater detail in Chapter 5.

SUMMARY

As superintendent, you are responsible for moving the district forward. It is a cycle of continuous improvement with each year building on the successes of the previous one. During your first year it is critical to set in place the elements for this forward movement. Of primary importance is the focus you place on teaching and learning. This can only be achieved through good decision making, goal setting, and evaluation processes.

The following are the major points you need to consider as you make plans to move a district forward.

- Learn how decisions are made in the district. Review management job descriptions and the formal and informal lines of authority and responsibility.
- Involve others as you make decisions. Validate and build on the positive accomplishments of those who preceded you.
- Work toward developing a culture of "no surprises."
- Master the district's budget. Understand how it drives the instructional program.
- Understand the relationship that exists between human resources and business departments and the importance of position control.
- Focus on teaching and learning in the district by gaining a thorough understanding of the district's curriculum and instructional policies and practices.

- Learn how to use assessment data to improve teaching and learning in each classroom.
- Keep abreast of changes in modes of student learning. Learn how to effectively translate this knowledge into strengthened district instructional policies and practices.
- Understand the role goal setting and evaluation play in moving a district forward. Review the district's strategic plan or long-term goal-setting process.
- Set annual district goals and ensure evaluations are based on achieving those goals.
- Prepare for your evaluation as superintendent by understanding the board's expectations and performance goals. Learn how to respond to evaluations.

Effective decision making, goal setting, and evaluation procedures assist you in your work. They help you establish clear lines of responsibility and accountability, as well as focus the district on its mission of improved student learning.

Completing Year One, Planning Year Two

A Continuous Cycle

Planning for the future and transitioning from year to year is a never-ending process of continuous improvement. There are no time-outs. The work of the current year lays the foundation for future years. You build on the strengths of the district and your accomplishments while addressing the district's weaknesses. You use the eighteen-month planning process to set goals, allocate resources, design and implement strategies, assess progress, and revise goals once again. The cycle continues from year to year.

Preparing for your second year is challenging. While you are still learning the job, familiarizing yourself with the district and working tirelessly to achieve the current year's goals, you must start planning for succeeding years. Do not think that next year will take care of itself or that it is merely a repeat of the first. Effectively planning is the only way to achieve the district's long-range goals.

In addition to preparing for next year, there is work to complete before the school year ends and you take summer vacation. Again, what you do during the next five months affects what happens over the next few years. This is also the time when you think about where you want the district to be in the next four to five years. The greater your clarity of expectation, the more likely you will achieve success.

This chapter focuses on how to develop your personal long-range goals while ending your first year as superintendent and planning for the second.

DETERMINING YOUR LEGACY GOALS

You accepted the superintendent position based on a set of beliefs and assumptions about the district. Once hired, you started learning about every aspect of the district's climate, culture, functions, and operations. You may have inherited a set of district goals, or even a strategic plan, from your predecessor. Or, you may have led the board and the district through an attenuated goal-setting process for the current year. In either case, these goals were based on your understanding of the district and its short- and long-term needs at that time.

Since becoming superintendent, your understanding of the district has changed, perhaps substantially. You have a clearer sense of what works and what does not work. You understand the board and its expectations for you and the district. You better understand the board's individual and collective strengths and weaknesses. You have made inroads with your employee unions. You have worked closely with your cabinet and the leadership team. As with the board, you understand their individual and collective strengths and weaknesses.

You are now familiar with the district budget and finances, and you are thinking of how to better use resources to achieve district goals. You have delved more deeply into the instructional program for students and have greater clarity as to what is needed if all students are to achieve at the highest levels.

Now step back and carefully reflect on where you want the district to be in the next three to five years. This is a personal visioning process driven by your need to lead the district forward. As district leader, you want a clear vision and a plan for achieving it. If you do not know where you are going, you are unlikely to get there, or anywhere.

Successful superintendents plan three, six, eighteen, and sixty months ahead. They know decisions made today affect where they want to be at the end of this school year or the next. They see their work as part of a giant, multiyear complex jigsaw puzzle. Every piece is carefully placed to build the whole. Successful superintendents do not make random decisions; they make decisions consistent with the board's expectations and their personal plan for the district.

Ask Yourself

- If I leave the district at the end of five years, what do I want to have accomplished?
- If I leave earlier, what can be accomplished?
- How will the district be better at the end of my tenure?
- How will my actions improve teaching and learning?

Consider all aspects of the district in answering them. Some guiding areas of focus include the following.

✓ Do current instructional practices support student learning?

✓ Does the district have high expectations for all students and strong accountability to support these?

✓ Is the instructional program effective? If yes, what should we continue doing? If no, what must be changed?

✓ Does the district need a bond to upgrade student facilities or build a new school?

✓ Does the district need a parcel tax or other stable source of funding for increased revenue?

✓ Should the district be looking at a foundation to assist with revenue for student programs?

✓ Does the board function effectively? If yes, how should I support its work? If no, what steps must I take to improve its work?

✓ Does the district have infrastructure systems in place that support our work, or must there be substantial changes?

✓ Does technology support and provide instruction?

✓ Are district and employee relationships working well? How do we need to improve our relationships?

✓ Does the district office need reorganization?

✓ Do I have the right administrative team, or must I make changes?

✓ Do current state or federal mandates assist or hinder the district's progress? If they do not assist it, is there anything that can be done to either modify them or better work within their frameworks?

Your responses to the questions above will help you identify your legacy goals. Limit yourself to five or six.

For example, your district may have a board-approved goal that states, "By the end of five years, our students will have increased their performance in math and reading." Your private legacy goal may include a standard to assess this goal. "English language learners will improve more than 20 percentile points in standardized tests in math and reading." Or, another legacy goal might be, "By the end of five years, the district will have passed a bond measure to fund the full modernization of all the science labs."

Legacy goals drive your work. Place them on your computer or in a notebook. Review them frequently. They inform the district's strategic planning and goal-setting process.

The district's formal goal-setting process also informs your personal legacy goals. For example, if your board approved an annual goal of a 2 percent increase per year for English language learners, you know it will be a great challenge to achieve your personal goal of 20 percent over five years. This information helps you further refine your work with staff and the board; you need to expand their vision for improving student achievement.

Every superintendent leaves a legacy, regardless of whether they develop personal legacy goals. Everyone remembers what you did, or did not do, for the district. You want to be remembered for your accomplishments. You do not want to be remembered as the "superintendent during the big strike" or worse, with "When was he here?" Identifying your legacy goals helps you shape your tenure into something you can be proud of long after you leave.

Revisit your legacy goals on a regular basis. In Chapter 10, this topic is addressed from the perspective of an experienced superintendent.

PLANNING THE FINAL SIX MONTHS OF THE SCHOOL YEAR

In January, in addition to developing your legacy goals, identify what needs to be done before the end of June. You want to successfully meet your performance goals and end the year well. You also must take some actions to make a smooth transition to next year. While some of this work appears routine, it is crucial to your long-term success.

1. Review the Eighteen-Month Planning Process

The steps of the eighteen-month planning process were introduced in Chapter 4. Now, at mid-year, work with your executive assistant and cabinet to plan for the completion of any remaining steps in the process. Plot out due dates based on scheduled board, cabinet, and leadership meetings. Determine if additional meetings are needed. Delegate responsibilities to your cabinet. Pay particular attention to next year's budget development and district goal action plans. Everyone should know what is expected to complete all the steps.

2. Determine Mid-Year Adjustments to District Goals

It may not be possible to meet all the district goals for the year. Changes in the internal and external environment may have affected the availability of human and fiscal resources. Substantial challenges may have arisen after the goals were approved.

Meet with your cabinet to review the action plans for each current district goal. Identify challenges not included in the district goals. Place the work in priority order. Identify activities that will not be attempted or completed. Repeat this process with your leadership team.

Bring recommendations for changes in district goals to the board as part of your mid-year goal report. Where appropriate, in closed session, recommend changes in your performance goals. The board approves any mid-year adjustments to district goals or your performance goals.

Once changes are approved, clarify performance expectations with your leadership team and any affected administrators. Your team will appreciate your clarity, especially if you have recommended mid-year changes based on principal requests.

Your personal legacy goals guide you throughout this mid-year planning process. For example, if one of your legacy goals is to improve student math performance, you are not likely to recommend a delay in the implementation of a new math curriculum or text. More likely you will agree to delay the implementation of some other noninstructional goal instead.

3. Address Changes to the Management Team

Normally, the makeup of your management team will change between your first and second year. Some administrators retire, move on to other districts, or return to a nonmanagerial position. In difficult financial times, positions may be eliminated.

You are responsible for assessing the competence and suitability of individual administrators. Provide each administrator an opportunity to demonstrate competence in the job. Most administrators strive to show the new superintendent they are competent and even indispensable. They are aware that the potential for job loss or reassignment is greatest with changes in district leadership.

You also may find that the district goals call for skills and knowledge not previously required. Your standards and expectations may differ from those of your predecessors. You may have inherited underperforming administrators on a performance improvement plan or administrators who resist your leadership or cannot or will not perform even with substantial guidance and support.

You may discover a recent hire is not working out as intended. It may be someone you promoted or reassigned from within or someone you hired from outside the district. It also may be someone you worked with in a previous district. Sometimes someone is not a good fit for the district or the position. Other times the person may not have as good a set of skills as you first thought. Whatever the reason, do not hold on because it was your hire.

Example

A new superintendent in a high-performing district hired an assistant superintendent from outside the district to replace a retiring and highly regarded assistant superintendent. It was a disastrous hire for the district from the start. Principals met and voted "no confidence" due to his performance and interaction with them. This vote was presented to the superintendent, who chose to ignore it based on a past working relationship with the person. Needless to say the superintendent's tenure in the district was shortened.

Based on your ongoing supervision, the mid-year evaluations, and your review of your team's work, you may decide to recommend administrative changes for the coming year. Share your concerns with the board before taking action. This is crucial as your board may have strong feelings about individual administrators—good or bad.

Superintendents beginning their tenure in July have about eight months to assess their administration before notifying administrators of a change in assignment for the following year. Superintendents who begin mid-year normally have little time to make these assessments. In these situations, check with the board, as the previous superintendent may have initiated changes the board continues to support.

You learned how individual board members and the board as a whole view your management team and individual administrators through the interview process, your transition meetings with board members, and comments made during closed sessions. Some board members have loyalties to particular administrators and may resist making changes. Others expect you to make changes and even direct you to make a particular change.

Ultimately, you determine the composition of your team based on your values, standards, perceptions, and judgments. Recommend changes when needed. It is untenable for the board to hold you responsible for achieving the district's goals when key administrators are not performing.

In most districts, the board must approve changes in organization and administrative assignments, particularly if your recommendations increase costs. Carefully process proposed administrative changes so the board understands, accepts, and supports what you are doing. Bring your recommendations to the board as early as possible, giving the board substantial time to deliberate. You may need to schedule several closed sessions before the board is prepared to make a decision. Boards do not appreciate being rushed to make decisions that may have substantial political impact for them, you, or the district.

This is especially important when individual administrators have served a long time in their current position, are well-known, and have community support. Sometimes the least competent principal has a legion of supporters. As with any major change, expect resistance. Board members are helpful in anticipating the political consequences of administrative changes.

Some superintendent contracts include provisions giving them full authority to make changes in their management team without board approval. Even with this authority, fully inform your board about the changes you are making and why.

Each state has differing requirements for changing administrative job assignments, including horizontal moves, demotions, and dismissals. These requirements can be quite complicated. Different laws, policies, and procedures may apply to assistant or deputy superintendents, principals, managers, and directors.

In addition to state law, many districts have approved policies or agreements with their management group that further define the rights of individual administrators and the process required for demotions, transfers, or return to nonadministrative positions.

Guidelines to Follow When Making Administrative Changes

- Work closely with legal counsel and adhere to state guidelines, procedures, and statutes.
- Meet district policies and approved management agreements.
- Keep your board informed. It is easier for board members to approve changes if they fully understand the circumstances.
- Take action sooner rather than later. The more you try to accommodate an incompetent person, the more difficult it is to make the change and the more everyone suffers.

> Example. In one large district, a superintendent waited more than three years to release a highly placed administrator who was an alcoholic. Excuses were made, work was distributed to others, and the administrator in question began to backstab the superintendent. By the time the person was terminated, the administrator's drinking problem had worsened. Intervening sooner may have assisted the administrator in dealing with his alcoholism and assisted the super-intendent in working more effectively within the district, rather than always working around this person.

- Assume that any forced change will engender resistance. Every administra-tor has a following.

One of the most difficult responsibilities you have as superintendent is to terminate, reassign, demote, or ease into retirement an administrator who is not performing up to your expectations and district standards. Only the most heartless superintendent fails to recognize the impact of the deci-sion on the administrator. These decisions are even more difficult when the person in question is kind, warm-hearted, well-meaning, and popular with staff, parents, and students.

This responsibility does not get easier over time. You learn early on in your career that changing the status of an administrator affects you and the organization. A dismissal or reassignment reminds members of the management team that you and the board have power over their lives. Your management team may treat you with greater deference. Teachers and support staff may comment about the lack of trust in the district. They may state or feel, "If this could happen to Joe, it sure could happen to me."

In some situations, the public and the management team recognize that the individual was not performing well in the job and appreciate that the change was made. They were watching to see if the new superintendent "had the guts" to do something.

A poorly performing administrator weakens your ability to move the district agenda forward. In addition, there is a cost to continuing to employ a poorly performing administrator. In times of scarce resources, when districts are eliminating positions or reducing important services, an administrator performing at 50 percent of capacity is a waste of 50 percent of her or his total compensation costs. If an administrator's total compensation is $150,000, working at 50 percent capacity is a loss of $75,000, or the cost of a full-time teacher.

More often than not, administrators and the public are not aware of the reasons why the change was made. They only guess. Frequently the decision to dismiss or reassign is made for a number of differing reasons that are not readily apparent. In almost all situations, regardless of how poorly you or the board thought the administrator performed, some good things were accomplished and some students and staff were helped. Rarely can you expect universal approval for your action.

While most administrators accept the decision to demote or dismiss them and move on with their lives, some do not. Even when you make every effort to support the administrator and provide opportunities for improvement, an administrator may perceive the change in status as personal or vindictive. In many instances they fight back by taking their situation to the public.

As the dismissal or reassignment of an administrator is a personnel action, in most states neither you nor the board is permitted to comment on the reasons in public. The administrator and their allies can stand before you and the board at a public meeting and challenge the decision and criticize your leadership. You and the board can only respond by saying "No comment—this is a personnel action." If you do provide details, the administrator could sue you or the district for defamation of character.

Example

At the superintendent's recommendation, a board agreed to terminate the employment of a principal. The main reason for the decision was consistent poor judgment exercised by the principal in working with parents, students, and staff. The superintendent received numerous complaints and worked with this principal for two years, providing counseling, guidance, and support. The principal failed to improve. Notified by the superintendent of his impending termination, the principal chose to go public.

> This resulted in a series of board meetings packed with angry parents and staff criticizing the board and the superintendent for their decision. People expressed their gratitude to the principal for his many kindnesses. Both the board and the superintendent assumed that everyone knew that the principal was performing poorly. Those supportive of the decision did not attend the board meetings. All they could do was sit and listen.

Even if you follow all legal procedures and board policies, the administrator can file a grievance or even a suit against you and the district for wrongful termination. You can be accused of discriminating because of race, religion, gender, or sexual orientation. The newspapers can write stories and editorials critical of you and the district for dismissing or reassigning the "wonderful Mr. Jones."

Experienced superintendents, reflecting back on what they have learned over the years, frequently cite the failure to remove inadequate administrators as one of their biggest mistakes. There are arguments for giving the person another chance. Many of these center on avoiding internal or external political consequences or on the mistaken belief that "with one more year of help the person will improve." In almost every instance, giving them one more year proves counterproductive.

The harm a person may do to the organization or students during that year far exceeds any political harm the superintendent or board may incur as a result of the dismissal. If you are questioning what to do about an administrator, simply ask yourself the effect this person is having on the improvement of teaching and learning in your district. You need the best people you can find to move the instructional program forward for every student. If those people are not present, you need to find them.

Work with and support administrators struggling to meet your standards. Provide assistance, but maintain your expectations. If a person is retiring or moving to a new district, celebrate their accomplishments. If someone is demoted or leaving due to a forced resignation, provide what support you can within the law. Treat everyone with dignity.

Filling Vacancies. Conduct a thorough review of the district hiring procedures before filling a vacancy. Each district uses a different process based on tradition, board policy, or management agreements. Decide the role you wish to play in the process. Depending on the size of the district, some superintendents manage the process for all administrative hires, while others delegate the responsibility. Some districts have elaborate posting, screening, and interviewing procedures involving a broad spectrum of staff and community. The most important piece of the process is recruiting exceptional candidates.

Whatever the process, meet with the finalists prior to making a recommendation to the board. You have the right and the obligation to make the final determination. Do not recommend a candidate who is not a good fit or who fails to meet your expectations. It is far better to repeat a search or appoint an interim than to hire the wrong person.

Example

One superintendent who rejected a finalist was told by the assistant superintendent for human resources that not hiring the person was a mistake. The superintendent requested the assistant to do more reference checking on specific issues that had emerged during the final interview. If these checks were good, then the superintendent was willing to reconsider her decision. A week later the assistant superintendent reported that the candidate had been released from two previous positions and was about to be released again due to poor performance.

Review all proposed changes to the district hiring process with your cabinet and management team. There may be long-standing reasons for the current process. Avoid demeaning the existing practice, as most of your administrators were hired using it.

Make certain the district provides an orientation and training for all newly hired administrators. A carefully planned introduction to the district or a new position results in a far more productive employee. This orientation provides an opportunity to clearly delineate the district's vision and goals.

Determine if Changes Are Needed in the Administrative Organization. An important challenge for new superintendents is determining if and when major changes are needed to the organization of your district administration. This includes managers, directors, and other district-level employees. This is especially important if the board, staff, or community have expressed concerns about the administration.

Most new superintendents gather information in their first year and recommend changes in their second. This is due to the amount of work to be completed in the first year, your lack of familiarity with the staff, and the political consequences of making changes. Only proceed with a major reorganization if there are compelling reasons to do so, such as the following.

- Many Vacant Positions
- Ongoing Issues of Confidence in the Administrative Staff
- Required Reduction of Administration Due to Budget Cuts
- Substantial Criticism of the Size of the Administrative Team

Under these circumstances, recommend an administrative audit be conducted by an outside consultant. Administrative audits are discussed in Chapter 10.

4. Set Calendars, Dates, and Meetings

In the spring of your first year, a number of important planning decisions must be made for the following year. As noted in Chapter 3, many of these activities were already planned when you started your tenure. Now you are now responsible for overseeing all of them.

Vacations. In January or February, starting planning your summer vacation. Every superintendent needs some time off, preferably away from the district and the day-to-day demands of the job. You may be tempted to skip a vacation at the end of your first year because you feel "way too busy" or that the "district needs me here." Do not fall for the temptation. You need to get away. This is as true now as it was at the start of your tenure last June.

If you have a family, you owe them time as well. A week sitting on a beach can do wonders for even the most hardened workaholic. What you do is modeled by others. If you elect not to take a vacation, others in your district office might think this is the new norm. A workaholic district office is not healthy for anyone. People who are regularly overtired make mistakes.

Work with your cabinet to develop a summer vacation schedule that ensures at least one higher level district office administrator is present or immediately available throughout the entire summer. You never know when an emergency will arise. If you have summer school or are in the midst of a large construction effort, you must have someone in the district.

Most superintendents also require cabinet and leadership team members to provide telephone numbers or e-mail addresses where they can be reached throughout the summer, no matter how distant they may be. The days of the quiet summer with little happening in school districts is long gone. Emergencies occur that require the immediate attention of principals and district office administrators. These individuals may have information necessary to resolve an issue before it becomes a crisis. In some situations, especially those involving special education and student discipline, deadlines and timelines are statutory and make no exceptions for summer vacation. Be sure you also leave your phone number and e-mail.

Ensure the vacation schedule brings administrators back to work in time for the August management retreat, which was discussed in Chapter 3.

Meeting Calendar. As a new superintendent, you probably inherited your predecessor's meeting calendar. You now set the calendar based on your needs and experience in the district. In February or March, have your administrative assistant prepare a draft calendar showing the days, dates and times of all cabinet, leadership, and management team meetings. Share the draft with the cabinet. Include projected dates for other important meeting groups. Then share the calendar with your full leadership team, make modifications as needed, and have your assistant distribute a final version. Many districts now develop this calendar using interactive online software programs. Share this calendar with the board.

Management Team Work Calendar. In March or April, review next year's work calendar with your management team. Clarify dates for the start of their work year, as well as the dates of the management team retreat and summer meetings. In larger districts, you may not find a date that includes all members of the team due to differing responsibilities and length of work years.

Management Retreat. Building on what you learned during your first retreat, begin planning in March or April for next year's. Form a small volunteer committee to assist with this. The committee should represent the management team. Starting the retreat planning process early allows you to secure the services of desired speakers or consultants and to secure a good location for the retreat. Use the guidelines discussed in Chapter 3.

Occasionally, administrators ask permission to miss the retreat for some personal reason.

Example

In one district, a middle school principal wanted to take her high school daughter away to a cheerleading camp for two weeks; another wanted to take a three-week cruise to an exotic location. Both promised to make up the days during the school year.

The challenge is that you need everyone to attend the retreat but do not want to appear callous to the needs of your team. To avoid this dilemma, plan the dates as far in advance as possible. Inform everyone of your expectations for attendance. It is appropriate to say no to those asking for exceptions. Administrators have opportunities for vacations and should plan accordingly. Be consistent.

Starting the new school year without your full team may lead to problems later in the year. When key staff miss out on a retreat constructed to further the work of the district, it is difficult or even impossible for them to catch up with everyone else. They will not have shared the same information, engaged in the discussions around the upcoming work to meet district goals, or met the new administrators. They will have an incomplete sense of your expectations.

However, there is a caveat. Sometimes not making an exception will cost you more than making an exception.

Example

The parents of a long-term, highly successful principal invited their entire family to take a two-week cruise in August to celebrate their fiftieth wedding anniversary. This was a one-time, extraordinary event. While the superintendent could deny the principal the right to attend, he was concerned that the team would find him rigid and unfeeling. He understood that leaders must exercise wise judgment and he gave permission to the principal to attend.

End-of-Year Cabinet Planning Meetings. In April, schedule end-of-year meetings with your cabinet in June. Use these meetings to finalize the current year's work, validate cabinet members' accomplishments, plan for the management team retreat and opening of school, review next year's district goals, and determine goal-setting meeting dates. Ideally, host the meeting in your home and provide lunch. These end-of-year meetings provide an opportunity to meet with district leaders in a more relaxed setting to problem solve and further strengthen your team.

Next Year's Board Meetings. In April, recommend next year's meeting dates for board approval. Events frequently occur at the end of summer that substantially affect the district and the opening of school. You want board members in attendance at these meetings as their decisions may be crucial to the success of the school year. If necessary, change meeting dates to accommodate trustee vacations.

Many boards avoid July meetings. Yet you may need to schedule an emergency or special meeting to approve construction contracts, hire staff, or respond to new legislation. Your executive assistant should track trustee vacation dates, locations, and phone numbers so you can contact them to schedule a meeting. Some districts schedule a July meeting with the expectation that the superintendent will cancel if the meeting is not needed. A majority of the board must attend these meetings to make a legally binding decision.

Board Workshop. Schedule a workshop in August before the management team retreat. Use this informal meeting to review district goals and action plans, affirm or finalize your performance goals, review plans for the retreat, and introduce newly hired district administrators. Discuss unanticipated changes in enrollment or revenue projections and possible staffing changes. This workshop provides an opportunity to review events on the state level that may affect the district. It brings the board up to date and prepares them for the start of the school year.

5. Prepare for Student Promotion and Graduation Ceremonies

You are expected to attend student promotion and graduation ceremonies. If you have many schools in your district, attend as many as possible in your first year and rotate attendance the next year. This is particularly important if you have more than one high school. You also want board members to attend these events. These ceremonies are of great importance to the students, staff, and parents.

Normally, middle school and high school principals are responsible for planning graduation exercises. Some districts also have kindergarten promotion ceremonies or fifth or sixth grade transition ceremonies to middle school or junior high school. The elementary school principal organizes these events, working with the parents and teachers.

If you learn that a school's graduation ceremony is problematic, share your concerns with the board. Meet with the principal early in the school year to review tradition and your expectations. Work with the principal to develop a graduation improvement plan. Unfortunately, in some districts a wild ceremony is a long-standing tradition. Changing it involves considerable effort as you have to change community values that support the inappropriate behaviors.

In some districts it is traditional for the superintendent to give a speech at the high school graduation. In others the superintendent's role is to hand out diplomas or do nothing more than attend and sit on the stage. Many superintendents prefer a passive role at graduations as they wish principals and students to be in the limelight. Here are some helpful guidelines.

- Learn your graduation role early in the year and add all graduations to your calendar. Ask board members to attend graduation ceremonies as well.
- If you are asked to give a speech, find out what is expected. You do not want to spend weeks preparing a twenty-minute oration only to find out at the event that you were allotted five minutes.
- If you give a speech, keep in mind that the purpose of the graduation is to honor the students and parents. It is not a time to lobby the community for a facility bond to build a new gym or to expound educational theory.
- Clear your calendar for several days prior to the end of school and graduation. This is particularly important if your district has a high school. High school students have a tendency to go down to the wire in meeting their graduation requirements. Some just do not

make it. Or students find a senior prank too tempting to ignore. This places them in a disciplinary situation, barring them from participation in the graduation events. Parents appeal to the principal, then the superintendent, and even to the board, if allowed. This process is emotionally wrenching for all involved and takes considerable superintendent time to resolve.

Your high school and district should have policies and procedures for adjudicating these challenges. If not, work with the principal, parents, students, and staff to put them in place. Everyone should know the rules governing graduation eligibility and attendance at the prom, senior breakfast, or other graduation-related activities.

Even when these are in place, no superintendent can ignore desperate and hysterical parents who have just been informed that their child has lost an appeal and will not be "walking down the aisle" as expected. No matter how tight your schedule, of necessity you will meet with these parents.

Your End-of-Year Reflection. At the end of your first year, set aside quiet time for reflection. Reflect on your legacy goals. Identify your accomplishments and consider your goals for next year. Look at the big picture and consider how your work improved the lives of students. Quietly celebrate your accomplishments. Think ahead to your well-deserved vacation and the challenges ahead. You are now a second year superintendent.

SUMMARY

Just as you feel you are getting started in your new position, planning for the next school year begins. Work in a school district is a continuous cycle, with each year building on the preceding one. This planning involves assessing what is working well and what needs to be changed. It is integral to success, as nothing happens by chance. The achievement of district goals and improved student learning depends on effective planning.

The following major points will assist you as you begin this planning cycle.

- Understand the importance of setting legacy goals for yourself and the process to use.
- Learn what you need to do during the last six months of the school year to prepare for the coming year.
- Assess the strengths of your management team and determine if changes are needed for the coming year. Meet all formal and legal requirements.

- Assess existing hiring procedures and implement changes as needed. Realize you make the final determination about which candidate to bring to the board for approval.
- Set calendars in the spring for the coming year, including dates for the August management retreat and cabinet and all other routine meetings.
- Work with the board to establish the following year's board meetings.
- Establish vacation schedules and ensure that the district has adequate coverage at all times.
- Prepare for student promotion and graduation ceremonies.

Once you complete a full year as superintendent, you have a better understanding of the ongoing management cycle. You also have systems and staff in place to face the inevitable challenges that arise. At the end of each year, take the time to reflect on what you have achieved and what you want to improve. Use these reflections to refine your legacy goals.

Working With a School Board

Working effectively with a school board is a challenge every superintendent faces. Learning this skill allows you to use the systems you developed to meet the district and your legacy goals. Begin by learning your state's laws governing school board operations. Develop strategies to work with the full board, factions of the board, and individual members. The school board is your employer. A simple majority can reject your recommendations or remove you from your position. While each chapter addresses a piece of this unique relationship, a complete overview sets this work in context.

Members of a school board, or trustees, are elected by the community or appointed by a mayor. Successful boards and their superintendents recognize the primary functions of the board are to set policy, to approve and oversee the budget, and to hire and, if necessary, fire the superintendent.

Boards serve as a public face to the communities that elect them. They use this position to promote and support the work of the district. They only have authority when a majority of the members are in agreement and an action is taken at a regularly scheduled board meeting in adherence to prescribed state laws. Board members have no legal authority outside a board meeting.

In a number of states over the past few decades, school funding shifted from the district to the city, county, or state. This shift diminished the authority of local school boards, causing unintended consequences. In effect, mayors, city councils, legislatures, or governors often mandate how district funds may be expended. This power comes at the expense of the authority of local school boards.

In turn, with their traditional authority usurped, local school boards may view their role as that of a superintendent. Some micromanage their districts at the expense of the superintendent's authority. Another unintended consequence is the election of one-issue board members or board members supported by teacher unions.

Superintendents need to be aware of the political context within which they work. Whatever that context, recognize that you, and not the school board, are responsible for the day-to-day management and leadership of the school district and for maintaining appropriate board and superintendent roles. Work with the board to establish appropriate parameters for board members' work. Respect the authority they have and appreciate their individual strengths.

No board member needs to contribute forty to sixty hours a week. No matter how talented a board member may be, no matter what position she or he may hold outside the district, no matter how educated, you are the CEO of the district and the expert in how to accomplish the district's work. You are the professional, not the board member. Not understanding this creates conflict with the board and eventually a parting of the ways.

Just as superintendents differ, so to do board members. Some are dedicated to the welfare of all the students, some have particular issues they wish addressed, while others are interested in specific segments of the student population. Except in rare instances, almost all school board members have something positive to contribute to the district and its work. Some are easy to work with and others are not. You need to work with all of them.

The following are strategies, guidelines, and protocols that successful superintendents use in working with boards. They can be helpful as you begin to master the intricacies of board-superintendent relationships.

THE BASICS

1. Board Members Vote; You Do Not

Superintendents bring recommendations; boards accept, modify, or reject them. Boards also initiate their own proposals. While you have substantial day-to-day authority and responsibility, ultimately, the board has final authority. Once the board takes an action or sets policy, you are responsible for implementing it as the board intended. If you come to believe you are as powerful as the board and either ignore or poorly implement the board's decisions, you may find yourself looking for a new position. Conversely, if you are in grave disagreement with the board's policies, you may wish to look for another position.

Formal board action on any proposal must occur in a properly noticed meeting. Many states have open meeting laws. They require discussions between and among board members to occur in public. Every state has rules governing how meetings must be publicly noticed, what discussions can take place outside the meetings, and how many votes are needed to pass a motion.

Become familiar with these laws. One of the best sources can be the state school boards association. These associations have a vested interest in making sure their members understand and adhere to state laws. Law firms also provide workshops for superintendents, their executive assistants, and board members.

Prior to becoming a superintendent, you may have reported to one person. Now you are reporting to five or more people. Be aware of this and do not overstep your bounds. You also may be working with board members from differing cultures, ethnic backgrounds, and education levels. Respect each board member and the board as a whole. They are the ones who vote.

2. Working With Your Board

Treat all board members the same. Each is an elected official, and together they are your employer. Whether or not you like board members, each deserves the same respect, access to you, and receipt of information given to other board members. For example, if one board member requests information about the cost of a particular program, copy that information to all board members. This keeps the board from thinking you favor one member. More importantly, it gives them all the same information needed for decisions.

The board president plays a unique role. Most are elected by the board at its annual organizational meeting and serve for one year. Not all districts define the role of board presidents or chairs in the same way, just as most districts have differing bylaws that govern their actions.

Responsibilities of Board Presidents

- Assist in the formulation of the board agenda.
- Chair both closed and open sessions of board meetings.
- Serve as the spokesperson for the board to the public and the press.
- Appoint board members to committees.
- Manage the superintendent evaluation process and provide guidance where appropriate.
- Communicate concerns or questions raised by other trustees or even members of the community.

An experienced and competent board president is of immeasurable value to any superintendent, especially new superintendents. You want a cordial and respectful working relationship with your board president. Schedule a weekly meeting with the president or exchange e-mails, or phone calls. The president is frequently contacted by the press, district and community leaders, as well as irate parents.

Provide your board president early notice of any controversial communication you are addressing in your Friday letter, which is discussed later in the chapter. The president needs complete, up-to-date information in order to appropriately respond. In turn, you need the guidance, wisdom, and support of an experienced board member. As you learn more about the district, these communications may taper off. In your first year, err on the side of more rather than less communication with the president.

Board members are community members who give countless hours with little recompense. Many also work. Respect the role of all board members. If you cannot, it may be time to assess your relationship with the board using an outside consultant. This is discussed at greater length in Chapter 10.

3. Boards and Micromanagement

The very nature of school boards makes micromanagement an issue in the best of districts. There is a saying: "Nature abhors a vacuum." This is particularly true when leading school districts. If the superintendent does not provide leadership or the type of leadership the board expects, individual board members or the board as a whole will step in and provide it.

If you succeed a weak superintendent, it is likely your board has moved away from setting policy and is involved in day-to-day operations.

It takes time to move the board back to its appropriate role. Do not be surprised if some members resist returning to a policy-setting role. Some board members may not understand or even recognize the difference between setting policy and micromanaging.

Often board members perceive that they were elected to carry out a specific mandate, such as lowering the drop-out rate, improving the science curriculum, or building more schools. They believe they know the best way to accomplish the goal and work tirelessly to achieve it. They continuously seek support for their goal from their fellow trustees.

Staff are affected by board micromanagement as well. If staff members see every goal of the district is of equal importance and every board member's request is a to-do item, they begin protecting themselves. They take only surface actions and avoid tackling an issue in a meaningful way. They know another directive is on its way. Setting priorities is essential.

It Takes a Majority of the Board to Approve an Action. One board member, no matter how enthusiastic, committed, and focused, may not set board policy. A majority of the board must agree. Once a majority is reached and the goal becomes district policy, it is your responsibility to determine how best to achieve the goal. Where majority support is not achieved, recognize the efforts of the minority. Spend time meeting with these members and work to channel their interests into other, more productive areas.

If one board member gets his or her way through aggressive or inappropriate support for a goal, other board members may replicate that behavior. The district can quickly drift from striving to meet a set of integrated and coordinated goals to meeting the random expectations of individual board members. Be concerned when a board member overtly offers support for other board members' individual goals in return for their support for a particular goal.

Board members must learn to respect the district's decision-making systems. No school district can be run effectively if board members expect you to address their goals immediately and before all others. You cannot do everything at once and be effective.

While it is normal to have differences of opinion on the board, you want to avoid a serious split. Often serious splits occur when board members do not like one another, hold conflicting views, or do not share common values. Sometimes these splits magnify when new members join the board. If you have a serious split on the board, work with your president to develop protocols that will facilitate the work of the board. If this fails, encourage the board to retain a consultant. You do not want the conflict to result in a dysfunctional board.

Listen to Board Members. One way to avoid this issue is to listen to board members with a personal agenda. Help them learn about the district. This is an important role of the board president as well. It is especially important if a new board member has an area of specialized interest or focus. Provide information on any financial, contractual, legal, or state issues that may be involved.

Often new board members may discover that the district has accomplished far more than they realized. In turn, you may find that not enough communication on the topic has occurred. Share this information with all board members. If a board member is still dissatisfied with what the district is doing, explain the annual goal-setting process and how this issue can be addressed through the established process. The board member may have an excellent goal that does need to be addressed by the entire district but it is important that it be addressed in a systematic way.

Find Areas of Outside Interest for Board Members. Another way to work with board members with agendas is to identify areas of interest to them that further the work of the district. For example, if board members are interested in policy review, state legislation, or fund-raising, assist them in channeling their strengths and interests into this work. Encourage them to attend workshops and conferences or assume leadership roles in state or national associations. If you cannot accompany them, send a district office administrator instead.

In many districts, new board members, along with senior members, are assigned to district committees. This gives teachers, principals, and parents an opportunity to get to know them. Their participation means you are likely to have board member support of the committee's recommendations. Informed board members are far more likely to support your initiatives. This work also may engage board members who came on the board with agendas. Through committee work they gain a broader perspective of the district.

Ensure the Board Has Ongoing Training. Provide ongoing training to the board on the role of the superintendent and board. Your board must recognize and respect your responsibility to make recommendations and implement policy, while you recognize and respect their rights to pursue policy goals. Use the eighteen-month planning process to maintain board enthusiasm while keeping the board focused on commonly held goals.

Include in board training a thorough understanding of the state laws regulating the work of school boards. Some states, like California, have laws governing everything from the length of time needed to notice a meeting to where it can be held and what can and cannot be discussed. Others, like Oregon, have laws that allow the press to sit in on closed sessions to gather background material for stories. Other states allow for negotiations and personnel decisions to be discussed without press present. No matter the state laws, learn them. Make sure the district adheres to these laws. If needed, request counsel to assist you and your staff in doing this.

Board Protocols. As noted in Chapter 3, some district protocols affect both management and the board. One of these is expectations for management team attendance at board meetings. In most districts, cabinet members are expected to attend all board meetings, with principals and other administrators only attending if there are agenda items pertaining to their responsibilities. Review your expectations with the board so it is comfortable with your approach, especially if your expectation differs from the previous superintendent's practice. Help board members to respect the needs of administrators, particularly principals.

Set expectations for board-administrator communications. In districts with very active boards, individual members want access to your staff. Some superintendents are comfortable with board members communicating directly with members of the management team while others prefer board members to address questions and concerns directly to them. This is important to resolve as board members often intimidate administrators or even attempt to direct their work.

Board members need information to make good decisions for the district. They want to be part of the district and get to know administrators and staff or continue the relationships they had before being elected. Often, when grappling with contentious district issues, they turn to the staff they know. Experienced superintendents know that board members want to talk with principals and other district administrators.

What is critical is that you lay out your expectations regarding these conversations. You do not want surprises. You want to be kept informed. Work with your board to develop an understanding of when and under what circumstances it is appropriate for a board member to contact a member of your cabinet or leadership team for information or an opinion.

Some experienced superintendents make it clear before signing a contract they are to be informed whenever this happens. Some boards even develop protocols for this purpose. Others simply come to an understanding with their superintendent and work together to maintain consistency in implementing it.

Whatever the agreements, it is never appropriate for a board member to contact an administrator and direct that person to take action. You are responsible for directing staff, not board members. Further, it causes great angst for the administrator, who becomes torn between you and the board member. If this is an issue, provide training to the board and staff to clearly delineate roles and responsibilities.

In turn, clarify with administrators how to keep you informed of their conversations with board members. In most districts, superintendents want board members to meet with the assistant superintendents or chief business official (CBO) to clarify their questions. They simply expect the administrator to let them know when this occurs. You do not want to be surprised at a board meeting by a trustee who says, "Well, the assistant superintendent told me something different about the budget than what you just reported."

4. Board Policies

School districts are governed by board policies that are set by the board. Policies cover a number of topics, including personnel, student instruction, facilities, budgeting, class size, school size, and board meetings. Most states recommend topics for board policies, and most state board associations have sample board policy manuals divided by topic. In most districts they are now online. This makes them accessible to more people, but also requires you keep the manuals up to date.

While policies provide a framework within which the district is governed, they can cause difficulties if not reviewed on a regular basis. Many districts make the mistake of creating unneeded policies or making them so detailed that staff often violate them without knowing. It is the management team's responsibility to be familiar with district policies and to implement them correctly. The best policies are those that address the needed topics and provide guidelines, not parameters, within which to work.

Example

In one district, board policy dictated no elementary school have more than 600 students. When the majority of the elementary schools approached that number, some board members wanted to build a new school. This would require redrawing all elementary school boundaries, as well as passing a bond. A number of parents did not want their children moved from the school they currently attended. Further, the district had reached its projected peak enrollment and was expected to drop in enrollment over the next five years. If the board did not open a new school, it would be in violation of its own policy. It finally chose to amend the policy providing a range for the size of elementary schools that also took into account future projections. This saved countless hours at board meetings and parent frustration.

You and your staff develop the administrative regulations that implement policies. Some districts require board approval of these, while others simply want to be informed of them. Carefully craft these administrative regulations to provide the flexibility you need to implement the policy.

Another issue confronting the management of board policies is the continual passage of new federal and state legislation. This happens at least yearly and may affect existing policy. For example, when Title IX was passed, boards needed to change their policies governing athletics and access to other extracurricular activities. The same was true for the Individuals With Disabilities Education Act (IDEA), the legislation putting special education into place. Further, both of these continue to be amended, requiring further changes to board policies.

As superintendent, you are responsible for reviewing current policies to see if they are up to date, as well as recommending new policies based on district needs and changing legislation. Review the current policy manual, which may be online. You should have received one during your transition. If it appears your policies are up to date, you need only keep them that way. However, if a quick perusal indicates that most policies are out of date, recommend to the board that it undertake a policy review. This may be time-consuming and even costly, but having out-of-date policies opens the district to potential liability and is even more costly.

Most districts need a policy review. This is one of those jobs that rarely becomes a priority. Most state board associations have sample policies, as well as staff that can assist the district in reviewing and revising its policies to bring them into line with existing law. Another option is to have legal counsel review them. This is usually more expensive but may result in fewer, more streamlined policies.

Policy Review Categories

- Policies That Meet District Needs and Require No Change
- Those That Are Outdated and Need to Be Deleted
- Those That Require Some Change but Are Not Controversial and Can Be Done in a Short Time
- Those That Require Substantial Change and Will Be Controversial
- Those That Need to Be Added Due to Current Law or District Practice

Work with your board chair to develop a process to review the policies. In some districts, policies that need no change are acknowledged at one meeting. Policies that require minimal change or need to be deleted are reviewed at the next meeting and approved at a following meeting. That leaves only the policies that need an extensive rewrite and new policies. Time is then set aside at each meeting for policies until the task is completed. Where possible, similar policies are lumped together. The board sees progress being made at every meeting.

While some board members dislike doing this as it appears to be a review of the past, they will thank you when the process is over. This is their area of responsibility. Having good, up-to-date policies that reflect district goals and values makes it easier to govern.

Once this task is complete, it is far easier to bring revisions to the board as laws change or new policies are needed. Work with legal counsel to keep abreast of needed changes. Work with your cabinet to bring forth policies that further the work of the district. Always remember that it is the board, not you, that approves policy.

5. Board Elections

Usually no board elections occur during your first year as superintendent. But there are exceptions. Be prepared should elections happen during your first year.

One superintendent was hired in November with an official contract start in January. Between the time he was hired and when he began his tenure, a board member resigned and moved to another state. A new board member was appointed until elections were held the following November. At that time the new board member lost his seat. Within one year the superintendent worked with two board members out of five who had not hired him.

Avoid personal involvement in the election process beyond your legally prescribed duties. This is particularly true during your first year as superintendent. Superintendents who become political players have much to lose, especially if their preferred candidate loses. However, you play an important informal role in this process.

As you become involved in your community, you meet people who would be excellent board members. If these individuals ask your opinion about running, it is appropriate to encourage them. Explain you cannot endorse them or any candidate. Superintendents, irrespective of where they live, should never endorse board candidates, even incumbents.

If you see prospective candidates at an event, you may comment on how fortunate the community would be to have them on the board. But do not approach them and ask them to run. It is appropriate to meet with any community member who is interested in running for the board and needs more information about the position. Many districts schedule workshops for potential board members prior to the sign-up deadline and have the superintendent as a major speaker.

One or more of these candidates will be elected to the board. During the campaign, model how you will work with the candidates after the election. There are certain things you can and should do for all candidates once they become official candidates.

Working With Board Candidates

1. Make every effort to treat and respond to each candidate in a positive, nonpartisan manner, even if you dread the election of one or more candidates.

2. Call each candidate and thank that person for his or her interest in serving the students of the district.

3. Provide each candidate a comprehensive district information packet.

4. Schedule a meeting of all the candidates. Have cabinet members provide an overview of the district from the staff perspective. If the board president and vice president are not up for re-election, have them attend this session.

5. Schedule one-on-one meetings with candidates only if you offer to do the same with each candidate.

6. Send each candidate a full board packet for each regularly scheduled meeting prior to the election, excluding only confidential material.

7. Answer questions candidates might have about board packet materials. Where appropriate, provide the other candidates the same materials and information.

When the election is over, contact the candidates who lost and thank them for their commitment to the district. Encourage them to continue their involvement in district issues and activities. Losing candidates frequently try again at the next election.

Call and congratulate the candidates who won. This is important even if a candidate was not supportive of you or the board during the campaign. Be gracious and professional. Offer to meet with them to begin a formal orientation. You want to learn their expectations and perceptions of the district's strengths and challenges. If you do not hear from them in a few days, persist in setting up an orientation process.

If an election results in a substantial political transformation of the board, it may be time to reflect on whether you will remain in the district. When new members join the board, it is a critical time for the board, you, and the district. More about this is discussed in Chapter 10.

Provide an Orientation for New Board Members. Plan an orientation for new board members. Most state school board associations have annual training sessions that coincide with the state's election cycle. Encourage new board members to attend this training and other workshops during the school years. You and your board president should attend as well. In addition, many boards schedule an annual meeting with a consultant to develop working protocols. Having new members participate in this review allows for a much smoother transition as all trustees recommit to the protocols.

Include funds in your district budget to support the training of board members. Too often districts are "penny wise and dollar foolish" when it comes to expenditures for board development. These are legitimate district expenses and well worth the cost. Boards need training and support as much as teachers, principals, and superintendents do. The goal is to have a board that works with you to meet the needs of the students.

COMMUNICATING WITH THE BOARD

Communications are central to superintendent-board relations. Be responsive, proactive, and knowledgeable. Do not try to boss board members or overwhelm them with information favorable only to your positions.

- ✓ Respond in a timely manner to board member e-mails or phone calls.
- ✓ Communicate information prior to its appearing in the paper or local news.
- ✓ Communicate information prior to its being brought up in public at a board meeting.
- ✓ Prepare and present board reports, which provide information and data for making decisions, including opposing views.

Board communication includes both informal and formal interactions. This is further compounded by electronic communications and paperless meetings. If you and your board members use computers or other electronic devices for most of your communications, learn the public records' laws pertaining to these communications. Also ensure all electronics used by your board members are secure and free of viruses.

Some districts supply each board member with this equipment. If equipment is provided, it is on loan and returned to the district when the board member leaves the board. The advantage to providing equipment to the board members is that it is easier to keep these devices "clean." Also, there is less chance that a family member or friend of the board member sees sensitive information. However, there is a downside. The district needs to purchase, set up, and maintain this equipment. Find out your district practice. Work with the board and district staff to determine what works best.

1. Informal Communications

Informal communications occur at any time through meetings with individual board members, phone calls, texting, tweeting, or e-mails. Informal communications occur in many settings, including formal meetings, conferences, or community events. Treat all your communications as informed and official. Casual, off-hand comments may have consequences. This is particularly true if you assume you share values and beliefs with people you hardly know. Your words have an impact, so carefully consider what you say.

Meet Regularly With Individual Board Members. A good way to keep abreast of the ideas and issues of individual board members is to meet with them on a regular basis. This gives board members an opportunity to discuss ongoing work of the district. You learn more about them and their interests. The board member can provide valuable information on what is happening in the community.

In turn, you can answer questions about staff reports or what board members have observed on a recent school visit. Questions are addressed that may save hours of staff time. This is also an opportunity to direct the board member's interests to projects of importance to the district, such as bond elections, fund-raising, or lobbying for state or federal legislation. Keep informal notes.

Schedule these meetings monthly until you get to know all board members and their particular issues. Inform your board that you wish to initiate these individual meetings and have your assistant schedule them for you. Most board members appreciate an opportunity to talk one-on-one with you. If a board member works or cannot get to your office easily from his or her place of work, schedule a breakfast, lunch, or coffee. Be willing to meet early mornings, evenings, or on weekends. Board members have as complex a schedule as you do.

If you hold meetings over a meal, follow district protocols or those outlined in your contract. In some districts, board members expect the superintendent to pick up the tab and submit the cost for reimbursement. In others board members either pay out of their own pocket or submit for reimbursement. There are even districts in which board members expect the superintendent to pay even though there's no expense reimbursement provision in the superintendent's contract.

Even if you are in a district that relies mainly on electronic communication, set up face-to-face meetings. These allow you to gain information not just from the words but also from tone and body language. Going back and forth on e-mail does not provide you with the same information you gather from a visit with the board member. You also run the risk that an e-mail is passed on to others.

Informal Drop-In Meetings by Board Members. Develop a protocol on how to respond to informal drop-in meetings by board members. This requires close superintendent-assistant coordination. While you should treat board members with respect at all times, you are not obligated to drop everything you are doing to meet with them on a moment's notice. Nor should they expect you to do so.

It is not appropriate to ignore previously calendared meetings or events. Oftentimes your scheduled appointment has an equally challenging and tight schedule. Respect everyone in your community. Do not arbitrarily cancel meetings or keep people waiting in the hallway.

When board members drop in, have your assistant attempt to assist the board member before interrupting you. If you cannot be interrupted, the assistant can schedule a specific time for you to respond by phone or meet personally.

If a board member consistently drops by to see you or other members of your cabinet, talk to the board member to determine her or his issues. If the board member's concerns are policy driven, you may need to schedule more frequent meetings. If they are more operational or even personal, discuss this with the board president. The board president may need to meet with the board member to clarify the roles of the board and the superintendent.

Example

A board member constantly dropped by the offices of the superintendent, CBO, and assistant superintendent of instruction. The superintendent then scheduled two one-hour meetings each week with the board member to keep the board member away from staff. The superintendent spoke with the board president, who brought up the issue to the board member. After a discussion of board and super-intendent roles, the board member agreed to contact the superintendent when she needed more information. The twice weekly meetings were reduced to one.

Phone Calls, E-mails, and Texting. Phone calls, texting, and e-mails are other forms of informal communications with board members. In many districts these are a growing part of communications between and among board members and staff. Board members often see this as less intrusive but fail to understand that their insistence on a same-day response can be more frustrating to staff.

Example

During one year, a board member sent over one thousand e-mail requests to staff for information. The superintendent copied the rest of the board on each response. He also talked with the board president. Finally, the board president met with the board member to limit communications. The rest of the board was pleased this was done.

Guidelines for Responding to Board Communications

✓ Treat the board member with respect and courtesy no matter the subject of the call.

✓ Be aware that what you say may be shared with others, including the media.

✓ Work with your board president to reduce excessive requests from board members.

✓ Always share the content of the calls, texts, and e-mails with the rest of the board.

An exception to sharing the content of messages is when board members share personal issues they do not want made public. Even then urge them to share the matter with the board president.

Set limits with the board on when it is appropriate for them to call you at home, after work, or on weekends. As superintendent you are on call 24/7 in case of an emergency. However, you are entitled to privacy and a life outside the office. Some board members are night owls and think nothing of calling at ten or eleven in the evening or even at midnight. Others think that every concern of theirs constitutes an emergency.

Establish expectations on when e-mails or phone messages will be returned. Too often an immediate response is expected. Unless it is an emergency or a need for information for a meeting that is about to occur, board members should not expect a response until the following day. Further, that response simply may lay out the amount of time needed to gather the requested information.

Also establish protocols for the use of tweeting, texting, and Facebook communications. These forms of communications are in the public domain. Protocols should include when it is appropriate to use these venues and how and when they will receive a response. Avoid ongoing discussions on Twitter and Facebook unless you want the entire community involved.

Given the emergence of 24/7 communications, establish parameters for both staff and board members. Whatever protocols are established, a best practice is to ignore the occasional violation of your privacy for an "urgent request" from a board member. Review yearly the established communication protocols and, if necessary, use an outside consultant.

State Laws Governing the Attendance of a Majority of the Board at an Event. Boards must adhere to state law governing attendance at community events. Superintendents and boards are often invited to events such as foundation parties, city celebrations, holiday parties, or Chamber of Commerce lunches. While these are social events, state law prevails. In some states this means that if a majority of the board attends a community event, the event must be publicly noticed. Most boards coordinate attendance to avoid having a majority present. In situations where a majority must attend with proper notice, board members avoid discussing school business. If they do not, you need to remind them of this in a gentle but firm manner.

You may be invited to social events hosted by a board member. These can include weekend parties, birthdays, anniversaries, weddings, or christenings. As mentioned in Chapter 2, it is best not to develop personal relationships with board members and staff. You do not want to be perceived as having a special relationship with one board member over another. It can undermine your credibility. Avoid attending the social events of one board member unless all board members are invited.

You have no obligation to invite board members to your family events. You are entitled to a personal life. However, hosting an annual barbecue or holiday open house for the entire board and administrative staff provides an opportunity for everyone to get to know one another on an informal basis and to celebrate the district's accomplishments.

Learn about these annual traditions during your transition. Either maintain it or start a new one. These traditions are essential components of the district culture. You gain by maintaining them.

Example

A superintendent began her contract year in November. She was told that the superintendent always hosted a holiday party for all the administrative staff and board and their spouses or partners in mid-December. Everyone was waiting for her to pick the time and place and send out invitations. She had not even moved into her new home. However, she recognized the importance of the event. With help from her administrative assistant, who offered her home, she pulled it all together and hosted a great party.

No matter the event or how many board members attend, remember the board cannot take action anywhere other than at a publicly noticed board meeting. Review these protocols when new board members join the board.

2. Formal Communications

A superintendent communicates formally with the board in several ways: through board packets, presentations at board meetings, weekly updates, formal letters, e-mail correspondence, or other materials sent to all board members. Formal communications refers to information or data you want all board members to receive and read. In most states, formal communications, with the exception of materials relating to personnel and some limited liability and legal issues, are available to the public upon request. This includes e-mail and text messages. As a new superintendent, be mindful that most all of your written communications are public documents.

Example

In one district, during a hotly contested board race, a member of the public requested and, by law, received all communications sent to the board each week by the superintendent. This included all e-mails between the top-level administrative staff, the superintendent, and the board. The only materials not sent were those pertaining to personnel actions.

Weekly Board Communications. Most superintendents send weekly information packets to the board, usually on Friday. These are prepared by the administrative assistant. Some districts mail these packets, others deliver them directly to board member homes, and an increasing number send them electronically. Most superintendents also include in these packets a weekly memo or report to the board.

These *Friday letters* are an essential communication tool. They provide information about your work and the district between board meetings. This is especially important in districts where the board meets once each month rather than twice. Without this weekly communication, the board may lose track of what you are doing between board meetings to achieve the board's goals and any day-to-day management issues. The Friday letter is your lifeline to the board.

As these are public documents, they can be requested by community members or the press. If possible, avoid discussing these in public and caution your board about this.

One district has used Friday letters for more than sixteen years. It has had three superintendents, but never a public request for these letters. Board members like having their own communication and simply refrain from talking about it in public.

Use your Friday letter to provide the following.

✓ An Update on Your Weekly Activities, Including Meetings and Events Attended, Appointments With Community Group Representatives, Professional Development Activities, and Planned Travel

✓ Background on Work to Meet District Goals

✓ Updates on Staff Preparation of Reports and Recommendations for Upcoming Board Agenda Items

✓ Reports From Each Major District Division Summarizing the Week's Activities

✓ Reports on School Site Activities

✓ Copies of Letters or E-mails That May Be of Interest to the Board

✓ Summaries of Requests Received From Individual Board Members and the Response Given

Also include in the packet selected readings for the board; a calendar of upcoming district activities, especially those requiring board attendance; information materials from cabinet members; handouts from district activities or events; and correspondence received for individual board members.

Review reports provided by the school sites, key departments, and general communications. This is your communication to the board. You do not want to be surprised by what is being written by the head of one of the departments.

One superintendent failed to read the report from the technology coordinator and was taken aback when board members began calling about the lack of district funding for a particular technology program. Needless to say, this did not happen again and the budget issue was resolved.

This weekly communication helps the board understand the work that goes into running the district and preparing reports and recommendations included in the board meeting packet of materials.

Divide the letter into two sections. The first is the *public* report, containing the information that may be requested by the public and the press. If you are printing it, do so on the same white paper used for all other public documents. Do not include information about upcoming board meeting agenda items unless this information is included in the board meeting packet materials or presented to the board at the meeting as a handout. Doing so is likely to violate open meeting laws.

The second section is *confidential* and contains information that does not, by law, have to be shared with the public and press. The confidential section may include information on personnel issues, negotiations, discipline actions, staff and parent complaints, legal issues, and potential legal issues. What can and cannot be contained in this section depends on your state's laws. If printed, do so on the same color paper used for all confidential, closed session correspondence with the board. If sent electronically make sure it is marked confidential.

Some superintendents share the public portion of the letter with cabinet or other members of the management team, while others do not. Some superintendents share the confidential portion with superintendent-level cabinet members, while others do not. Either way, be certain your board is aware of and supports your practice.

Occasionally a new superintendent discovers the previous superintendent did not send the board a weekly letter. If this is your situation, inform the board of your intended practice. Send one and ask for feedback. Almost all boards appreciate receiving this timely correspondence. As time goes by, board members tell you what materials they enjoy receiving. You develop a format that works best for you and the board. Following are some ways to make the preparation of this letter easier for you and your administrative assistant.

❒ Write your portion of the letter either Thursday evening or early Friday morning so corrections can be made before it is distributed on Friday afternoon.

❒ Establish a 9:00 a.m. Friday deadline for receiving all staff materials to be included.

❒ Carefully review the letter before sending it. You are responsible for any errors, including those made by subordinate staff. Ensure no state open meeting laws are violated.

❒ Have your assistant set up a system for gathering materials for the packet during the week. Scan or copy material as it is received. Doing this as it occurs each day rather than trying to gather everything together on Friday morning will make the preparation more efficient.

❒ Provide options for how the board will receive the packet if it is not sent electronically. Some board members prefer to visit your office on Friday afternoons to pick it up directly; others want it delivered to their homes. If mailed, determine when the packet must be posted to ensure Saturday delivery. Most board members want to read and review the materials over the weekend so they can call or e-mail you on Monday with questions or comments.

BOARD MEETINGS

Board meetings are crucial events in the lives of superintendents. At these meetings you present reports and recommendations to the board. These focus on district goals, operations, and student learning. Presentations and recommendations inform not only the board but also the community. Work with your board chair and assistant to organize these meetings so the board can take timely action on decisions. A board meeting encompasses the development of the posted board agenda, the preparation of documents supporting each item on the agenda, the presentation of these materials in a public board meeting, and necessary follow-up.

These are meetings of the board conducted in public and not "public meetings of the board." This is an important distinction. The public has every right to attend the meetings of the school board, review materials, ask questions, and voice their opinions. Public participation at meetings is determined by state law and board policy. However, it is the board that set the agenda and determines the actions it wishes to take.

The public does not have the right to disrupt meetings but can attempt to influence the board in legally appropriate ways. If the public disagrees with board decisions, members of the public can state their case at the next board meeting. Community members who disagree with the board also can run for office, get elected, and change board policy.

1. Frequency, Time, and Place

Districts Vary on the Frequency of Board Meetings. Most boards meet either once or twice each month, with additional meetings scheduled as needed. Both schedules have advantages and disadvantages. Meeting twice a month is more costly and requires substantial preparation time. The more time spent preparing board materials and attending lengthy meetings, the less time there is to do the work of the district—educate students. Monthly meetings reduce public access to the board, disrupt the continuity of decision making, and usually require the scheduling of additional meetings. It also requires lengthier Friday letters to keep the board informed.

Many board policies require two meetings before a recommendation on a nonroutine matter can be approved. At the first meeting the recommendation is received and discussed by the board. The recommendation is approved at the second meeting, and time is provided at both meetings for public comment. Two meetings per month facilitate this process.

Even districts with twice monthly meetings normally meet only once in December due to the holidays. Also many boards schedule no meetings in July due to staff vacations and preparations for the opening of school. Some districts even limit the August calendar to one meeting. The board approves the meeting schedule, usually at its annual organization meeting when newly elected board members are sworn in and board officers are elected. If you want to change the meeting calendar, review your reasons with the cabinet and board chair before bringing your recommendation to the board for approval.

Special Meetings. As noted in Chapter 5, your annual board meeting calendar should include a July or August meeting date in case a need arises to address issues such as construction, hiring of staff, or changes to the budget. It can be canceled if not needed. Special meetings must adhere to public notice legal requirements.

Topics for Special Meetings

- Student Expulsions
- Interdistrict Transfer Hearings
- Parent, Student, or Staff Complaints
- Emergencies, Such as a Natural Disaster
- Bid Approval Needed for Ongoing Construction

Except in an emergency, a school board should not meet on a weekly basis. Frequent meetings are a sign of a board losing confidence in the superintendent or micromanaging. If this is occurring, have a serious discussion with the board and, if necessary, bring in a consultant.

Time and Place for Meetings. The time and place for board meetings varies among districts. Schedule board meetings in the early evening so community members can attend. If possible, televise meetings on the local community channel so community members can view them from home. Most people simply want to know what is being discussed and will not attend meetings unless there is a crisis or topic of interest. Usually a few regulars attend the meetings, including parents, staff, some students, and the occasional community observer. In larger districts, there even may be a regular reporter assigned to the district.

The board chair is responsible for running an efficient meeting. Ideally, if the board meets twice each month and is well-prepared, the public session of the meeting takes two to three hours. Meetings should be concluded by 10 p.m. Some boards set time limits for meetings into their policies and require a board vote to lengthen the meeting. Exceptions occur when the board is confronting controversial issues such as school closures, boundary adjustments, or changes in district curricula.

Lengthy meetings exact a price on everyone who attends, as most attendees work the following morning. Consistently, lengthy meetings lead the community to conclude that the district is disorganized or the board is divided or incapable of making a decision.

Some districts move their meetings from school to school to encourage local parents to attend. While well intentioned, this practice has more negative consequences than positive. For example, it disrupts schools that have limited custodial staff to help prepare for the meeting. In addition, it increases the workload of district office staff as recording and other equipment must be moved, including individual computers for each board member if packets are sent electronically.

Ways to Increase Community Attendance

- Televise the meetings.
- Use Constant Contact or another Web-based system to distribute agendas to the public.
- Begin each meeting with a student, staff, or parent recognition activity.
- Schedule student presentations.
- Schedule the instructional and controversial community issues early in the agenda.
- Treat the staff and public with respect and provide time for public comment on agenda items.
- Conduct time-efficient meetings.

With proper planning, having a set time and place for board meetings will encourage attendance. In addition, holding board meetings in a district office designated room permits cabinet members and your assistant to retrieve supporting materials from their offices should the need arise. You have immediate access to copy machines and your computer. Your assistant can prepare last-minute changes to important documents needed for the meeting. Closed sessions can be held in your office.

2. Preparation

The administration and governance of the district intersect at public board meetings. Successful board meetings require good preparation, beginning with the board agenda and supporting documents. A poorly designed agenda disrupts your work, as well as colors public and staff perceptions of your leadership ability and the competence of the board.

Boards want the public to perceive them and their superintendent working together to achieve district goals. They do not want to be viewed as rubber-stamping everything the superintendent recommends, micromanaging, or being disrespectful to staff. Superintendents do not want to be perceived as docile or controlling. These issues converge in the board agenda and the subsequent meeting.

Agendas. Sections of board agendas are determined by board policy and state law. For example, the public noticing of closed and open session agenda items is usually in state law and requires the use of specific language. You and your administrative assistant are responsible for this.

In most districts the superintendent's administrative assistant is authorized to contact legal counsel for advice on this topic.

What can and cannot be discussed in closed session without the public present is usually the biggest issue regarding agendas. Place the discussion of closed session items before the start of the open session rather than at the end of the meeting.

- The board should review personnel decisions in closed session before approving them in public session.
- Sometimes you will need legal counsel to attend. However, you do not want highly compensated attorneys sitting through the meeting waiting for the closed session to start.
- Some board members come directly from work. Provide a light meal before the meeting begins. A hungry board member is unlikely to sit patiently through a meeting.
- The board can meet and greet, and then shift into board member mode.
- You can assess the mood of the board.
- If allowed by state law, you can brief the board on potential issues or problems that might arise at the meeting.

Boards often have bylaws or policies outlining the agenda-setting process. Agenda formats include a number of sections that may vary in order. Templates for agendas are readily available as most districts post board agendas online. The most common sections include the following.

- *Date, Time, and Place of the Meeting.*
- *Closed Session.* This session lists the education codes allowing for closed session but includes no individual names.
- *Calling the Meeting to Order and Pledge of Allegiance.*
- *Agenda Approval.* Board members can request a change in agenda order or remove an item from the consent calendar.
- *Listing of Closed Session Actions.*
- *Public Comment.* The public may comment on items not on the agenda. The board listens but cannot respond as to items not on the agenda. It should be noted that most boards limit public comment to three minutes or less so they remain in control of the meeting. Others place this item later in the agenda so board business can be done in an orderly fashion. A set time such as 9:00 p.m. is established and adhered to for public comments. A board majority does have the authority to direct staff to follow up on an item or to have

it placed on a future agenda. Always request that speakers fill out a card listing their names, addresses, phone numbers, and topic of comment. It allows staff to follow up with speakers and ensure they are community members. Check with legal counsel on the procedures to follow.

- *Superintendent, Committee, Parent Club, Union Reports.* These highlight activities of interest to the community.
- *Student or Staff Recognitions.* These are usually ten to fifteen minutes and placed early in the agenda so participants may leave after the presentations. Honoring students for their work in music, art, athletics, math, science, technology, writing, community service, or other endeavors sets a wonderful tone and focuses the meeting on students and instruction. Many districts honor outstanding teachers, parent-teacher organizations, foundations, or support staff members as well. The board raises district morale by demonstrating its support and appreciation for those who contribute to the education of students.
- *Consent Calendar.* It includes routine items not needing board discussion, such as monthly expenditure reports.
- *Discussion Items.* These include major recommendations that are brought to the next meeting for approval. They also can include items that require no action, such as a discussion of student assessments. The public is allowed to address this item for a set time prior to the board discussion. After that, public comment is not accepted.
- *Action Items.* These require approval by a board majority. Most of these items were discussed at previous meetings, unless there is a district emergency. Again, public comments occur prior to board action.
- *Information Item.* These items require no discussion or action, such as district enrollment reports, but are included so that the board and community are informed.
- *Board Correspondence.* It includes correspondence sent to the board from community organizations or local, county, and state officials, or the state department of education. Normally, letters of complaint are not included.
- *Board Reports and Requests.* This is when board members report on their activities and make requests for staff reports. Requests usually require a majority vote of the board. Listen carefully.
- *Future Board Meeting Dates.* Board members review meeting calendars and future agenda items.
- *Adjournment.*

As with all district operations, before recommending changes learn why the agenda is structured as it is. If agendas are poorly constructed, resulting in dysfunctional board meetings, work with your board president to restructure the agenda. Do not change the organization or structure of the board agenda without board approval. These are board meetings, not superintendent meetings.

Develop a Yearly Calendar of Routine Agenda Topics. As noted earlier, this calendar includes both open and closed session items. Once developed it guides the preparation of each board meeting agenda. Include routine items such as budget presentation and adoption, personnel reports, assessment reports, eighteen-month planning process actions, adoption of board goals, approval of the board calendar, audit reports, and approval of expenditures.

Your assistant can prepare this calendar by reviewing board agendas from the prior two or three years. Identify annual items, and add any specific reports required by the district goals. Distribute these reports throughout the school year so each meeting is equally balanced. Review the proposed agenda calendar with your cabinet and leadership team. This also helps them organize their work for the year.

Review the preliminary calendar with your board president and vice president for comments and feedback, then share it with the full board. Let them know the calendar serves as a flexible guideline with target dates. As the year progresses, one or more board members may ask for additional reports. If the majority concurs, include the report in the calendar. Review the board's expectations with your cabinet so the affected administrator can plan accordingly.

Have the administrative assistant update the calendar as changes are needed. Include any changes in your Friday packet. Consider this calendar as a superintendent work product. It does not need formal board approval but it is a public document. Review this with your administrative assistant and cabinet on a regular basis. Plan at least two meetings ahead.

As noted in Chapter 3, adhere to your meeting group sequencing. On Monday morning your assistant provides a draft of the upcoming board meeting agendas based on a review of the agenda calendar and an assessment of what occurred at the previous board meeting. Modify the drafts as needed and present them to the cabinet at your Monday meeting. Clarify assignments and expectations. Share these agendas with the board president at your Tuesday agenda planning meeting. Where appropriate, share the agendas with your leadership team at your Wednesday meeting. Include a brief summary of the key agenda items in your Friday letter. In this way, everyone plans ahead. Encourage the cabinet to identify problems in meeting the board's expectations so you can address them.

Finalize the Agenda With Your Board President and Vice President. Meet with the board president and vice president to finalize the agenda. If one cannot attend, ask the board president to select another member. If necessary, have another member participate by phone.

- This avoids the perception that you are too close to the president.
- It provides a second opinion if there is disagreement about what was approved at the planning meeting.
- It gives the other member experience in agenda planning.
- And it gives the other member knowledge of the agenda should the president not attend the meeting.

Agenda planning meetings frequently turn into informal strategy sessions. They provide an opportunity to test your arguments in support of initiatives and alert the board to potential political issues. You receive a broader perspective and identify potential board or community questions that might arise at the meeting. These meetings also identify information or other materials needed by the board.

Finalize the order of agenda items. Adjust the timing of the meeting based on your assessment of expected public concern or attendance. Place the most controversial items early on the agenda so the public knows when their item is to be addressed. If need be, when the agenda is formally approved in open session, move a controversial item to the front. You do not want to place these items late in the meeting as it angers the community. They may decide to vent their hostility on issues they otherwise would have ignored. Once the controversial item is complete the crowds will leave.

Also place items addressing curriculum, instruction, and students early in the agenda. These issues speak to the core of the district's work. They can be followed by any budget or operational issues, with board comments and reports at the end.

Some districts post times when the board will take up an agenda item so community members can judge their arrival. If the meeting runs ahead of schedule, you cannot start that item until the posted time. Other districts note an estimated time for each item on the agenda to help the board maintain a meeting flow. Then, if discussion takes longer than anticipated, the chair asks board members if they wish to extend the time.

At the planning meeting, review the closed session agenda. Determine its length based on the number of issues to be covered. Adjust the starting time accordingly. Your executive assistant should contact all board members to inform them of the meeting time and post it in the agenda. Notify the board if an attorney or consultant will be present for particular items.

Board Agenda Expectations

- If items are not grouped by category, identify whether they are for *discussion* or *action*.
- Number each item to correspond with the supporting material.
- Identify the administrator presenting the item so the board and the public can call or e-mail questions prior to the meeting.
- Adhere to appropriate state law for the language required to post closed session items, and list the education or legal code authorizing it.
- Only include position titles, not employee names, in the personnel report.

Once the agenda is finalized, your executive assistant posts it. Usually *posting* means distributing the agenda two or three days in advance of the meeting so the community knows what items the board will be discussing and acting upon. Today most districts post agendas on their websites and distribute them by e-mail to anyone requesting them.

If circumstances change after the agenda is posted, the board may change the agenda order or delete an item at the meeting. This requires formal board action. However, the board cannot add an item, unless there is a defined legal emergency, or change the time of an item if the time was included in the posting. Most districts only post starting times for agenda items if they are public hearings or items of great interest, such as boundary changes or significant budget reductions.

Preparing Board Meeting Materials. Board packet preparation is critical. Packets reflect your standards and expectations, as well as your knowledge of district issues. For many, these packets are the "face" of the district. You are the educational leader of the district. Ensure your packets and board materials reflect this.

Cabinet members prepare most board reports. At cabinet meetings, review the key issues of each report or recommendation and ensure they are finalized at least two days prior to the packet's being completed. Answer questions and clarify expectations for cabinet members' roles at the board meeting. Identify questions or concerns that the board, other staff, or community may raise. Consider this review a dress rehearsal for the board meeting. This provides time to make revisions or adjust the presentation.

Ultimately you are responsible for the content and quality of all materials, reports, and recommendations that go to the board. This applies equally to student athletic reports submitted by a first-year high school assistant principal or budget reports presented by the CBO. All reports must adhere to your standard format and be concise, informational, data driven, and free of grammatical error.

Many new superintendents find that they are given reports filled with grammatical errors or misspellings. Review your expectations for formatting, spelling, punctuation, grammar, and style with the leadership team. Inform everyone you have mandated your assistant to return substandard reports or materials. This should eliminate the problem.

Write board recommendations clearly and ensure they are supported by the backup material. It is better to pull a report than to submit one that raises more questions than it answers. In addition, if materials are to be handed out at the board meeting, note this in the written report to the board. The only reason for this should be data that is publicly released after packets are distributed; for example, state testing results. New materials distributed at the last minute reflect poor planning on your part and may be in violation of some state public information or *sunshine laws*. The public has a right to review materials used by the board in decision making.

Usually your assistant is responsible for pulling together all the materials needed for the board packet and distributing it to the board and public. Some larger districts have an employee who is responsible only for board packets and meetings. Whoever has this responsibility, it is a complex, time-consuming process. Establish clear guidelines and standards for the timing of the submission of final versions of all materials. Be sensitive to your assistant's workload on board packet preparation days.

A final packet review is essential, whether it is done in hard copy or electronically. Sign off on any materials sent in the board packet, even if you are not the author. Anything you send to the board is presumed to be *yours.* If an error is revealed in the report at a board meeting, you and not the staff member should take responsibility for it. Never denigrate staff in public. The staff member is already embarrassed. Address the problem in private after the meeting.

In your Friday letter, provide the board a preview of the upcoming meeting. Identify politically sensitive agenda items. Usually board members receive their packet along with the Friday letter. This gives the board the weekend to read and prepare for the meeting. They should call or e-mail you if they have questions about any item.

Just as the board does not like surprises, neither do you. It is better to know board member concerns in advance so you can work with staff prior to the board meeting. Often the questions are helpful and the answers to them can be included when you introduce the agenda item.

If a board member expresses substantial concerns about an issue and you are unable to resolve it, contact the board president prior to the board meeting. Work with the president to avoid confusion or disruption at the meeting. In addition, if you discover an unexpected problem with the agenda materials after they are distributed, notify the board president. If necessary pull the agenda item.

No matter how well you prepare packets, there may be some board members who do not read them. This occurs more often than one thinks. In turn, other board members read the packet as if they are grading a student paper and point out every misplaced comma or typo, often sending you e-mails prior to the start of the meeting. Bring these and similar issues to the attention of your board president, especially if they occur on a regular basis. These behaviors undermine staff and can erode public support. Over time, these behaviors also negatively affect the board meeting.

3. Management

Meet privately with the board president at least twenty minutes prior to the start of a closed session. Address any issues pertaining to the upcoming meeting. For example, if the assistant superintendent for instruction informs you a contingent of teachers is coming to the meeting to hear the board discuss the new math curriculum, suggest the board president move this item up on the agenda. Depending on your state's laws, you also may be able to inform the rest of the board at the end of closed session. If you cannot, at least the president is aware and can request this item be moved up when agenda approval occurs.

Closed Session. Normally you have a limited amount of time in the closed session. State laws govern what the board can discuss. In some districts the superintendent leads the board through the closed session items, while in others the board president assumes this role. In smaller districts the superintendents attends closed sessions, with cabinet members joining only for particular issues. In larger districts, cabinet members attend all or part of the closed session. Typically, personnel administrators, CBOs, and counsel attend for personnel and negotiations updates.

Some boards prefer to hear only from the superintendent. Even if this is the case, provide opportunities for directors and assistant superintendents to participate in closed sessions. They have information and expertise that can assist the board in its discussions. However, prepare staff if they lack experience working with boards in closed session. The experience can be unnerving for the novice.

Open Session. After the closed session, the board adjourns to the open, public session. At the posted time, the board president calls the meeting to order. The board president then moves through the items on the agenda.

As noted earlier, the board may limit how long each person speaks to items that are on the agenda. A time limit is essential for meetings when controversial issues are discussed or voted on. In some districts 50 to 100 people may wish to address the board. The time quickly mounts so that decisions are reached very late when everyone is tired and not at their best. Some boards call special meetings to address controversial issues so as to give the community sufficient time to express their concerns and opinions.

The Superintendent's Role at Board Meetings. The superintendent plays an important role at board meetings. You met with the board president to develop a cohesive, organized agenda. You prepared a detailed and complex packet of materials for the board to review and included recommendations for board action. You want the meeting to go well and the board to approve the recommendations. While boards have differing expectations of their superintendent at board meetings, the following guidelines apply in most situations.

✓ Provide a brief introduction for each agenda item after the president announces it. This gives the board and public necessary background information and frames the issue being discussed. Keep your comments concise. Then introduce the staff member responsible for presenting the item or report.

✓ Once you make your comments, do not speak on that item again unless asked or you raise your hand and are called upon. Do not dominate the conversation. Respect the board's role. It is their meeting, not yours.

✓ Intervene if staff members are attacked by the board or public. Staff, even cabinet members, need to feel safe attending board meetings and making presentations. Do not leave them "hanging in the wind" when they are attacked. Exercise judgment in determining whether to answer the question or deflect the attack away from the staff member and onto the subject.

✓ However, if you are the one under attack, do not respond. Be professional, calm, and poised and never respond to accusations. Answer reasonable questions, ignore those that are not. You, not the attackers, are expected to set the tone for the district. This is particularly true if it is a board member attacking you. Show grace under fire. When the board member is through, you can make a statement of fact or you may choose to do nothing. If such attacks persist, work with your board chair to address the problem. If more than one board member consistently undermines your work at board meetings, consider that your tenure may be drawing to a close.

✓ Consider where you sit. Some superintendents sit next to the board president, while others prefer to sit at the end of the table, next to their administrative assistant. In some districts, assistant superintendents sit at the board table, while in others the assistant superintendent or higher level cabinet members sit at tables adjacent to the board. Every arrangement has advantages and disadvantages. Confer with your board president to determine what works best for your situation.

An advantage to sitting next to the board president is that you can confer and advise the president during the meeting. This is particularly helpful if board packets were sent electronically and board members use computers during the meeting to refer to the packets and their notes. A disadvantage is that the public may perceive you as controlling the board.

An advantage to sitting next to your administrative assistant is you can confer with him or her. This is important, as you may need the assistant to return to the office to pick up materials or run off additional copies of important materials. Sometimes the assistant can provide the names of people in the audience or speaking, or can pass on other important information to you.

An advantage to sitting at the end of the table is that you can observe board members, cabinet, and audience. You can assess the body language of the board and members' response to your comments or public comments. It is difficult to do this if you sit next to the board president.

Example

One district has the superintendent and the assistant superintendent at either end of the board table connected to an electronic chat room. It is amazingly effective for gathering information and responding to questions. The board president has eye contact with the superintendent and uses signals to initiate communication with the superintendent. This requires sophisticated technology not available to all districts.

✓ Always have a notepad and take notes. Maintain a to-do list based on the discussions. Staff or the board may not remember what information was requested or what actions were approved. You do not want to rely on the memory of others for these follow-up tasks.

You do not want to wait until the minutes are completed or rely on the memory of others for these important follow-up tasks.

✓ Pay attention to your appearance. Your attire should be formal and professional. This is especially true if your meetings are televised.

✓ Pay attention to your behavior. Members of the audience are observing you and the board. They read your facial expressions. Avoid conveying your thoughts through facial or body language. You make a statement if you are bored, yawning, or fidgeting during a presentation. Stay alert even if you need caffeine. Also, do not allow yourself to be distracted during presentations and discussions. If you become distracted, you may miss an important statement or question. As a result you will be unable to respond when asked to by the board president. This is embarrassing.

✓ Help the board look good. Board members are elected officials. You work for them. You want the public to perceive you and the board as receptive, competent, professional, and productive. Do not criticize or otherwise denigrate them or their decisions in any way.

4. Follow-Up

Follow-up to a board meeting sets the stage for future successful board meetings. The day after the meeting, examine the impact of the previous evening's meeting on the next board agenda. If needed, begin the process for making changes. Your to-do list made during the meeting is helpful. Send an e-mail to the cabinet with highlights of this list and any immediate actions you are taking. If your executive assistant attends the meetings, ask for feedback.

Some superintendents even have short, regularly scheduled cabinet meetings the morning after each board meeting. These are particularly useful if the meeting was a difficult one. They can always be cancelled but are hard to schedule. Having these meetings in place permits venting, debriefing, and moving forward. This is particularly helpful for cabinet members with concerns over the meeting.

Call your board chair and review the meeting. If need be, call or e-mail other board members, the press, or community members. If you promised materials or further information to the board, work with your administrative assistant to ensure it is included in the next Friday letter.

It is a time for reflection on what went well and what did not. These reflections form the basis for any needed changes. In particular examine actions that occurred against the progress you wanted made for students and the achievement of the district's goals. Based on these reflections, decide what you want to accomplish at the next meeting. Prepare what you want to discuss with the cabinet in regard to this and the next board meeting.

Validate cabinet and staff members for their work. Send thank-you notes to those who presented. For staff members who had a difficult time, it is important to provide feedback and support. Review with them or their immediate supervisors what can be done differently in the future.

SUMMARY

Working effectively with a school board is challenging. You and the board should function as a team, knowing and respecting each other's roles. The board is your employer and you are responsible for running the district. You also are responsible for preparing information the board needs to make decisions and conduct meetings.

As you work with a board, always be respectful. Use the information gained from each meeting to further inform your work. This is a never-ending process as board members come and go.

The following will assist you as you begin working with a board.

- Learn the role of the board and state laws pertaining to school governance and board authority. Remember, it takes a majority of the full board to approve an action.
- Treat all board members the same, listen carefully to them, and keep them informed.
- Understand the difference between micromanagement and governance.
- Ensure the board has ongoing training.
- Understand the difference between board policy and board regulations. Keep board policies up to date.
- Know how to conduct yourself during board elections.
- Understand the public nature of e-mail, tweeting, texting, and Facebook when communicating with the board.
- Schedule informal meetings with board members to gain a better perspective on their views and needs.
- Use formal communications with the board, such as Friday letters, to present district information.
- Work closely with your board president and understand the uniqueness of the president's role.
- Prepare carefully for board meetings. Work with your board president and vice president to finalize agendas. Develop a yearly calendar of routine agenda items.

- Determine with the board the frequency, time, and place of board meetings a year in advance. Realize the pros and cons of the decisions surrounding this.
- Learn what is included in a board agenda and board packet. Understand the difference between open and closed session. Learn the role of the public at the board meeting.
- Prepare board meeting materials thoughtfully and carefully. Review and approve all documents sent to the board.
- Understand the superintendent's role at board meetings and the need to be prepared for each item on the agenda. Follow up on each meeting and the decisions made.

As time goes by, your work with a board will become more instinctual. You will understand the individual and collective needs of the board. This does not mean you will avoid conflict. Rather it means you develop a good working relationship that allows the district to progress toward meeting its goals.

Working With Employee Groups

All superintendents must master negotiations, or *collective bargaining,* as it is more formally known. In almost every state, public school employees have the right to bargain wages, benefits, and working conditions. This right usually covers teachers, support staff, and, in some instances, administrators.

Employee compensation, including benefits and mandated employer costs, consumes between 85 percent and 95 percent of a district's unrestricted general fund expenditures. Employee work rules can affect student instruction and staff development. Your success in managing negotiations affects your success in achieving your goals and the district's educational mission.

Collective bargaining is not confined to negotiations. It includes your daily work with unions, the board, and staff. By mastering a wide range of complex and often interconnected skills, you can manage the complexities of the collective bargaining process. Learn state law, contract management, finance, and budgeting. Demonstrate good judgment and develop a deep reservoir of trust and confidence with your board, community, union leadership, and their constituents.

Also learn to balance the needs of students, staff, parents, and community. These needs include the following.

- For students and parents, a quality education.
- For staff, equitable compensation and supportive working conditions.
- For the community, fiscally sound and educationally successful schools.

Achieving this balance requires strong leadership skills. Problems arise when the balance is lost and one group believes that the district is meeting the needs of another group at its expense. Use a common set of core values to address this issue. These include the following.

- Honoring staff members for their work and commitment.
- Respecting the integrity and value of the collective bargaining process.
- Acknowledging that student instructional needs are paramount.

Your employees must believe that you, the board, and the community support their need for a fair and equitable wage and positive working conditions. They expect to be viewed as partners in the education of the students and respected for their skills and knowledge. Employees who feel poorly treated and underpaid are less inclined to implement new programs or work harder at already challenging jobs.

Many new superintendents have little or no collective bargaining experience. They are thrust into negotiations or contract management issues from the moment of their arrival. Situations arise that do not appear to be negotiation issues, yet require district-union collaboration and problem solving. Failure to manage these issues has a long-lasting, negative impact, but their successful resolution earns the respect of staff and affirms the board's good judgment in hiring you.

Mastering the collective bargaining process begins with working with unions and their leadership. This involves time, attention, and a willingness to learn from experience. The information that follows provides an overview of what is involved. The negotiations process is covered in Chapter 8.

ESTABLISH RELATIONSHIPS

Your first step is to create or maintain a positive working relationship with employee groups. You are judged by what you and your administrative team do throughout the year. If you lead from a foundation of absolute integrity and trust, the staff is likely to trust you in negotiations. If you are perceived as untruthful, untrustworthy, or sneaky, unions will treat you as such at the bargaining table.

There are no time-outs for integrity and trust due to extenuating circumstances; no permission to take shortcuts. Trust crumbles rapidly if you say one thing to teachers and another to the board, community, or parents. This is especially important during times of crisis. Staff members look to you for strong leadership and adherence to principle. If they lose confidence in your integrity, they will not respond positively to your recommendations or leadership.

1. Respect the Integrity of Agreements

Negotiations work best when staff is confident that you respect the integrity of negotiated collective bargaining agreements. Confidence grows as you work with the management team and board to ensure contract provisions are known, understood, and followed. Staff should view you as the *keeper of the contract,* the one who honors the bargaining process. Do not ignore or demean contract provisions you, the board, or administrators find inconvenient. If you do not like a provision, seek to change it at the bargaining table.

Provide workshops on contract management for the management team whenever there are contract changes. Administrators must know who to contact for contract management questions. They need to know you hold them accountable for contract management and will not blindly support them if they fail to adhere to contract provisions.

Conversely, the administrative team and, in particular, principals expect you to work with them to resolve contract implementation issues. You want to know how the contract impacts student instruction or impedes the management of the district. Set aside time at leadership team meetings for administrators to voice concerns and problem solve. This helps you determine what issues the district may wish to negotiate.

2. Meet Regularly With Union Leadership

Schedule monthly meetings with union leaders to discuss matters of mutual interest. Union participants may include the president, executive committee members, or the head of the negotiating team. Include your human resources (HR) person or a principal. These are not negotiations sessions and do not require public notification.

Note-taking practices vary. If notes are not taken, encourage the practice. Informal notes help you refer back to what was discussed and any agreed-on follow-up actions. These notes are not meant for general distribution.

These meetings are a time for frank discussions. They provide an opportunity to communicate areas of possible concern, resolve problems, and generally keep each party informed of needs and expectations. Either side can identify situations in which the other side is violating contract provisions. You can review district goals and identify how specific contract provisions are hindering instruction. The goal is for each side to understand and respect the others' view and to work toward a resolution.

Sometimes issues arise that should be shared with your leadership team. For example, if union leadership reports that principals are not implementing a new contract provision correctly, inform the principals by e-mail and schedule a discussion at your next leadership team meeting. Let union leadership know you are following up on their concerns. In turn the union should inform you of how it is following up on concerns you presented. This builds mutual trust. These meetings serve a variety of purposes.

Purposes of Meetings

☐ Get to know union leadership better in an informal setting.
☐ Communicate about the state of the district and the impact of new or proposed state or federal legislations.
☐ Discuss ways the district and staff can better work together to improve student learning and achievement.
☐ Exchange contract implementation challenges for both management and the unions.
☐ Problem solve site-level contract management issues.
☐ Discuss issues that may need to be negotiated.
☐ Respond to questions about management decisions.

Example

One new superintendent in a small district with a history of acrimonious negotiations asked the union presidents to identify the most difficult issues they had with the district. Both the teacher and support staff leaders mentioned concerns with the board's decision-making process. The superintendent proposed scheduling meetings with the presidents prior to each board meeting to review agendas and board packet materials. This deepened their understanding of the board's role and the factors influencing its decision making. Relationships soon improved.

Some districts schedule meetings of the superintendent and teacher or support staff representatives from the schools. The purpose of these meetings is to narrow the gap between the district and the schools by sharing information and problem solving. Agendas are mutually developed. These are not negotiation meetings, although minutes usually are taken. Unresolved problems are then discussed at the union's executive committee and the superintendent's cabinet. Some issues eventually end up in formal negotiations.

Remind your leadership team to inform you of union conflicts. Use your Friday letter to inform the board of contract issues, as the board also does not appreciate surprises. If necessary, allocate time in a closed session to review substantive issues.

3. Respect the Union

Respecting union leadership is an essential strategy for district success. No matter how union leaders behave, they are the elected representatives of your employees. Some have a global perspective and are eager to work cooperatively with the district; others may be aggressive and oppositional. Either way, cultivate a positive relationship with union leadership. The following are some things you can do.

- ❒ Provide them advance notice of important district events.

- ❒ Inform them of issues so they are prepared to respond to calls from their membership.

- ❒ Introduce them at meetings.

- ❒ Invite them to participate in important district committees.

- ❒ Seek their advice and counsel when staff-related problems arise.

- ❒ Seek their advice and counsel on issues that affect their constituents.

Union leaders usually work full time. Many are outstanding employees dedicated to their work, schools, and district. They volunteer to serve in a leadership role to support their fellow employees. In some districts the union may negotiate and pay for a release period or extra preparation time for the president or chief negotiator. In many districts the unions provide a stipend for the union president and chief negotiator for all the time and work they put into their roles.

Union leaders receive support from their state unions usually through a full-time county or regional representative. Many state organizations provide training and workshops for presidents and chief negotiators, usually during the summer. They provide newsletters and bulletins, and they also provide additional support during contentious negotiations or grievances.

Even with this support, union leaders lack the time or resources to be as knowledgeable about issues as you and your staff. It is not in your best interest to stand by while the union takes a position that you know is counter to its best interests. Where appropriate, provide the advice and information needed for the union to self-correct and make a better decision. Do so even if the union leadership fails to treat the district in the same manner.

If you take advantage of the union, ultimately it will realize the error and resent you for not helping it avoid the mistake. This greatly weakens the trust relationship. Playing "gotcha" is counterproductive. Always act with the utmost integrity. Maintaining trust is essential. Union leaders report back to their peers and constituents, through e-mails or newsletters. You can lose the respect of your employees if you fail to maintain the highest levels of professional behavior.

It is easy to forget the union leader you work with on a day-to-day basis is actually a third grade teacher or a bus driver who wants to perform his or her job well and with integrity. Union leaders do not have the same flexibility of schedule that you have.

How to Show Respect to Union Leadership

- Use e-mail, text messages, or voice mail to contact them so you do not interrupt their workday.
- Recognize that it may take them awhile to get back to you as they probably lack a secretary to assist them.
- Offer to meet them at lunch or after school at their work site instead of your office.
- Anticipate a need and send them information prior to their having to request it.
- Send sufficient numbers of copies of important materials.
- Thank them when they provide you with a heads up.

Many unions negotiate a provision in their contract requiring the district to provide a small office where the union president works so she or he can conduct business more efficiently. These offices may include a dedicated phone line, fax machine, answering machine, shredder, and a small copier. It is in your interest to arrange for this space. It facilitates smoother communication between union membership and the district.

Also, recognize the difference between how decisions are made in a typical union as compared to how districts make decisions. You have considerable independent decision-making authority; union presidents do not. Respect the time and communication limitations of your union leadership. Do not expect them to move as quickly as you are prepared to do. For example, you and a union president identify a problem and are recommending a solution. You contact your board president who agrees with your decision and approves your moving ahead. In turn, the union president first must communicate or confer with an executive committee before making a commitment. Executive committee members in turn may need to confer with their membership. This takes time.

Almost all districts provide full board agendas and packets to union leadership. If your district does not, instigate this practice. Either you or your assistant should notify the union president when items are on the agenda that are of importance to the union. Oftentimes the packet comes to the school and gets to the president the day of the board meeting. The packet may be available online only a day or two before the meeting. This limits the president's ability to review the material in advance and consult with the executive committee. Providing a heads up is appreciated and develops respect.

Provide Accurate and Timely Data. In most states, districts are legally bound to provide accurate and timely information to unions for collective bargaining purposes. Nothing ruins union relationships faster than providing inaccurate data or refusing to respond to requests for information.

Ask the unions if they receive what they request. If not, work with your executive assistant and cabinet to review your expectations. The district should respond to requests in a timely manner. Carefully review the materials, as unions may use this information to make decisions about what to negotiate. Offer to meet with the union to answer questions.

The district benefits by having an educated union, one that knows and understands how the district operates. Unions are particularly interested in the financial state of the district. They need accurate information about the district's revenues, expenditures, and long-range financial projections to make informed choices about salary and benefits. In addition to financial information, unions frequently request information about enrollments, class sizes, health benefit programs, and staffing. Check with counsel if you have questions about what you must provide.

A Receptive District Office. The district office environment affects employer-employee relations and the negotiations process. If employees feel respected when they visit the district office, they are far more likely to believe you have their best interests in mind.

You are responsible for establishing the district office environment. You want employees to perceive the office as a pleasant place to visit, where everyone works hard supporting the district mission. This sets a tone for the entire district.

When you first become superintendent, bring together all district office employees. Thank them for what they do and convey to them your expectations for how visitors should be treated. Assume they are already doing this, even if they are not, and reiterate how important it is to treat all visitors with respect.

District office staff should greet everyone promptly and courteously and help resolve immediate problems. This is especially important for staff members who rarely visit the district office. They will share with their peers if they were treated poorly. Before long, the district office and the superintendent have the reputation of not caring. Employees who are uncomfortable visiting the district office are less likely to respect you and follow your leadership.

AN OVERVIEW OF COLLECTIVE BARGAINING

Your working relationships with the union leadership and members will assist you at the table. You also need a thorough understanding of collective bargaining issues prior to beginning negotiations. Having this knowledge and the appropriate systems in place facilitates negotiations at the table.

1. Learn About Negotiations

During your preparation to become a superintendent, you learned about collective bargaining by participating in your district's collective bargaining process, talking with your superintendent and HR administrator regarding their experiences, attending workshops, and reviewing state and federal laws governing the collective bargaining process. What you learned included the following.

- How a Superintendent Prepares for Negotiations
- The Role of the Superintendent or District Negotiator at the Bargaining Table
- The Role of the Board and the Relationship Between the Board and the Superintendent During Collective Bargaining
- The Relationship Between the Superintendent and Union Leadership
- The Relationship Between the Superintendent and the Other Members of the Negotiations Team
- Strategies Used by Districts and Unions

Even if your state does not engage in collective bargaining, understand these issues. You never know when you may move to a state or district that does use this process. These basic concepts also assist you in working with any employee group.

Build on your knowledge by continuing to review negotiation advisories distributed by law firms or state organizations and by attending pertinent workshops. Keep abreast of state finances, especially if the state budget directly impacts your district's revenues for the current or upcoming school year. Inform the board of any changes in funding that affect the district's ability to provide salary increases to employees. Attend county or regional superintendent meetings in which superintendents share negotiations experiences. These are helpful sources of information about potential issues you may face. Share what you learn with your board. For example, if superintendents from districts similar in size and resources to yours report their teachers settling for a 3 percent increase in compensation, it is likely your teachers know this and expect a similar settlement.

You are responsible for maintaining your finance, budget, and negotiations skills. This is an ongoing process as circumstances change rapidly. Maintain this focus throughout your tenure.

2. Collective Bargaining History

In most districts, one union represents all teachers, counselors, and librarians. Another union represents all nonteaching support staff, such as secretaries, custodians, bus drivers, groundskeepers, instructional aids, and district office personnel. Many large districts have separate unions representing food service workers or bus drivers. Some may have as many as eight recognized unions.

Learn the unique history and culture of negotiations in your district. Support staff negotiations may differ considerably from teacher union negotiations. One unit may be far more militant than the others. Institutional memories are long, and even ancient.

Example

In a district where a strike occurred thirty years ago, some support staff still refuse to work with members who crossed a picket line.

Learn the historic bottom line or "over our dead body" issues for the district and each employee group. These are issues that are considered nonnegotiable.

In one district, moving from a seven-period to six-period workday at the high school was an "over our dead body" issue for the board. In another, not reducing the number of night custodians was a "bottom line" issue for support staff.

Respect these positions. Learn why they are critical to each party. This information helps determine the viability of proposed changes and negotiation strategies. Making substantive changes in bargaining practices is risky at best and even more so if you lack understanding of the history and culture of the district. You will gain respect for your leadership if you take time to learn.

During your transition you reviewed the contracts for each employee group. As negotiations approach, schedule meetings with key board members, cabinet members, and administrators who served on negotiations teams.

Questions to Ask Each Employee Group About Negotiations

- Are there well-established protocols?
- Does the process differ for teachers or support staff?
- Who sits at the table for the district and who represents each employee group?
- What is the role of the chief business official (CBO) and the HR administrator?
- What is the role of board members?
- Who speaks for the district?
- Does legal counsel sit at the table?
- What were last year's issues?
- Are there unresolved issues?
- Are there contract provisions limiting the instructional program? Other operations?
- Are there any unusual provisions in the contract? If so, why?
- Are negotiations conflict-driven or nonadversarial?
- Who takes the minutes and what kind are taken?

When meeting with board members, ask them to critique the last negotiations cycle.

> ### Questions to Ask Board
> ### Members About Negotiations
>
> - Were they satisfied with the negotiations outcomes?
> - Were they kept informed of progress at the table?
> - Did they have enough time in closed session to discuss the issues?
> - What worked or did not work for them?
> - What are their expectations for this year's negotiations?

At the end of this fact-finding process, you will have a much better understanding of your role in negotiations and any needed changes. Review proposed changes with the board before bringing them to the cabinet, as the negotiations process represents the board's interests.

3. Nonadversarial Bargaining

Many districts have a strong history and commitment to nonadversarial, problem solving, or win-win negotiations. These districts moved from adversarial or positional negotiations to a form of negotiations in which the parties respect each other's needs and positions and develop solutions to commonly held problems.

The underlying value is "What's good for the district is good for teachers; what's good for teachers is good for the district and its students." Some districts plan for the transition by having both district and union leadership participate in a training program. These districts also may retain a neutral consultant to guide them through their first nonadversarial negotiations.

Moving to nonadversarial, problem-solving negotiations requires strong district and union leadership. Often this is in response to a series of negotiations that both parties felt were acrimonious or unsuccessful in addressing their interests. There may be a history of conflict between the board or superintendent and the union. A rigid board, weak district leadership, poor contract management, and negative union leadership all contribute to acrimonious relationships.

Districts mired in contentious, conflict-driven positional negotiations often lack resources to provide competitive compensation. Nonadversarial negotiations work best when a district has sufficient resources to adequately compensate staff so the resolution of other issues does not become problematic. Many districts use problem solving for noncompensation issues but revert back to positional bargaining to address salary issues. In these situations the compensation bargaining is likely to be less adversarial.

In some, rare districts, the superintendent meets yearly with the union leadership and negotiations are completed in a few hours. The CBO or HR head may be present or on call. This approach flourishes in districts with commonly held values, trust, communication, and abundant resources for salary increases. Work closely with the board and your unions to monitor the efficacy of this model for the district. One or two changes in the internal or external environment can result in a deterioration of the relationship and the start of adversarial negotiations.

In some states or districts, negotiations are held in public. The press, community members, and interested staff attend the sessions and listen to negotiations. This presents a unique set of issues and challenges. Learn about the process before the start of negotiations.

4. Role of the Board

The role of individual members in negotiations varies from district to district. Following are three of the more common models used by districts.

❏ *Two or three board members serve as negotiators for the district, with the superintendent playing a subordinate advisory role.* This occurs most frequently in small districts where the superintendent also serves as principal. This model works well when teachers meet with the board to discuss wages without the support of a union. It is now a less viable model, as most small district staffs are represented by unions. It is further complicated by state funding formulas and legislation.

For this model to work, the board members must be as well-versed and trained as a superintendent. A consequence is that teachers view the superintendent as less powerful and go directly to the board when issues arise.

❏ *One or two board members take turns serving on the negotiations team.* They sit at the table, with the superintendent serving as spokesperson. The role of board members is to listen carefully, advise the superintendent, and report back to the board. Districts using this model are often small and more affluent. Some board members serve for years and are knowledgeable and skilled members of the negotiations team.

These board members have considerable training or sophisticated financial or budgeting skills. They are trusted by the board and work closely with you. They provide valuable advice and guidance, especially during your first negotiations. However, if resources are restricted, there are contentious issues, or the board itself is divided, you may find yourself negotiating with the board as well as the unions.

❑ *No board member sits at the table. The superintendent or other designated administrator, such as HR, serves as spokesperson.* This is the most common model for most middle to large districts. Here you negotiate within the parameters set by the board and keep the board fully appraised of what occurs at the table. No board member is put in the position of tentatively agreeing to a settlement later rejected by the entire board. However, you may have board members who would like to participate more actively.

Learn your district's practice and support it. Review problems or concerns with the board and develop protocols outlining the board's role and involvement. Hold off making major changes until you complete one full year of negotiations.

All board members, especially those new or sitting at the table, should receive negotiations training. Almost all state school board associations provide this service. Attend these workshops with your board and discuss how the training content applies to your district.

If the board members sit on the team, avoid having a majority of board members on the team. Once a tentative agreement is reached at the table, the agreement must be approved by a majority of the board. If a majority participates at the table, a union could rightly hold that any agreement reached is final. This disenfranchises the remaining board members, leading to possible internal board conflict.

Having board members serve on the negotiations team does not guarantee full board support. For example: board members on a team believe they have reached a fair agreement. When the full board reviews it, they and the superintendent cannot convince a majority to support it.

5. Composition of the Team

In most small districts the superintendent is responsible for managing the entire negotiations process. You serve as the head of the negotiations team and determine its composition, and you select the district's spokesperson.

In larger districts the superintendent delegates key aspects of the negotiations process to another cabinet-level administrator, usually the head of HR. The superintendent confers with the designee to select the negotiations team. If there is more than one union, several teams may be assembled. Review contracts, as some may include language limiting the composition of these teams. Most district negotiation teams are fairly small in number and may include the following.

- ❑ Superintendent or Designee
- ❑ Board Members (as Discussed in the Previous Section)
- ❑ Human Resource Administrator
- ❑ Chief Business Official
- ❑ Site Administrator(s)
- ❑ Legal Counsel

Team composition varies depending on past practice, district culture, contract language, and the union. In some districts the superintendent only sits at the table for teacher negotiations. In other districts the CBO joins negotiations when finances are discussed.

If your district has a long history of contentious and time-consuming negotiations, your board may mandate that you delegate table responsibility to counsel and a cabinet-level administrator. Work closely with your designees, as you are ultimately responsible for any settlement proposal submitted to the board.

Cabinet Members. CBOs are key players in negotiations because they prepare and present fiscal information for both the staff and the district. They prepare spreadsheets and analyses for board discussion in closed sessions. They also meet with union representatives prior to the start of negotiations, as well as during the year, to review the district's finances.

Everyone must perceive the CBO as competent, honest, and forthcoming. Trusting the numbers is absolutely essential for successful negotiations. Skilled CBOs understand this role and avoid partisanship wherever possible.

Most districts include a cabinet-level HR person on the team. This person is knowledgeable about hiring, contract implementation, and other personnel issues. If your HR person is a mid-level manager with limited authority or negotiations experience, ask that person to attend only when background or data is needed on a specific issue with which she or he is familiar.

Site Administrators. Including principals provides a needed site perspective to counterbalance the staff perspective. It gives principals broader experience in preparation for districtwide responsibilities. Principals are usually supportive of having one of their members on the team.

A downside is their absence from school for a considerable part of the school day. This concerns some parents and staff. And their role can become politicized if negotiations become contentious. To mitigate this, some districts rotate this responsibility among interested principals.

Legal Counsel. The district's legal counsel is an important member of the team. Counsel provides guidance on contract language and the legality of recommended provisions or agreements, as well as advice on strategy and tactics. The role of counsel differs from district to district. Some sit at the table and lead the negotiations, some attend as observers, while others are on call to respond to concerns. In many districts, counsel meets with the board in closed session to provide the board an opportunity to review complex issues.

Many unions request support from their state organizations, as they feel they are overmatched by the district. They perceive the district as having highly educated and trained, full-time administrators representing the interests of the board and the district. They want state or county representatives to even out the playing field. These representatives may help or hinder settlements. The more contentious the representative, the more likely the district counsel will sit at the table. Be sensitive to this issue.

Example

> The support staff union president informed the superintendent that negotiations were bogging down because of the district's aggressive counsel. He proposed that both sides "go it alone." The superintendent agreed. Immediately, negotiations became less contentious and more productive.

Having an attorney at the table may force the union to have a similar outside representative. It may undermine your role and authority as well. In many situations the presence of an attorney makes negotiations more formal and adversarial.

Explore the issue of counsel sitting at the table with your board and cabinet. Make changes with board approval. If an attorney sits at the table, make every effort to have the attorney play a subordinate role.

Consultants. On occasion, both the district and a union may agree to bring a special consultant into the negotiations process. This occurs when the topic is so specialized that both parties lack sufficient information to make an informed decision. Examples of this include negotiating new health plans or annuity programs. Both parties should agree on the consultant's role.

Executive Assistant. An important role of your assistant is providing support for you and the board during negotiations. In larger districts the assistant to the HR administrator may do this. The assistant serves as an invaluable resource and guide throughout the process. Meet with the assistant to review the previous superintendent's negotiations files, notes, session minutes, and binders.

Assistants provide materials for negotiations sessions and for the board. They communicate regularly with board members who call in to find out how things are going. In smaller districts, the assistant serves as a confidential sounding board during negotiations. In all districts your assistant always has up-to-date information about negotiations. Meet regularly with your assistant during negotiations.

Unions select their own negotiating team. The number of staff on the team is outlined in the contract. Usually the team is representative of the differing schools or divisions. Normally it includes the union president, the lead staff negotiator, and several other staff selected by the union's executive committee or council.

When there is a long history of amicable negotiations, unions are likely to include experienced problem solvers. As might be expected, if negotiations are confrontational and difficult, the unions are likely to select their more positional members. State-level union representatives often serve as the union's chief negotiator.

6. Support Staff Negotiations

In many districts, support staff negotiations differ somewhat from teacher negotiations. Superintendents delegate responsibility to a cabinet-level administrator. The district team also may include mid-level managers and site administrators interested in support staff negotiations experience. Frequently, board members do not participate.

Make certain your board treats support staff and their unions with respect. They are central to achieving the mission of the district.

A district facing a large budget reduction due to an abrupt change in state support worked with the support staff union to establish a pay freeze. The teachers' union refused to do this, even though it meant a great many staff layoffs. Facing pressure from the support staff, the teachers reluctantly agreed to the freeze, saving jobs.

In many districts, support staff unions wait until teacher negotiations are complete and "ride" the teachers' salary increase. This strategy assumes, often rightly, that teachers will leverage a stronger settlement. In these circumstances, negotiations may start at the same time as teacher negotiations, with all issues resolved save compensation.

Support staff unions often feel that the district places a higher priority on the needs of teachers and administrators: "We are the last hired and the first fired." This perception may be based on a historic reality. In tough economic times, support positions are often eliminated before teaching and administrative positions.

Nonrepresented Support Staff. In many states, support staff members who work with administrators responsible for negotiations are not permitted to join unions themselves. This is because they are privy to confidential collective bargaining information. In some states these support staff are considered *confidential* employees. The term *confidential* does not pertain to keeping secrets, although confidential employees may not discuss their inside knowledge of negotiations.

Each district determines which employees are considered confidential. The number of designated employees varies with the size of the district, the number of bargaining units, and how many cabinet-level administrators are responsible for negotiations. In most smaller districts, the superintendent's assistant is a confidential employee, along with one or two staff members who work in the business office. In larger districts, confidential employees will include secretaries and support staff from human resources.

Confidential employees receive the same rights and benefits of support staff union members through board policy. The superintendent or assistant superintendent represents their interests before the board. In many districts these employees are considered members of the management team for compensation purposes. In larger districts, confidential employees may have their own bargaining unit.

There is a natural tension between the district and support staff unions regarding the number of confidential employees a district may designate. This is because these employees are usually some of the more highly compensated support staff. The unions want these positions as part of their bargaining units.

Unions pay close attention to the work of the designated employees to make certain they participate in collective bargaining support work. If not, they petition to have the position returned to the bargaining unit. As a new superintendent, conduct a review of your district's confidential employees to make certain they should be exempt. This will build trust with your support staff union.

7. Management Negotiations

Many states have differing laws governing certificated administrators (those requiring a teaching certificate) and support staff administrators (those not requiring a teaching certificate). This is particularly true for tenure provisions. Review these laws with counsel. Support staff administrator positions may include lower level, nonunion transportation or food services supervisors, as well as nonunion district office level confidential employees.

Most administrators in smaller districts are not represented by a union. In some states this is not even permissible. If you are in a district with no formal administrative representation, you *meet and confer* with representatives of the management team to address compensation, benefit, and working condition issues. They have no right to bargain with the board.

In some districts the management team representatives include both certificated administrators and support staff administrators. Or, you may meet with representatives of both groups separately. In much larger districts, administrators may have recognized bargaining units.

Meet-and-confer conversations take the place of formal negotiations. Usually they occur after the district has completed formal negotiations with the teacher and support staff unions. Your role is to listen, problem solve, and accurately and fairly represent issues and proposed resolutions to the board.

Encourage administrators to identify issues of concern and present their positions or requests to you. After a full discussion, thank the management team representatives. Review the pros and cons of the issues and present your recommendations to the board in a closed session. Unlike teachers or support staff, administrators must accept whatever decision the board makes. The board may accept or reject your recommendations, or they can ask you to present a different resolution for the administrators to consider.

Your role is challenging. While the administrators expect you to serve as their advocate before the board, the board expects you to help them make good decisions. If the board turns down an administrative request, the administrators may think you sided with the board or didn't fight hard enough. This can impact your relationship with the team.

Schedule sufficient time with the board to fully explain the importance of the administrators' requests. While the board has the authority to turn down your recommendations, doing so repeatedly may have consequences.

A board repeatedly rejected a requested reduction in the administrators' work year. The administrators blamed the superintendent for not representing them well. After three years, the administrators formed a union. They began formal negotiations and soon achieved their goal.

Meet with representatives of the management team on a regular basis to review their issues. Bring these to the board throughout the year. This will make the resolution of complex issues less challenging and enhance your leadership role with both the board and your team.

As superintendent, you should work with the board and management to develop policies governing working conditions. These polices normally mirror the contract guarantees afforded teachers and support staff. They address such issues as leaves, work year, paid vacation, professional development, promotions, demotions, and other related practices, such as compensation for assistant principals supervising sporting events on evenings and weekends.

Review the policies and agreements that govern management team employees. Give special care to administering these agreements. Respect these policies at the same level of rigor and integrity as you do union contracts.

A board's authority to change management compensation or working conditions is limited. The board may not unilaterally modify management team policies during the course of the school year. Any modification must occur with the consent of those affected. However, the board can unilaterally modify policies governing nonrepresented administrators during the current year for the following school year. As with all policies and agreements, review proposed changes with counsel. Usually changes are not needed during a school year unless a fiscal or some other crisis arises.

Respecting Management. Some district cultures are decidedly anti-administration. People complain about the cost of the district's "bloated bureaucracy." Usually the issue is the size of the district office, not the number of administrators at the schools. Others claim that administrators have it easy compared to the teachers or administrators don't do much when the kids aren't in school. Some boards tacitly or overtly support these contentions by treating administrators as "second-class citizens."

Many districts view administrative compensation differently than teacher or support staff compensation. Boards and other staff claim that because the total amount of an administrator's salary is greater, they do not need nor deserve the same percentage increase as lower paid teachers and support staff. While this strategy may validate teacher and support staff, it builds resentment when administrators fail to receive the same increase as other employees. This makes it difficult for you to motivate your administrators to higher levels of performance.

Assess your district's attitude and values pertaining to administration. Determine if any or all of the criticisms are accurate. An important task for a new superintendent is to gather data on the size, organization, and cost of the management team. Be prepared to communicate your findings in a positive manner.

Information to Gather About Management Team Compensation Issues

☐ Show the growth of management over time as a function of the number of students, staff, and size of district budget.

☐ Show the same for teachers and support staff.

☐ Show administrative salaries as daily (per diem) rates as well as the annual total.

☐ Compare administrative per diem rates to the per diem rates of teachers with similar experience and degrees.

☐ Adjust teacher work year days to those of administrators and then compare total salaries.

☐ Compare the number of full-time equivalent (FTE) district administrators in your district with the FTE of other, comparable districts in your area, as well as at the state and national level.

☐ Compare your district percentage of budget for administration with that of other districts and your state.

☐ Fully disclose all administrative compensation decisions made by the board.

☐ Clarify the role and responsibilities of administration through updated and publicly available job descriptions and organization charts.

☐ Meet with union leaders to review impending changes to administrative organization, job descriptions, and organization and compensation changes.

☐ Hold all administrators to a high standard of performance and accountability.

☐ Listen carefully to concerns expressed about individual administrators or the management team.

Review your findings with cabinet and the board to determine if changes are needed. Data and transparency are central to supporting the cost of administration. People expect you to make an independent judgment and not just support the status quo.

Example

A new superintendent joined a district where everyone complained about the size of the district office. The superintendent reviewed data about the size of the management team over the previous ten years. He discovered that contrary to public opinion, there were fewer district office administrators proportionally than ten years ago. After reporting this information at a public meeting, the grumbling ceased. The data is updated and reviewed annually.

In successful districts the relationship between the administration, the superintendent, and the board is a positive one. The superintendent fairly and accurately serves both groups. Your administrators should perceive you as caring as much about their needs and interests as you do those of the students, teachers, and support staff.

Both boards and superintendents have a vested interest in making certain that the district administrators are respected and appreciated. Your management team's hard work, dedication, and expertise guide the smooth implementation of district policies and goals. Work with your board and school community to honor and respect the needs of these dedicated staff members.

ISSUES INFLUENCING COLLECTIVE BARGAINING

Several issues directly influence your work with unions and influence the negotiations process. Understanding these concepts assists you in working more effectively with unions, staff, and the board. You gain insight into the dynamics at play within the district. Over time what you learn assists you in developing strategies to improve relationships.

1. Management Rights

The board is elected by the community to serve as the district's governing body. It is responsible for the education of the district's students. The board makes decisions and acts within the confines and limitations of state and federal laws to ensure this work is done. Within that context, the board has *all rights of management,* unless otherwise limited or defined through self-imposed policies or contracts negotiated with employee group unions.

As superintendent, you are responsible for knowing and implementing these laws, policies, and contracts. You also are responsible for understanding and protecting the *rights of management,* or *management rights* as they are most commonly known. If you or your board want to change the rules, you can lobby for changes at the state and federal level, review and modify your district policies, and negotiate changes in your union contracts. You do not have the right to make arbitrary or unilateral changes or fail to implement any aspect of the rules governing your actions. Failure to adhere to the rules will result in adverse consequences for you, your district, and your community.

In most districts the needs and interests of the district and the employees have much in common. Both sides may share commonly held values and expectations. However, even in the most nonadversarial district, there is an inherent tension between the board's need to maintain its management rights so it has the full authority to make decisions to best educate students and the union's need to improve working conditions and provide comparable compensation and health benefits for its members.

Giving away or watering down management rights may work in the short run to resolve negotiations conflicts. However, in the long run giving away management rights is a losing strategy. It negatively impedes the ability of future boards and superintendents to lead the district. In hard times, do not trade off valued contract language. When times get better, future boards will lament the decision and wonder, often out loud at a public meeting, "How could they have given this away?"

2. Contract Language

Contract language and what it represents is important to both the district and the employees. Once a provision is in a contract, it can be difficult to remove or modify. The language in a particular section of an agreement may appear innocuous but in reality reflect a hard-won right or a standard highly valued by one of the parties. A simply worded provision may represent a huge financial cost. For example, a district wants to increase the high school average class size by one student, while the teachers want to increase the K–3 classroom aid hours from three to four per day.

An increase of one student does not sound substantial. Yet, to the teachers, adding one student per class means larger class sizes, fewer teaching sections, and the potential loss of teaching positions. To the district, increasing aid hours means a large hourly cost, with part-time aides now eligible for health benefits.

Past Practice. Learn the difference between formal contract language and what is traditional past practice or "the way we've done things." Past practice is a powerful force in most districts. Be sensitive to what constitutes past practice. Not every work rule is memorialized by contract language. A work rule is an expectation that has been in place for some time and is mutually respected by both management and employees.

Do not unilaterally attempt to make a change to work rules without communicating in advance with the union. This is especially important at the site level, where inexperienced principals may not recognize a situation where consultation with the union is an important precursor to making a change.

A newly hired first-year principal decided to revise a long outdated teacher handbook. He worked hard over the summer and eagerly placed a copy, complete with a shiny new binder, in the mail box of each teacher the day before their return to work in August. Shortly thereafter, the school's senior teacher entered his office, closed the door, and sat down to chat. In a kind and motherly way she informed him that he had unilaterally changed the working conditions of each and every teacher in the building and that if he didn't gather up all the binders by the next morning, he would receive his first formal grievance. This was a lesson the new principal never forgot.

Before making changes, review the issue with your cabinet or leadership team and the union. Find out why the practice is in place and whether the union is comfortable making the change without needing formal negotiations. You may actually have to negotiate the change at the table. Seek advice of counsel if you question whether the change is negotiable.

Givebacks. Districts and employee groups abhor giving something back they previously worked hard to negotiate. Even in the most nonadversarial, problem-solving negotiations, if you want a union to modify or *give back* a highly valued provision, you must be prepared to trade something substantial for it.

Some unions will agree to a giveback for a substantial increase in compensation. Or, in difficult financial times they want givebacks instead of receiving increases in compensation. Districts with substantial resources may hold off agreeing to a large raise until they gain back some management right. Conversely, unions seek protections and working condition concessions if the district does not have adequate resources for a raise. Do not give up what is good for students.

Sometimes particular contract provisions must be changed for the sake of students. This may occur whether or not there are adequate resources to "buy back" this provision. A good example is the need to increase instructional minutes or time spent on district-led professional development. In these instances it may take several rounds of negotiations to accomplish your goals.

Start the process by building trust and effective communications. Approach these issues with a problem-solving approach and respect the union's position. Just because you feel righteous about a change—it's good for the kids—do not expect the union to immediately agree.

Meet with the board to review the proposed change and determine a strategy to achieve your goal. In more adversarial districts you may need to give to get. In a more problem-solving district you will need to convince the union that the proposal is in its best interests as well as the district's. Even then you may need to "sweeten" your proposal to bring them to agreement.

Work closely with your team and the board, as well as legal counsel, to work through your strategy. You may need to increase compensation to achieve your goal. For example, you may provide a stipend to teachers for attending the professional development classes.

3. Good Faith Negotiations

Negotiating in good faith is an important term with multiple meanings. One is that while neither side has to agree to any particular negotiations proposal, each side has a responsibility to hear, discuss, and consider the proposal before making a decision on its merits and saying no. It is not appropriate to say, "No, we won't discuss this at all!" and shut down the conversation.

Another meaning is that it is not appropriate to negotiate as though a possibility of agreeing exists when there is no such possibility. Also, it is not appropriate to use the negotiations on one item as a springboard for negotiations on another, more contentious item. In all situations, the expectation is that you are negotiating in an honorable manner.

Clarify team member roles before negotiations start. Have everyone commit to negotiating in good faith and behaving appropriately. Making negative comments outside of negotiations can be as damaging to good faith as making them at the table.

4. Compensation Issues

Compensation is always the major issue in any negotiations. Employees expect to be compensated as well or better than employees in comparable districts. Other issues may be important, resolvable, or even contentious, but in the end, concerns about money drive most negotiations. This is why affluent districts with wonderful union relationships often find themselves in bitter negotiations when resources become scarce.

Fully Loaded Costs. Compensation includes all district costs for an employee. Often this is referred to as *fully loaded*, or salary plus salary-driven benefits. Total compensation includes salary, all district-paid mandated benefits based on salary, such as social security, Medicare, state retirement contributions, workers compensation, unemployment insurance, and health benefits. Some districts annually provide employees an accounting of their total compensation.

An important tool for negotiations is determining the projected cost for a 1 percent increase. Employees tend to view compensation as salary only. This vastly understates the true cost of each 1 percent increase.

Make certain that the district and the unions use the same terms. If you fail to understand the fully loaded cost of a 1 percent increase, you will vastly underestimate the cost of a salary increase. This will undermine your relationship with your board and potentially place your district in financial risk. It is not uncommon for a fully loaded salary to exceed the actual salary by 30 percent.

Normally, this 1 percent is calculated separately for each classification of employee or bargaining unit and then collectively for all district staff. In determining the districtwide 1 percent, include any nonrepresented group that usually receives the same percentage increase as teachers and the support staff, such as crossing guards, hourly employees, substitute teachers, and staff funded by state, federal, or local contributions. Use the collective figure for multiyear cost projections.

Other information needed before compensation increases can be determined include the following. Your CBO provides this information for you, the board, and the unions, and it is all public information.

- ❏ Current and Future Year State Funding Projections
- ❏ Multiyear Revenue and Expenditure Projections
- ❏ State and Federal Categorical Funding Projections
- ❏ Size of District Reserves
- ❏ History of Projected Versus Actual Ending Balances
- ❏ Inflation Rates for Your State and Area
- ❏ Multiyear Enrollment Projections
- ❏ Comparison of Enrollment Projections to Actual Enrollments
- ❏ Number of Full-Time Equivalent (FTE) Teachers and Their Placement on the Salary Schedule
- ❏ Projected Number of Resignations, Retirements, and Leaves of Absence
- ❏ Health Benefit Costs
- ❏ Cost of Mandated Salary Benefits
- ❏ Cost of Other Related Compensation Expenditures, Such as Stipends

Ask your CBO to remind the board that the total costs for an increase in employee compensation are ongoing. They become the base upon which other costs are added—year to year. This is why multiyear revenue and expenditure projections are so important.

5. Health Care Costs

Perhaps the most volatile ongoing cost facing school districts has been health care coverage. School districts are not alone in this. The cost of health care benefits has increased dramatically over the past few years. The recent passage of health care reform is intended to stabilize these costs over time, but this will not alleviate the need to negotiate health care costs with employees. Irrespective of what happens with health care reform, negotiations about health benefits will continue to be complicated and most likely contentious.

Districts have varying costs, depending on the coverage they provide to employees and their dependents. In most districts, the district and the employee share the costs in some way.

Examples of Employee and District Cost Sharing

- Employees pay a co-pay for medical benefits, doctor visits, and hospital visits in order to reduce the district paid premium.
- Employees pay a portion of the monthly premium.
- The district provides coverage for the employee while the employee pays for coverage for the spouse and children.
- Districts pay for medical benefits, with employees paying the full cost of dental or vision care.
- Districts provide full coverage for a lower cost plan, with employees paying the difference in cost for a higher cost plan.
- Districts provide a specific amount of money per month for the employee to purchase a health plan.

The cost of health care premiums rises despite the sharing of costs. Unions want districts to assume the cost of these increases and not consider the increased costs as part of compensation. Some employees believe their health benefits are a "right." They expect the district to cover all costs increases independent of any increase in salary. Districts view the increased costs as part of the total compensation package.

In some districts, past boards agreed to assume the health benefit costs for retirees until the age of 65, when they become eligible for Medicare. A few districts even provide lifetime coverage. Boards agreed to this when health care costs were relatively low, or as a trade-off against a lower compensation increase. These retiree health benefit costs increase annually, diminishing the funds available for employees currently working or the instructional program for students.

Communicate the annual health benefit cost increases as a function of a 1 percent increase in compensation. For example, if the increased cost in health benefits for teachers is equal to one half the cost of a 1 percent increase in salary, inform the union that, should the district assume the additional cost, the district has provided a 0.5 percent increase in compensation. This is a good base on which to negotiate salary.

Health care provisions negotiated by the unions can be complicated and vary considerably between districts. The differences have substantial impact on their employees' total compensation.

Example

Two similar, equally funded neighboring districts have completely different health benefit funding mechanisms. In one district, contracts require the district to pay the full costs of a particular health plan, even if the cost of the plan increases substantially from year to year. Because the district absorbs these increased costs, it has fewer dollars for salary increases.

In the other district, the negotiated contracts call for a health benefit cap, or a fixed dollar amount the district will pay for the health benefit program. If the costs increase, the district contribution remains the same, with the employee making up the difference. Because the employees absorb the increased costs, the district has more dollars available for salary increases.

Managing a district health benefit program requires substantial knowledge and skill. It is a high-stakes responsibility, as all employees have deep concerns about health care costs, eligibility, and coverage details. Any proposed change that is not an enhancement will have a negative impact on some portion of a bargaining unit membership, including the superintendent and the management team. In many districts, board members are impacted as they too receive or purchase district health benefits.

Resistance to increasing the cost of the employee share of health benefit costs, or changing insurance carriers, can be severe. Work closely with your CBO or HR administrator to learn the history of your district's health benefit negotiations. Master the details of your benefit programs.

Today, many districts and employee groups work together to manage health benefit programs. They establish advisory committees that include representatives of all employee groups, the district CBO, and HR administrator. Some districts include board and retiree representatives.

In smaller districts the superintendent sits on the committee. It is often jointly chaired by the district and the union representatives. The committee meets on a regular basis throughout the school year to monitor and guide the district's health benefit program. Minutes are taken and distributed to all district employees.

This committee works best when the committee serves as a nonpartisan fact-finding group. It makes nonbinding recommendations to the district and the unions regarding modifications to the differing health benefit programs. Ultimately, decisions regarding changes to programs and the dollar impact of these changes must be negotiated with each union or employee group and approved by the board.

Exercise extreme caution before recommending changes to the health benefit program without substantial review and support by the committee, unions, and the board. It may take years to build consensus among employees that a particular change is needed and appropriate. In many districts the contracts with health providers may require all employees in the district to have the same health plan. This means all district bargaining groups must agree to a change at the same time. Strong leadership by the superintendent and union is needed to accomplish this.

If changes are recommended, carefully review proposed contract language with an attorney. Careless or ambiguous wording can result in conflicts with employee groups and substantial financial consequences to the district. Avoid extending district responsibility for health care unless there is an agreed-on *hard cap*. Educate staff so they understand the cost to the district of extending retiree benefits or adding a new coverage, such as an enhanced dental plan.

Many districts hire an experienced health benefit consultant or firm to advise the committee and develop the fiscal analyses needed for decision-making purposes. The more widespread the understanding of the complex health benefit challenge, the more likely it is that wise and informed decisions will be made.

In one medium-sized district, a superintendent convinced the committee that the district needed to hire a health benefits consultant. The result was a substantial reduction in the cost of benefits with no sacrifice in coverage. Staff appreciated the superintendent's judgment and leadership skills.

6. Grievances and Complaints

Grievances and how they are managed are a key indicator of the union health of a district. A grievance is a claim by an employee or the union that management violated a provision of the contract or board policy. As a new superintendent, you should review the grievance file to learn how many grievances have been filed over the past few years. Note whether the grievances are predominantly related to teacher or support staff contracts. Grievances are usually rare in districts where management respects the contract and is fully aware of contractual provisions, board policy, and the demands of past practice.

If your district has an extensive file of grievances, determine the root causes. Do not assume it is the district's or the union's fault. Meet with principals and the head of HR to better understand the nature of the grievances. You may learn that administrators are unfamiliar with key contract provisions or have little knowledge of how to process a grievance. Or, because of a lack of trust, unions use the grievance process to protest district actions or circumvent negotiations.

You may conclude that considerable work is needed to strengthen communications with the unions and management's understanding of its responsibilities. During your monthly meetings with the union leaders, discuss grievance issues to better understand the problem. Work with the union leadership to develop or strengthen an early warning procedure. Sometimes, a confidential call from the superintendent can make all the difference. If needed, schedule grievance resolution workshops conducted by counsel. Over time, increased trust, communications, and clarity of expectations should result in fewer, or even no, grievances.

Most contracts have very specific procedures and timelines for the processing of grievances. The general rule is that a grievance should first be addressed informally at the lowest possible level of the organization. The grievant almost always has the right to union representation during resolution meetings. If the problem is not resolved, the grievance proceeds to the next level outlined in the procedure and is treated more formally. An exception is when the union is filing the grievance against the district. In these situations the grievances process may start at the superintendent level.

You are responsible for making certain that the grievance procedure is adhered to in a timely manner. Provide guidance to principals or other managers adjudicating a grievance to ensure the appropriate procedural response. A helpful practice is to delegate responsibility for processing grievances to an appropriate member of your cabinet. This provides a buffer or level of appeal between the administration, the board, or the intervention of an outside authority.

Adjudicate all disputes in a fair and impartial manner. On occasion, principals or district office administrators, or even you, violate the terms of an employee group contract. Should this occur, intervene, accept responsibility for the administrative error, and correct any wrongdoing or misapplication of contract language or past practice.

Do not automatically side with administration for the sake of solidarity. Doing so will undermine your credibility with the union leadership, staff, and even your board. This is especially true if the grievance proceeds to the board level or arbitration and either party supports the union position.

If the district is in error, meet with the responsible administrator to explain the error, as well as why you must override the administrator's decision or action. Give the administrator the opportunity to make the change. If needed, review the grievance outcome with your leadership team as professional development opportunity. Fully inform your board of what you have done.

Contact your counsel when the grievance is filed by the union against the superintendent or the board, or the grievance has complicated legal or policy implications. This is especially true if your district is committed to binding arbitration as the end step in the grievance process. As a new superintendent, you may not be aware of all the consequences of what appears to be a relatively simple problem.

Review the grievance language in district contracts with counsel to make certain they adhere to state law and provide appropriate due process guarantees for both the district and the union. Where possible, initiate changes or modifications during times of few grievances.

Complaints. How districts manage complaints impacts union relationships. Complaints differ from grievances as they are not limited to employee concerns over contract implementation. A complaint can be filed by students, parents, members of the community, and staff members against the district, an employee, the superintendent, or even a board member. Complaints address many behaviors and issues, including sexual harassment, employment discrimination, improper use or selection of instructional materials, assignment of grades, teacher favoritism, and application of student discipline, to name a few.

Many states have specific laws or expectations outlining how complaints should be processed. Some complaints, such as those involving harassment or employment discrimination, are covered by both state and federal law. Some states require boards to approve policies and procedures outlining a process for addressing complaints.

Review the district complaint policies and union contracts. If your district lacks complaint policies, work with your board and counsel to develop them. As with grievances, review the complaint files to determine how frequently complaints are filed and how they have been addressed in the past.

Discuss the complaint process with your cabinet and leadership team. Determine who is responsible for providing support to principals and who is responsible for adjudicating complaints at the district level. When needed, schedule a workshop led by counsel.

Complaints are often directed at employees. This is why most contracts have detailed provisions covering the complaint process and how the district can use complaints in an evaluation. If employees feel threatened by the process, they are likely to seek greater security through more restrictive procedures. Usually this means greater due process guarantees and limiting the district's ability to use complaint-related materials in evaluations.

Most complaints against staff members are managed at the school or department level by a well-trained principal or manager. Some complaints cannot be resolved at the local level or are against the administrator. These complaints then move to the district level for resolution. If possible, designate a district office administrator other than you to adjudicate complaints. If not resolved by the district administrator, the complaint will shift to you and possibly the board for final adjudication.

As with a grievance, when an unresolved complaint reaches your desk, adjudicate fairly and impartially. This can be a challenge. Often facts differ and cannot be verified. Yet the reputation of a teacher, support staff member, or administrator is being challenged. By the time it reaches your level, perceptions have hardened, people have taken sides, and resentment prevails. Everyone looks to you for "justice."

When Unresolved Complaints Become High-Stake Issues

☐ The reputation of one of your employees is threatened.
☐ The staff member has union representation and the complainant threatens legal action.
☐ Perceptions have hardened and staff and parents have taken sides.
☐ Anger and resentment prevail.
☐ The parents contact your board president and the union president asks to meet with you.
☐ A reporter from the local newspaper left a message and a letter to the editor criticizes the district's handling of the complaint.

The complaint process should be confidential. Unfortunately, confidentiality is almost impossible to maintain. Soon the complaint is a topic of conversation. Sides are taken. Everyone expects you to uphold justice and side with their people. The complainant expects you to support the integrity of the process and punish the inappropriate behavior of the staff member. Staff expects you to protect them from irrational accusations.

In many districts a hearing before the board is the final step of the complaint process. While your board expects you to resolve complaints before they rise to a formal hearing, sometimes, despite all your best efforts, the complainant may insist upon the hearing. These hearings can be politically challenging, time-consuming, and expensive, with both sides using attorneys to present their case.

It is crucial that you follow state law and your district policies in conducting these hearings. Most sides will accept decisions, even those not in their favor, if they believe those involved used good faith and followed established procedures. At the end of the complaint process, review every aspect of it to identify and address any areas of institutional failure to prevent a similar occurrence.

The complaint process demonstrates the complexity of your role as superintendent. Everyone depends on you to make certain all are treated fairly and justice prevails. This requires having knowledgeable and competent administrators, up-to-date and carefully crafted board policies, supportive legal counsel, positive working relationships with employee unions, a wise and well-trained school board, and a firm understanding of legal process. Even with all that in place, in some situations there is no clear right or wrong answer. You simply do your best.

The role of the superintendent is not for the faint of heart. You must have a strong ethical foundation and confidence in your ability to make fair and impartial judgments in the face of political opposition and adversity. Over time, if you act with integrity and respect, your staff, the unions, and your constituents will learn to trust you.

All of this comes into play as you begin negotiations. Negotiations at the table are reviewed in depth in Chapter 8.

SUMMARY

Working with employee unions or associations goes beyond negotiations. By building relationships, trust, and communication, you better understand their needs, just as they will better understand the district's expectations for their performance and work.

The following points will help you work with employee groups.

- Understand and respect the competing needs of employees, staff, students, parents, and the community.
- Learn the importance of establishing relationships by respecting the integrity of collective bargaining agreements.
- Meet regularly with employee leadership and always provide accurate and timely data to them.
- Learn about collective bargaining in your state and its history in your district. Find out who sits at the table and the role legal counsel plays in your district negotiations.
- Know the difference between adversarial and nonadversarial bargaining.
- Examine the role your board plays in negotiations, as well as why you may wish to modify it.
- Understand issues important to teachers, support staff, and administrators. Recognize your unique role in representing administrators.
- Understand collective bargaining concepts such as management rights and negotiating in good faith.
- Learn the costs associated with compensation and what is meant by *fully loaded.* Pay particular attention to managing health care costs.
- Learn the importance of respecting employee leadership.
- Recognize the impact grievances and complaints have on negotiations.

The information covered in this chapter is only an overview. Continue to increase your knowledge through workshops, reading, and discussions with other professionals. Above all, appreciate the give and take that occurs between and among staff and employee groups. The more you do this, the better you will understand the needs of your staff. This strengthens your influence and leadership, helping you improve teaching and learning for students.

Negotiating Agreements

In Chapter 7 you learned about working with unions and collective bargaining. Now the focus is on leading your first union negotiations as superintendent. You understand collective bargaining is not just about employees' compensation needs and the ability of the district to pay for them. It is about improving the quality of education provided to students while balancing the needs of employees, parents, and the community. This is no easy task.

Becoming a skilled negotiator takes time. The work outlined in the previous chapter informs and influences what happens at the table. Each cycle brings new insights and better ways to negotiate. What you learn, or fail to learn, along the way will impact your relationships with staff and the unions.

State laws differ on how negotiations are conducted. Meet with counsel to review any questions or concerns you have. Address any knowledge gaps before your first negotiations. As stated in Chapter 7, it is important to understand this process, even if you work in a district not covered by collective bargaining.

GETTING STARTED

1. Contract Openers

Union contracts usually identify the number of changes to the contract each side can propose in any given year. In more adversarial districts these proposals are limited and the rules strictly enforced. These proposed changes are called *openers,* as you are proposing to "reopen" the contract.

In most districts, compensation and health benefits are contract provisions that are open for consideration on an annual basis. Usually there are one or two additional openers. Some contracts are specific as to whether an opener is a full article (chapter) of the contract or a specific provision within it. The latter is far more restrictive as you are limited to the identified provision.

In less adversarial districts, all issues of concern from both parties are listed and discussed. The belief is that reviewing all issues reduces impediments to a smoothly operating district. Both sides benefit from this flexibility and willingness to solve problems.

While you want to identify and resolve concerns as soon as possible, you do not want to renegotiate each section of the contract each year. You and your team must limit yourselves to negotiating only those issues most critical to achieving the district's goals. This means living with some minor contract provisions you otherwise would want to change.

The negotiating process officially begins when the union and the district publicly identify their openers, or what chapters or provisions they wish to change. In some states this process is called *sunshining,* as both sides "shine light" on what they are seeking.

This sunshine process occurs at a regularly noticed board meeting. It provides the public and the board an opportunity to ask questions about the proposals. This is usually the only part of negotiations that is open to the public until negotiations are concluded and the board approves the settlement.

2. Gathering Information

A first step in negotiations is to determine the district's openers or negotiations proposals. Reflect on what you have learned about the district since your arrival. Consider your legacy goals. Are there contractual impediments to implementing the district's goals?

For each union, meet with the management team to identify contract provisions of concern. Normally these discussions cover issues affecting the running of the schools and departments. For example, principals may be concerned that extra duty stipends are so low they cannot find teachers to take on important curriculum development work.

Work with the cabinet to prepare a comprehensive list. For each proposal or concern, identify a solution and potential costs. Determine if the solution requires a change in contract language, an interpretation of existing contract language, or an entirely new provision.

Review this list with the leadership team to prioritize the proposals. Let them know that the board determines which proposals they wish to negotiate. Review the leadership team list with your cabinet and refine the proposals. Prepare a report with your recommendations for negotiations for the board.

Avoid proposals with no chance of success just to "scare" or bluff an employee group. Union leadership is likely to view these openers as inflammatory and use them to rouse their constituents to a greater level of support for the union. Radical openers intensify feelings and make progress at the negotiating table more of a challenge. However, do not shy away from opening challenging provisions if they improve the district's financial stability or move the instructional agenda forward.

Query the management team about staff comments concerning the upcoming negotiations. Frequently, staff or union leaders speak openly to site administrators about their concerns and expectations. Principal perceptions of staff attitude and morale are invaluable in helping you recommend more realistic compensation parameters for the board.

As discussed in Chapter 7, proposed contract changes may make obvious sense to management. However, this does not mean your employees will agree. There may be unintended and unanticipated adverse consequences for merely proposing a change.

Example

A board proposed specific modifications to the district's health benefit plan to save money to improve the salary schedule. This angered the union, which assumed the board wanted to reduce health care coverage. Negotiations got off to a rocky start.

Experienced superintendents use general, nonspecific language in stating the district's openers to avoid these situations. Once negotiations begin, start with the problem and work toward the solution. Through negotiations the parties often come to a better solution than was initially proposed. They also identify problems not previously recognized or understood by administration. It is important to keep an open mind. Even in the most adversarial district, your goal is to solve a problem, not to win.

3. Decision Making

Meet with the full board in closed session to present your recommended proposals. Provide copies of all management team suggestions so the board better understands the full range of issues that you and your team face in leading the district.

Determining the district's openers is an important and strategic activity. You and the board must consider the district's interests and needs in relation to available resources and the likelihood of the employee group responding positively. Consider inviting your chief business official (CBO), human resources (HR) administrator, and legal counsel to these closed sessions. Having a number of perspectives is helpful. Deciding what to negotiate and what not to negotiate is a skill you need to be a successful negotiator. You must guide the board through a careful analysis, assessment, and decision-making process.

Inform the board that the unions go through a similar process. They ask their membership to identify needs and any contract provisions that need modification. Their executive teams meet to develop a strategy, and they assess the likelihood of a positive district response.

Frequently, state organizations provide support to local union leadership in developing the openers. In some situations the state organization may mandate a particular opener if it is promoting a statewide outcome.

Some union openers are based solely on difficulties union members have with supervisors or on the outcomes of grievances or complaints. It is not uncommon to find certain contract provisions nicknamed for a principal or supervisor.

Example

In one district the number and length of each school site staff meeting was left up to the principals to determine. One principal took advantage and scheduled two or three one-hour meetings weekly. After several years, with requests to reduce the frequency and length of the meetings falling on deaf ears, the teachers negotiated meeting limits. As a result all principals now have only ten one-hour meetings per year in which to conduct school business.

This is also an excellent example of why it is so important to meet regularly with union leaders to identify and solve problems before they appear as a negotiations proposal.

Unions sunshine their proposals first, followed by the district at the following board meeting. This provides time to assess the impact of their openers on your proposals and, if needed, make changes to your preliminary list of openers. Meet with your cabinet and leadership team to assess the cost and impact of each proposal. Involve other members of the management team as needed. Site administrators and middle management bring a unique perspective based on their day-to-day work with union leadership and members.

After analyzing the union openers, schedule a special closed session with the board for a final negotiations opener and strategy review. If you have many unions, you may need to schedule a full-day Saturday workshop or two separate meetings. Include the CBO, HR administrator, and legal counsel. You do not need the full negotiations team at this meeting. At the meeting, provide the following.

✓ An Assessment of the Impact, Cost, Consequences, and Likelihood of Achieving Agreement of All Major District and Union Contract Proposals

✓ A Recommended District Response for Each Union Proposal

✓ A Recommendation for District Openers for Each Union

✓ A Review of the District Budget and Several Alternative Levels of Compensation Settlement

Compensation. Compensation issues are the most difficult as they pose the highest degree of risk to the district. The board will ask any number of important questions. Even if it does not, know the answers to the following questions.

Compensation Questions

- What can the district reasonably afford this year?
- What is the impact on next year's budget?
- What are neighboring districts doing?
- Have sufficient funds been set aside for program improvement or strategic plan implementation?
- How much will the district's recommendations cost as compared to the unions'?
- How much are they likely to accept?
- Will the unions accept a one-time, off-the-salary-schedule bonus in lieu of an increase to the salary schedule?
- What is the cost to maintain current health benefits?

Be prepared to answer these and all other questions in great detail. You must have confidence in the numbers. Meet with your CBO prior to the meeting to review and analyze the data. Ask questions and insist on readily understandable and logical answers. Identify information to present and information to provide for the board to read.

Present financial information and projections in a consistent and coherent format familiar to the board. This is not the time to introduce an entirely new format unless the state requires it. The board is charged with making financial decisions that have an enormous effect on the district. If the numbers are wrong, or if you or the board fail to understand their meaning, any benefit gained by successfully completing negotiations will dissipate quickly. The board will lose confidence in your leadership skills.

Example

A first-year superintendent was hired by a relatively new and inexperienced board. Teachers requested a revision of their salary schedule. They had previously requested this change several times but the old board and superintendent had refused to go along. The proposal was complicated and included adding and consolidating steps and columns.

The new superintendent worked out the numbers and recommended the district approve the new schedule. He was eager to please staff and show his new board that he could make hard decisions. The board supported his proposal. After the contract was ratified, the CBO was charged with implementing the new schedule. Soon a senior accountant informed the CBO that the superintendent had failed to consider that many teachers had "piled up" at the last step of each column and would receive multiple step increases. As a result, the new schedule was vastly more costly than anticipated, causing the district to operate at a substantial deficit that year.

Provide budget projection spreadsheets illustrating the impact of differing levels of increase in employee compensation for the current and following two years. Build the spreadsheets based on a 1 percent fully loaded increase. Avoid presenting an infinite number of spreadsheets. Use a low, middle, and high projection; for example: 1 percent, 3 percent, and 5 percent. Include health benefit and other major expenditure projections.

Provide an analysis and assessment of the impact and risk of each level of increase. Make certain every board member understands the information you provide. Offer to meet with them privately if they need more information. If the board is confused, slow down and review the spreadsheets again. Their confusion may indicate that your numbers or strategy is faulty. Do not move forward until everyone is secure and comfortable with the numbers and what they mean for the district.

Sample Compensation
Scenarios and Consequences

☐ *Scenario One:* "If we offer a 1 percent to 2 percent raise, we can cover the increase in health care premiums and the projected three-year budget will be fine. However, the unions will not accept this and may view this offer as demeaning. They are likely to press harder for the staff development program changes they proposed in their openers."

☐ *Scenario Two:* "If we offer a 3 percent to 4 percent raise, we cannot cover the increase in health care premiums. We will be fine this year but will have a deficit in next year's budget. In addition, the union will only accept this if they receive all the contract provision changes they requested. These provisions limit the district's ability to provide staff development and are unacceptable."

☐ *Scenario Three:* "If we offer a 5 percent to 6 percent raise, we cannot provide any increases to the health care benefits. We will be in deficit spending this year and for the following two years. The union is likely to drop its request for the contract changes to staff development as this is the increase it wants for its members. However, we will need to negotiate the change in health benefits. The union is likely to oppose any change."

In some instances you may negotiate a one-time allocation. For example, if your district cannot afford to give a 3 percent ongoing cost of living increase to staff, you may propose to give a one-time, off-the-salary-schedule increase to every staff member. This is similar to awarding a bonus.

The cost for this one-time bonus will be the actual cost plus mandated salary-driven benefits. This amount only affects the budget year in which the bonus is given and not future budgets. If you offer one-time money, the following year the union is likely to want this amount added to the ongoing salary schedule. In addition the union will not want this counted as part of its new salary requests.

Each scenario allows the board to discuss its options and provide guidance for negotiations. The end result of such a discussion may be to offer a 3 percent salary increase with a one-time off-the-salary-schedule stipend to assist with rising health care premiums, if all contract provisions to staff development remain the same. This offer is then translated to total dollars and, with board approval, becomes a negotiations parameter.

In addition to authorizing openers, the board also should provide clear guidelines and parameters on all substantial language proposals and compensation increases. They may accept your recommendations, modify them, or even initiate recommendations of their own. Respond positively to their comments and suggestions. If you are not comfortable with their proposed changes, respond with objective arguments, not criticism.

The board expects you to work closely with counsel in developing contract language. They expect you to communicate progress on a regular basis. In turn, remind board members they must be available between negotiation sessions to review emerging proposals and counterproposals. Also remind the board that negotiating is an art, not a science. No matter how prepared you might be, expect surprises, challenges, triumphs, setbacks, and even heartbreak. The more experienced and confident you are, the more likely the board will permit you to exercise independent judgment at the table.

If you are not negotiating for the district, make certain you debrief with the lead negotiator at the end of each session. Send a report to the board outlining progress and identifying issues and problems. Have a public statement ready for the media or community. Meet with the negotiator to review strategy and the next steps. While you are not the lead negotiator, you remain responsible for the success of the negotiations.

ORGANIZING NEGOTIATIONS

After sunshining the openers, schedule a meeting with the union. In some districts the superintendent and a second member of the negotiations team meets with the union president and head negotiator. In other districts, this orientation may be the first formal negotiations session with the full membership of both teams participating. This is an organizational meeting. Some of the topics to be covered include the following.

- ❏ A List of Each Parties' Team Members and Their Roles
- ❏ A Schedule of Meeting Dates, Times, and Locations
- ❏ Where Negotiation Will Occur
- ❏ Availability of Copy Machines and Caucus Rooms
- ❏ The Role of Counsel or State Union Representatives
- ❏ How Progress Will Be Reported to Staff
- ❏ The Use of Joint Communications
- ❏ How the Tentative Agreement Will Be Used

1. Tentative Agreement (TA)

The TA issue is an important one. In some districts, once the parties reach agreement on a particular issue, it cannot be revisited. In other districts, any item, even one that has a TA, can be revisited at the bequest of either party until a final overall agreement has been reached. It is best to resolve this issue from the beginning.

Even when a TA is reached, both parties have to agree to formal contract language. In addition, a TA on a contract does not mean the contract is closed or done. It must be ratified and approved by both sides. The provisions then remain in place for the duration or term of the contract. For most contracts, the term is two or three years. No provision in the contract can change within that period unless both sides agree to the change.

2. Protocols

Review traditions that are part of the culture of the district or the negotiations process. These may vary from union to union. They also vary depending on how adversarial the negotiations; the more adversarial, the more formal and less flexible. Here are some examples.

- *Who pays for snacks or dinner?* In some negotiations each party pays for its own. In others, the costs are shared or the district picks up the full cost.
- *May observers be present?* Occasionally either side may want to provide a training opportunity for a union member or an administrator. In some districts, negotiations are open to the public.
- *Who chairs the meetings?* Most districts take turns, with the chief negotiators alternating. It is helpful to review the group expectations for the chair. Frequently the chair develops and distributes a negotiations' meeting agenda.
- *Who signs the TA agreements?* Usually the district and union's lead negotiator sign off. Each district does this differently. In one district the union president and superintendent sign off using a special red pen reserved for this purpose. This tradition is carried on from year to year to represent continuity.
- *Are there behavioral protocols?* Some districts develop a listing of protocols to guide behavior at the table. These may include respecting confidentiality, listening respectfully to the other side, no passing notes or whispering, and no table thumping.
- *Who speaks for the district?* In some situations, the superintendent or designee speak for the district but call on others to speak. Usually this

is prearranged. In a true nonadversarial, problem-solving environment, everyone at the table is free to contribute to the discussion and problem-solving process. If the goal is to solve the problem, everyone should feel free to express opinions. This means some team members may make points contrary to the interests of their own group.

- *Who calls for a caucus?* Either side is permitted to call for a caucus at any time. A caucus is a short time-out, during which both parties go to separate rooms to talk among themselves. A well-timed caucus allows both sides to reconsider, think through and discuss what the other side has proposed, or come up with an alternative proposal. Caucuses are essential during compensation negotiations. You may need to contact the board, especially when a proposal under consideration exceeds the authority of the negotiations team and a settlement may be close at hand.

3. Minutes

Most districts have abandoned formal binding minutes that require approval by both parties at the end of each session. Instead, the parties agree to informal action minutes that identify the decisions made at the table, agendas for the next meeting, and other needed information. These are distributed to members of both teams after each negotiations session.

In some districts, each side takes turns preparing these minutes, while in others, the district takes and distributes the minutes. As they are informal, they are not binding on the parties. Usually they are shared with the school board and the union's executive committee.

These minutes differ from notes that any member may take of what is said or discussed. These are considered *work product* and are not subject to review by either party. As with formal binding minutes, most districts no longer assign one of their members to note everything everyone says verbatim.

Carefully note what occurs at each negotiations session. Over time it is easy to lose track of what transpired during previous negotiations. This is especially important if a conflict arises about the interpretation or application of a contract provision. Sometimes notes are used by one side or another at a grievance meeting or in future negotiations.

4. Order of Negotiations

Each side must understand the other's proposals. This is important as frequently only contract articles are listed for public consumption in the sunshine phase. Sometimes this article is opened because of one item within it. Now both sides have the opportunity to seek information clarifying their openers.

Example

The teachers in one district opened the contract article on extra service stipends but were only interested in increasing the stipend for high school department chairs. In turn, the district wanted to discuss an increase in the rate paid to teachers for hourly work. After a brief discussion, both sides agreed not to bring up or discuss any item in that article but these two.

Instead of a broad, time-consuming review of every extra service stipend or payment, the parties agreed to a much narrower and manageable task. As with most aspects of negotiations, where an amicable problem-solving environment is in place, the parties make every effort to work together to make good, informed decisions. Where no such environment exists, every negotiations decision can become time consuming and stressful.

After reviewing the issues, the parties reach an agreement on the order in which items will be brought up for discussion. One strategy is to identify major and minor items. Major ones are items that are likely to be costly, challenging, or time-consuming. Minor items are likely not to be costly, challenging, or time-consuming to resolve.

There are a number of benefits to starting with minor issues and working up to the more complicated and challenging major issues, including compensation.

- Both sides get to know each other better and develop a feel for the negotiations environment.
- Both sides have more time to gather information and prepare for the more complex issues to come.
- Both sides can work out communication issues with their boards or executive committees.
- It provides an opportunity to start the negotiations with some successes.
- It can develop a base of communication and trust.
- It allows for an assessment of the financial cost for all resolved issues before taking on compensation.
- This strategy works best if there is a clear understanding that the costs incurred in the tentative agreements are part of the total compensation. This means that when compensation, including health care, is discussed, there may be a need to revisit these items to free up funds for a salary increase. This is where the "art" of negotiations comes into play.

Example

A district wanted to settle at a total increase of 4 percent. If the total cost of resolving all items other than compensation amounted to 0.5 percent, or an equivalent one-half of 1 percent increase on the salary schedule, the district would want to settle for a 3.5 percent increase in compensation. The union likely wanted the 4 percent increase as well as the 0.5 percent from the other items, for a total increase to the district of 4.5 percent.

Another strategy is to take on compensation first. The thinking is that by addressing the most difficult issue first, the other items will be easier to resolve. But this approach comes with a number of problems. Once you resolve compensation issues, there is far less interest in the other items, resulting in either poor decisions or no decision at all. Also, if you use all your discretionary resources for compensation, no funds are available for other purposes.

AT THE TABLE

No matter how well you prepared for your first negotiations, what happens at the table will be a challenging experience. Much is at stake for you professionally and for your district. As the face of the district, it is important that you exhibit openness and confidence. You must be professional, respectful, firm, unflappable, and ready for all contingencies.

Your board expects you to demonstrate skill and leadership, even if you are not the lead negotiator or spokesperson. The board also expects a positive end result for both the district and the staff. Board members are elected officials who want to be viewed in a positive light.

Speak clearly and with knowledge about all negotiated issues. Be prepared and familiar with substantial levels of detail and understanding of district operations. Take time between sessions to learn about all the issues on the table. You may need to schedule additional meetings with principals or other specific administrators, depending on the issue.

Example

A superintendent in a district with a high school had limited or no prior high school experience. So she met with the high school principal to better understand why the union was asking for an increase in the department chair stipend.

Do not delegate your authority to others because you are inexperienced. Over time you will master the art of negotiations and develop an instinct for what is possible. However, it is appropriate to take advantage of the knowledge and experience of your more experienced team members. Consult with board members, legal counsel, the CBO, the head of HR, or experienced principals. They will be pleased to support you.

1. The Process

Employer and employees meet at the bargaining table as legal equals. Both sides are held to a common set of procedural standards and expectations. However, the district holds most of the power, because no contract can be changed, no salary increase implemented, without the approval of a majority of the board. Ironically, districts frequently feel that the employees have all the power, while the employees feel the district to be all powerful.

Treat employee bargaining teams with respect, irrespective of how hostile, argumentative, or disrespectful the employees may behave at or beyond the table. You will work with these team members again when negotiations conclude. Do not take it personally. Always act with integrity and grace.

Example

In one district the support staff union president was consistently at odds with the superintendent and the district. While a tireless fighter for his constituents he was a huge "pain" for the district. One year he was selected as the state's Support Staff Union Leader of the Year. The superintendent was invited to the union's annual statewide conference and asked to give a short speech extolling the virtues of the president.

In many ways, negotiations are a form of theatre. People posture and play roles, emotions rise to the surface, body language communicates mood and expectation, and tempers flare. Even in the most nonadversarial district, each side may make statements that feel extreme, exaggerated, or even untrue.

Always strive for success without long-lasting harm to relationships. You worked hard to establish these during the year. What happens at the bargaining table is conveyed back to the full staff and known by everyone overnight. There is no room for losing your cool. A humble, next-day apology to all who were present may be too late to undue the damage.

Negotiating is a give-and-take process. Rigidity is rarely a successful tactic; compromise is always a viable option. However, do not compromise on issues that jeopardize the district financially or impede your, or the board's, ability to lead the district. In some situations, the only appropriate response is to negotiate in good faith and eventually say no.

Always be mindful of the negotiation parameters approved by the board in closed session. It is not appropriate to exceed those parameters without consulting with the full board. If needed, table items until the next session. This gives you time to review the issue with the full board.

At the same time, employee unions must believe you have the authority to negotiate. You will undermine your authority if items are frequently tabled and caucuses called so you can check with the board. Unions will demand to negotiate with the full board as you appear to lack the authority to negotiate on the board's behalf. Not sitting at the table provides you an opportunity to meet with the team and develop responses without compromising your authority.

If the discussion of an item becomes contentious, mutually agree to bring the item back at the next meeting. Usually when this happens, both sides need more information and time to cool off. Before leaving the item, agree on what information is needed and who will provide it.

If progress is made on other, less contentious issues, both parties may be more inclined to compromise the next time around. Sometimes one side may simply drop an item if it is too contentious. When this occurs, the decision to withdraw the item should have a TA or be noted in the minutes.

2. Formal Contract Language

Once a TA has been reached in principle on a particular item, both parties must reach an agreement on the formal contract language. How this is done depends on the trust relationship and culture of the district. The less formal approach is for the superintendent to develop the formal contract language reflecting the understandings reached at the table. The formal language is then sent to the union leadership and reviewed and approved at the next negotiations session.

In a less trusting environment, the language is hammered out at the table with everyone participating in the "wordsmithing" process until a consensus is reached. This is a far less productive approach as consensus language can be poorly constructed. It is difficult to get everyone to agree on the same language.

Another approach is for both sides to agree to the concepts to be contained in the formal language, and a joint committee is appointed to develop the actual language. The committee meets and returns to the next scheduled negotiations session. This approach may delay the final resolution of the issue and the approval of the agreement, but it builds trust and support.

Irrespective of the approach, do not sign off on contract language until legal counsel reviews and approves the language. The union also will run the language by its legal counsel or state organization representative.

Do not rush the final ratification of an agreement until both sides are comfortable with the language. It is best to go slow to have clear and concise contract language in place to avoid problems of interpretation in the future. After language is in place and ratified, it is very difficult to change it. The only way to do this is to renegotiate it the following year, unless both sides agree a mistake was made. Even this may take a union member vote.

3. Prepare for the Next Session

At the conclusion of each session, before adjourning, the parties should do the following.

✓ Review and approve formal minutes, if taken.

✓ Determine the date, time, and location of the next session.

✓ Agree to the agenda for the next meeting.

✓ Determine who will chair the meeting.

✓ List the information either party is to provide at the next meeting.

Usually both parties agree not to communicate with the general public, including staff, on the progress of the negotiations. If there is to be a joint communication, it is reviewed and approved by the parties. Between sessions the parties may discuss the negotiations with their respective board or executive committees. The parties also may consult with their constituents to problem solve, gather information, or obtain or verify information.

Each new negotiations session usually starts with a half hour caucus for both sides to meet and get organized. When the session starts, the chair reviews the agenda agreed upon at the end of the previous session. Negotiations sessions are scheduled until negotiations are complete and all matters are resolved, or an agreement has been made not to resolve the item at this time.

After each session, meet briefly with the district negotiations team. Assess everyone's perceptions on what went well. If needed, ask different individuals to provide backup information or new data. You also may determine that you need to schedule a meeting to review specific proposals with site administrators. Thank all parties for their work, especially if the session was difficult. If board members sit at the table, meet with them for a few minutes after the others have left.

4. Board Communications

Ongoing communications with the board is essential during negotiations. After each session prepare a detailed memo to the board outlining what occurred. Identify both resolved and unresolved issues. Outline the agenda for the next session. You can send a separate communication or include this information in the confidential section of the Friday letter. Send a copy to legal counsel, even if counsel sat at the table. In some districts, the board receives this update in closed session with no written communication. If negotiations are particularly difficult, schedule a special closed session.

Provide opportunities for the board to meet between negotiations sessions. A good strategy is to identify dates for extra closed session meetings to discuss negotiations. This extra meeting time is needed to permit a full review of the issues.

Board members must recognize the need to devote considerable time to this process, especially during the first round of negotiations. The more experienced board members understand this and support these meetings. They will help you with the less experienced or more difficult board members.

SETTLING COMPENSATION

After settling other issues, negotiations move on to compensation. You must have a clear understanding of the board's expectations and the parameters of your authority to negotiate a salary settlement. This information must be specific.

After each closed session, make certain your parameters are clear, understood, and approved by all. This will clarify your range of authority. For instance, after discussing teacher stipends you might say, "Let me be clear. My understanding is that you prefer an increase of $500 per year for department chair stipends but are willing to go as high as $650 if absolutely necessary? Please nod if you agree." Take notes so you can refer back to the board's agreement.

1. Expectations

Compensation negotiations are difficult and stressful for both sides, even in the most nonadversarial districts. Employee unions want the highest possible salary and benefit increases they can obtain for their members. However, for most responsible unions, there is an underlying expectation that the board and the superintendent will exercise sound judgment and not make a decision that will undermine the financial stability of the district.

Responsible union leadership knows that financial instability leads to more difficult working conditions and a loss of jobs. Most unions will pressure the district at the table to shift more resources to compensation and benefits. But there is the expectation that the district will not let itself be pushed to give more than it can.

This expectation does not apply equally in all districts, especially for districts with long histories of adversarial and conflict-driven negotiations. Where there is no trust, or if employee compensation is low compared to neighboring districts, unions may disregard this expectation. They may push the district to come up with ways to increase revenue or decrease expenditures in other areas to pay for large salary increases.

This places you, the new superintendent, in a challenging position. You must do everything possible to maintain the parameters set by the board. You have a responsibility to your community to manage the district's resources wisely and to your employees to make certain they have an equitable level of compensation.

You also have a responsibility to students and their parents. You are the students' voice at the table. Unions may not want to put the district into financial chaos, but they may be willing to sacrifice programs or members of other unions to obtain increased compensation. Courage is needed at times to protect the education of students, and even to protect the unions from themselves.

Example

A district provided a 5.5 percent salary increase to its teachers and then all staff members. The multiyear projections supporting this increase were based in part on the state continuing to provide high levels of per-student financial allocations. When the state found itself in a fiscal bind the following year, it reduced the size of the allocations. The district was then forced to cut its budget by reducing teachers and other staff. Tensions between the board and superintendent, superintendent and staff, and district and community increased substantially.

In most situations the board wants to be fair. The board does not want to "give away the ship," jeopardize a balanced budget, or limit funds available for initiatives and instructional support. Teachers and other union members want a salary increase as large as comparable districts in the county or region. They may want even more in times of financial abundance, but rarely "give back" in times of fiscal shortages. You want a satisfied board, contented teachers and staff, and sufficient funds to maintain and improve the program for students. Maintaining this balance is a huge responsibility.

2. Strategy and Tactics

Because there are many factors to consider, it helps to develop a compensation strategy with the board. Take time to review these factors with your board before you begin negotiations.

Comparability. A powerful practice to ensure employee harmony and avoid substantial conflict over time is for the district to award all employee groups the same increase in compensation. So if teachers receive a 4 percent increase in total compensation—including salary, salary-driven benefits, and health benefit costs—the board provides the same increase in total compensation to all other groups, including administration.

How this increase is distributed depends on the group. For example, teachers may want all their increase applied to the salary schedule, while support staff may prefer some of the increase be applied toward health benefits. This approach supports the philosophy that all district employees are valued members of the district team, each in his or her own way supporting the education of students.

In some districts, teachers receive the lion's share of available resources, with both classified employees and administration receiving less. This practice is divisive and problematic. As superintendent, advocate for all employees. Each group plays a key role in the education of students and is entitled to an equally proportionate share of new resources for compensation.

An exception arises when the total compensation of one group falls disproportionately behind other groups. Use additional resources to even out these disparities. You may need a number of years to achieve this goal. Be aware that the other employee groups are not likely to appreciate or understand what you and the board are doing. Be prepared to provide a full explanation including backup data on comparative salary studies for all employee groups.

Treat all employees with the same level of respect and intensity of involvement. You want all employee groups to receive their proportionate share of the district's resources. However, take care that you not place the needs of your employees over the needs of your parents and students or your community.

Tactics. Even in nonadversarial environments, unions start out high and the district starts out low. Usually districts come up faster and unions come down slower. In most nonadversarial districts, teachers do not come in with an irresponsibly high number and the district does not start with an insultingly low number. The range is narrower but can be equally as daunting as both sides creep slowly to an acceptable compromise.

Where you settle depends on any number of factors. You are likely to settle on an increase similar to other comparable districts. If everyone is settling for 3 percent to 5 percent and you can only afford 2 percent, expect long and challenging negotiations. Another major factor will be the cost to maintain your current health care benefits. You may have enough resources for a 4 percent raise but can only afford 3 percent due to the projected premium increases.

When discussing compensation at the table, pay close attention to what unions request and say. Treat their proposals and arguments with respect and an open mind. While the district might not be able to afford a 10 percent increase, your employees may deserve such an increase. If you mock or scorn their proposal, you are mocking or scorning their hard work, integrity, and commitment to students and their jobs.

Make every effort to cost out their expectations and attempt to find a middle ground without working against your board's interests. This is important, even if you or the board oppose what is proposed. Often in the costing out of proposals you can provide information that had not been understood or appreciated.

Be mindful that unions do not have full-time CBOs to cost out proposals, even their own proposals. Once you demonstrate how much a particular proposal will cost, and show that cost as a proportion of a 1 percent salary increase, unions may reappraise their commitment to their own proposal.

Example

Teachers requested a 3 percent salary increase and an increase to department chair stipends. The cost to the district for increasing department chair stipends was equal to 0.5 percent salary increase. The superintendent asked the teachers if they would prefer to receive the 0.5 percent as an increase to the salary schedule or as an increase in department chair stipend, because the district could not afford both. If the teachers preferred the latter, the district would provide a 2.5% salary increase and the 0.5% increase in stipends.

In most instances the teachers opt to increase the salary schedule. This increase affects all members of the unit rather than the stipend, which only affects department chairs. However, the union will do its best to get both, for a total increase of 3.5 percent.

Sometimes, both the district and the teachers have an interest in approving a change with substantial cost. For example, if high school department chair stipends are substantially below the levels provided in comparable districts, high schools will find it difficult to find qualified teachers to assume these important roles. This works to the detriment of both the teachers and the district. In this instance both the district and the union would be in agreement.

However, just because both sides want this increase, the cost must be part of the total compensation package. Unions may request that it be in addition to whatever is approved. The union appears to have the upper hand as you need agreement on both compensation and stipends.

In these situations you may have to spend several years moving toward this goal. You cannot spend what you do not have. If you can "find" additional monies for this, the union may suspect you always have extra funds hidden. This may negatively impact negotiations in the future.

Compensation negotiations are often easier when there is stability among the teams over time. This is more likely to occur in less adversarial districts. In these districts the overall negotiations process is shorter and less stressful. Negotiations have a familiar rhythm and tenor with both parties readily reading the intentions and expectations of the other. Each side recognizes when the other has gone about as far as it will or can go and they soon reach a settlement.

In more adversarial situations, or when resources are scarce and the teams less familiar to each other, the process may move very slowly or stall. When compensation negotiations heat up, call for a lengthy caucus and give both sides time to cool off. If necessary, end the session and schedule another session in a week or two to provide time for reflection and gathering more data.

Sometimes, no matter what you do, negotiations reach an impasse. Most states have specific legal procedures to follow when negotiations stall. Alert your board and work with counsel to prepare for the next steps.

Helpful Negotiations Strategies for Compensation

1. Avoid trading off important contract language provisions for a lower salary increase.

2. Use one-time off-the-salary-schedule payments only as a last resort. In hard times an off-the-schedule payment may be appropriate and appreciated by the staff. Staff can use the funds to pay their bills. However, unions tend to view off-the-schedule payments as a debt to the schedule and will seek to restore the payment once good times return.

3. Avoid complex contingency agreements that affect salary schedules. Contingencies are confusing to implement and rarely anticipate all the changes that can, and usually do, occur. If contingency language is necessary, make certain a side letter includes several examples of how the contingency language will be applied, as well as copies of the different salary schedules and when and under what conditions they are to be implemented. In addition, identify how implementation conflicts will be resolved. These letters are time-consuming to prepare but will save time and spare misunderstandings and grievances.

4. Caucus with board members only if you are considering exceeding approved parameters. In many districts, administrators receive the same salary increase as other employee groups. With administrators in the room, board members may be reluctant to hold the line. If board members do not sit at the table, this is not an issue. You can discuss this at your next closed session.

5. Scrutinize carefully any changes to the structure of the salary schedule beyond a neat across-the-board percentage increase per step. Once an agreement is approved by the district and union, any changes are considered givebacks. If you make a mistake you need the union's agreement to fix the problem. The union may not be sympathetic, especially if it had a difficult time selling the agreement to some of its constituents.

Even when making a simple increase to the salary schedule, pull out your calculator and do the math yourself on a few salaries. Double-check the work of your CBO. While computers rarely make mistakes, humans do. It is better to find the error before formal ratification takes place.

Most districts want to complete negotiations prior to the start of the current school year. Due to budget reductions and resource scarcity, it is far more likely that negotiations will take place during the current school year for the current year. This means that salary agreements are usually retroactive to the start of the fiscal year. This provides room for timely, and in difficult times, lengthy negotiations.

The district CBO must monitor payroll carefully for accuracy as everyone employed in the district from July 1 onward is likely to be eligible for a "retro check" once compensation negotiations are completed and the contract is ratified. This includes employees who left the district after July 1 but before the contract ratification.

RATIFICATION AND NEXT STEPS

Finally, after a long and informative negotiations process, an agreement is reached. There is now a TA on the entire contract. This is a symbolic moment and should be treated accordingly. Copies of the final TA should be made for both parties to keep.

The agreement addresses all issues brought forward in the openers and others that may have arisen. The end result reflects compromise on both sides. You may even have some issues that you mutually agreed to put aside for next year so further study can be done. However, the negotiations process is not over until the contract has been ratified by the union and approved by the board in an open session.

1. Communications

Notify the board as soon as you reach agreement and schedule a closed session to review the contract changes. Prepare a press release announcing the conclusion of negotiations and the beginning of the ratification process. As the contract is still not ratified, no specifics should be included in the press release. A joint press release with the union is preferable but is not always possible.

Meet with the union president to review all the specifics that were negotiated. Make certain you are both in agreement. In larger districts the union president will do this with the CBO and the head of HR. Develop a list of the agreements that both parties can use as you move through ratification.

Ensure that the documents are in agreement with those that have a TA. They must be accurate before any ratification occurs. If a change is needed due to awkward language or typographical errors, do not make that change on your own. This can undo all the good will generated through the negotiations process.

Example

A new superintendent was informed by his CBO that due to the particulars of the compensation agreement, each of the salary schedule cells was slightly off and needed realignment for the district's computer software to work efficiently. The superintendent gave his permission to make the changes that amounted to only a few dollars difference per year for each employee. The union president found out about this and was enraged at the superintendent for making a unilateral change to a negotiated agreement and threatened to file a grievance.

After the contract has been reviewed and the financial costs are finalized, schedule another meeting with the union president. You also may have the CBO or head of HR present, particularly if one of them was the lead negotiator. Review the documents, including any required minor changes. Have the union president sign off. Once this occurs, meet with the board in closed session to review the contract.

2. Union Ratification

The union schedules and organizes its own ratification process according to its bylaws. As a courtesy the union should inform you of its schedule and process for bringing the proposed settlement to its members. The union negotiations team reviews the settlement with their executive committee before scheduling ratification meetings.

In smaller districts, one meeting is held at a central location. In larger districts there may be a number of separate meetings. Union leadership attends these meetings and reviews the new provisions with the membership.

The union president should contact you with the results after the vote is complete. Always ask for a school-by-school tally, or at least one from the whole district, so you can determine how effective the union leadership was in representing the expectations of their membership. You may or may not receive this information. The board does not take formal action until the union has ratified the contract.

3. Board Approval

Just as the union was responsible for its ratification process, you are responsible for the board's approval process. Provide the board copies of the final, union-approved contract language and all the new salary schedules. Depending on the size of your district and how you are organized, these documents may come from the CBO and head of HR, or they may be prepared by your assistant.

Inform the board and negotiations team once the union ratifies the agreement. Schedule a meeting for the board's approval of the new agreement. Hold a closed session before the meeting to review the ratified contract one final time. Invite all members of both negotiating teams to attend the public meeting.

Many districts conduct a formal ceremony at which all parties sign original copies of the new agreement. Prepare a press release and have a statement ready for your board president to use with reporters. Thank all parties for their service to the district.

4. Follow-Up

Following the meeting, send each member of both negotiating teams a letter of congratulations and appreciation for their service. Include in your note thanks on behalf of the board. This demonstrates respect for the process and those involved in it. Do this no matter how contentious negotiations were.

If retroactive paychecks or one-time stipends were granted, determine when they will be distributed. Work with your CBO on this and inform the union president and board. You want these payments sent in a timely manner.

In some states the fiscal impact of the agreement must be reviewed by the county office of education or another entity to verify that the district can afford the salary increase and meet its fiscal responsibilities. In these states, no pay warrants may be issued until this is done. Keep the union apprised of the timeline.

Schedule a meeting of the management team as soon as possible to review the new contract. This is particularly important if it contains substantial contract changes. Everyone needs to understand the contract, any changes, and why they were negotiated. They have to be prepared to implement them appropriately.

Not everyone in the management team will applaud you for the final settlement. You may have consulted with the management team to develop the district proposals and to assess the impact of the union proposals during negotiations. However, the final results may differ substantially from what the team wanted and expected. You will not please everyone.

You may have to explain why a particular proposal was not negotiated in the way the team wanted. You may even have to explain why a teacher proposal was approved despite the concerns of principals. Be prepared for some push back due to various site or department concerns. Principals may need to vent. Provide an honest explanation of what happened and why.

Do not try to appease management by sharing inside information about discussions between you and the board. Remind everyone that collective bargaining is an ongoing process and that in a short time you will be back at the table once again. There will be other opportunities to make changes.

Whatever the outcome, and whatever may have occurred at the table or beyond, be mindful of the morale of your staff. Be positive about the direction of the district and the challenges ahead. Make every effort to reestablish or maintain a positive working relationship with the unions.

However, there are times, despite everyone's best intentions, when negotiations do not go well for either side or when the union membership rejects a proposed contract. There may be issues that one side or the other feels were not handled well during negotiations. Feelings can be hurt and egos wounded. Even if an agreement is reached, neither side feels particularly good about the results.

Schedule a meeting with the union president and negotiations head to debrief the negotiations and determine what can be done next year to improve the process. Do this even if negotiations went well. Review these conversations with your board and cabinet. Determine if changes to the process are needed. These may include changes to the composition of the district's team, how financial data was presented, how the district's openers were presented, or any other issues. Build on what went well and work to minimize what was problematic in the process.

In some situations, especially after contentious negotiations, union leadership may not recommend ratification. Or, the union membership may reject the contract. This happens in difficult financial times when compensation and benefit increases are either small or nonexistent, or if major changes are made in contract language or working conditions. If any of these scenarios occur, you will need to return to negotiations.

This is a difficult time for a district. Often one or both sides will request a mediator. Work closely with your board and legal counsel. Each state has different laws governing this process. Above all, demonstrate grace under fire. The education of students in the classrooms must be paramount as you work through the negotiations process once more. At some point, a new contract will be developed and ratified.

SUMMARY

Even with employee relationships based on mutual trust and integrity, your first negotiations as a superintendent are challenging. Staff, parents, and community look to you to meet their needs, even if those needs are in conflict. Your goal is to reach agreements with employees that enhance the lives of students while meeting the needs of stakeholders.

The negotiations process has several well-defined parts. Use the following major points as a guide.

- Understand what is meant by *openers*. Develop the district's openers based on information gathered from your observations, the board, and the management team.
- Review negotiations proposals with the board. Develop a district strategy with possible scenarios. Work with the CBO to prepare materials for the board.
- Develop with the board guidelines and parameters for negotiations. Know how to negotiate within those guidelines. Communicate regularly with the board.
- Learn the importance of operational issues such as tentative agreements, establishing protocols, and determining the use of minutes.
- Learn the pros and cons of addressing compensation prior to other items being negotiated.
- Develop knowledge about the actual process at the table. Learn the challenges in developing formal contract language.
- Learn the complexities of settling compensation issues. Understand fully loaded costs as you develop a strategy.
- Learn why trading important contract language for lower compensation is an inappropriate long-term strategy.
- Understand the steps involved in ratification for both the union and the district. Carefully review all final language against tentative agreements.
- Recognize negotiations as a give-and-take process. Not everyone will be pleased with the outcome.
- Understand that, even under the best of circumstances, some contracts are not ratified.

This chapter is a guide to the mechanics of negotiations. Learning the art takes practice. Negotiations can be contentious, no matter how good the relationships are between you and the union leadership. Your best strategy is always to demonstrate respect and integrity with all employees.

Communicating

Enhanced Decisions

The district's effectiveness at communicating is judged not only by what you do but also on staff and board interactions with the community. It influences how the community perceives the district. Effective communication is fundamental to the development of good decisions and integral to your work.

Irrespective of your district's size or the staff available to assist you, develop a general communications plan. This is particularly important if you learned during the transition that your district is perceived as not communicating well with community, staff, or parents. It is also important to develop a specific plan for issues such as a special election or fiscal crisis. The time to master your district's communication strategies is before an emergency arises, not when it occurs.

Begin by examining how communications are currently managed. Develop strategies to improve what you find. Work with your staff and board to identify the work you each need to do. You may wish to use an outside consultant to assist with developing and implementing the plan, including training. Many state administrative organizations provide workshops and consultants on this topic. Whatever format you use, the purposes of the plan should address the following.

- *Providing Information to Specific Audiences.* Examples include keeping the school community informed of meetings and events, announcing student and staff awards, and keeping the district website up to date.
- *Receiving Information From the School Community.* Examples include attending parent-teacher organization meetings to address questions,

responding to electronic communications and letters, and routine meetings with staff and association representatives. Even if you disagree with those you meet, listen to them. It costs nothing and in the long run assists you in decision making.

- *Engaging in Discussion.* Town hall meetings are an effective strategy for engaging the public in discussions regarding important district issues. Examples include proposed curriculum changes, grade reconfiguration, school boundaries, or increased taxes. A well-organized and well-attended town hall meeting may increase support for the issue being discussed. At the least, it assists those opposed to the issue to better understand the district's needs and proposals. Established avenues for providing and receiving information increase community support. No one likes being courted only for their vote and not for their opinion.

Every district communication, be it an e-mail, letter, bulletin, text message, tweet, or board report, may be repeated in the media the next day. No matter how much you, or any member of your staff, may want to write or say something imprudent, do not. Always take the high road. You set the tone for the district.

Consider the means available to you for communication. Video, meetings, e-mail, texting, Twittering, Facebook, and blogs can be used in addition to print media. Every district is in a different stage of technology development and, with rare exceptions, the students are far more advanced in this area. Use available technology to reach a wider audience. However, as you use technology, pay close attention to the following.

- ✓ The field of electronic communications is constantly changing and expanding. This can make it difficult to ascertain how to use technology effectively within the work setting. You may need consultants to assist you with this.
- ✓ The issues of privacy and inappropriate use of electronic communications are generating lawsuits, as well as new legal precedents, legislation, and school policies. For example, some districts are instituting policies that prohibit teachers from friending their students on their Facebook pages. This may lead to legal challenges. Work with the district's legal counsel to address these kinds of issues.
- ✓ Keeping up with the latest trends can deter you from doing your job, unless you set parameters on how and when it is appropriate to use electronic communications.
- ✓ Keeping district electronic systems up to date is costly. These costs need to be monitored.

Review these issues with the board and staff. Determine how you wish to use electronic communications. Clearly delineate the protocols you develop to staff and the community.

COMMUNICATING WITH PARENTS AND THE PUBLIC

1. District Websites

The public, especially parents, want up-to-date information concerning the district and board actions. Often this can be provided through a district website. However, if you elect to create a website, keep it regularly updated and its source of funding secure. If that is not possible, a website can do more damage than good. Out-of-date information is confusing to the public and sends a message of poor management.

A well-designed and managed website contains basic information on the district.

What to Include in a Website

☐ Information on the District and Each of Its School Sites, Including the Administrative Staff
☐ Board Information, Including Board Member Profiles, Policies, Agendas, Materials for Upcoming Board Meetings, and Minutes of Previous Meetings
☐ A Message From the Superintendent
☐ E-mail Access to Board Members and the Superintendent
☐ A Yearly Calendar of School Activities, Along With Highlights of Upcoming Events and Linkages to School Websites and Those of the District's Foundation, Parent Organizations, and the County and State Offices of Education
☐ Information on the District Budget and Student Assessment Data, as Well as Programs Unique to the District
☐ Student Health and Nutrition Information
☐ Information on Staff and Student Achievements and Awards
☐ Descriptions of District Programs and Whom to Contact by Phone or E-mail for Additional Information
☐ Up-to-Date Parent Bulletins
☐ Other Information Useful to Parents, Such as "Frequently Asked Questions," Including Responses and Directions to the District Office

---

You may wish to include additional information on school sites or district programs, or even a community blog. If you provide a blog, set ground rules so it does not become a place for anonymous complaints or unfounded rumors. One ground rule is a request that all participants identify themselves by name and indicate if they are a community member. A district-operated blog is a public forum.

Assign a staff member to monitor the blog's content and inform you of issues needing a response. Exercise caution before implementing a blog, as negative unintended consequences may exceed its benefits. An increasing number of school districts also use Facebook. If you choose to do this, follow the same procedures as for a website and monitor it as you would a blog.

If you have parents and community members whose first language is other than English, the website, blog, and Facebook page need to accommodate this. This is particularly important in districts with large non-English-speaking populations. Finally, keep tabs on the number of visitors to the sites and areas of interest to them. This assists in revising and updating the site.

While running a good website is complicated, it is relatively easy to learn about them. Browse the Web and view good district sites. Talk with vendors who specialize in district websites. Once you have the information you need, start with a small, manageable site you can keep updated. Expand the site only when you have the capacity to do so. In some districts, staff can assist in putting the site together, with individual departments held responsible for updating their areas. Designate someone in charge of overseeing the entire site so it is effective and useful, not a source of problems. A poorly constructed or maintained website reflects poorly on you and the district. It is worse than having no site.

Websites used by parents, staff, and the community can be cost-effective. Information can be delivered in a timely manner. For example, school registration packets can be distributed through the website. Principals no longer worry that information has not reached the home. However, for this to work everyone involved needs access to a computer. If you wish to move in this direction, work with your local community libraries and nonprofits to set up programs whereby parents are given access to computers and training on how to use the district website. Realize that parents with no computer access will not receive the information.

Relying on websites means your parents and community know the district is using its website to communicate important information. If possible, designate a day, like Friday, for important postings. Also let parents know that during an emergency the website may be down and they will need to turn to the media for updates.

2. Print Materials

Print materials on specific programs and districtwide newsletters can be of assistance in communicating with parents and community. For districts, especially those with families who fall near or below the poverty line, printed materials are a must. Most of these families have limited access to computers. Materials should be available in the dominant languages spoken in the community. Printed materials are your main access to these parents and one of the few ways you can use to invite them to meetings or other events.

Distributing the materials is another issue. Use mail to distribute important documents such as back-to-school information or letters concerning a particular student. Other materials, such as district newsletters, can be sent home with grade school students, with additional copies available at school sites, the district office, public libraries, and the local Chamber of Commerce. Avoid sending materials home with middle and high school students. The older the student, the less likely materials are to reach home.

Some districts use newsletters. They are distributed monthly, quarterly, or semiannually. To save on costs, districts often work with local newspapers. Papers may print the districtwide newsletter as part of their publications. Some even agree to include the newsletter as an insert. However, due to the high cost of printing and the proliferation of Web access, some newspapers are only online. If you use this venue, make sure the newspaper reaches all residents in the community and is not online only.

Print materials still have an important place in districts. They are more expensive than posting everything on the website, but until the issue of computer access for all can be addressed, these materials are needed.

3. E-mail, Cell Phone, Texting, and Tweeting

E-mail is a powerful tool for communicating with staff, parents, students, and the community, but not everyone has access to it. For those without e-mail access, make print copies available. Before deciding to use e-mail extensively, understand the work it entails. Many districts that use e-mail ask parents to provide both phone and e-mail when registering their students. However, these e-mail addresses need to be updated on a routine basis as users often change accounts. Arrangements must be made to keep e-mail addresses current at both the school and district level.

Once e-mail addresses are collected, groups can be developed and information routinely sent to them. For example, parents and community members interested in receiving board agendas or even board packets can receive these electronically. E-mail can also be used to deliver timely information, such as school closures due to weather conditions. However, these messages must also be delivered through radio and television. Often the media provide this as a public service and give districts access numbers to use. At the start of the school year, inform parents which stations carry this information.

Respond to e-mail you receive from parents and the community. Try to avoid using an automated response, though. A simple thank you for taking the time to write and a sentence on any action you may take is sufficient. Your response may be that you are forwarding the message to another staff member for response or that you will share the comment with the board at its next meeting. If the e-mails are on a controversial matter and you are receiving a large number of them, send an automatic e-mail response linking them to a detailed response that is available on the district's website. Remember, all e-mail responses can be made public. So exercise care in writing them.

If you receive great numbers of e-mails on a daily basis, set aside time every day to respond. Do as many as you can within that time. If you cannot do this in a timely manner or on a regular basis, work with your assistant to set up protocols. As part of these protocols, clarify which messages need to be responded to by you and which can be responded to by the assistant or sent on to other staff members. Make certain your staff understand that a timely response is expected. All staff members, including you, can be inundated with e-mail. It is preferable for you and your cabinet to develop a system whereby you each take responsibility for succinctly responding to all e-mails you receive.

Example

One superintendent responded to e-mails every evening before leaving. It allowed her time to unwind before going home to her family and provided an overview of what was happening in the district. Her responses were usually short, but the fact she responded in a timely manner, usually one to two days after receiving the e-mail, built up a reserve of goodwill for the district.

Some board members, staff, parents, students, and community members who have your cell phone number will prefer to send text messages. If you are comfortable with this venue, use it. However, given the nature of the work and your need to be reached in an emergency, it is best to limit access to your cell phone to administrators, the board, and your assistant. You may also wish to give your number to the union leadership. Have your e-mails accessible through your phone and respond to them as time permits using the above protocols.

Twitter has opened another avenue for communication. Some superintendents now use this, along with the district website, for communicating school emergencies or reminding staff and community of upcoming events. If you do this, be sure to include your Twitter address along with your e-mail address. Link your tweets to the website that contains additional information. Again, follow the above protocols.

Use these avenues of communication to your advantage, but do not be driven by them. Be aware that staff, parents, and community members who use these forms of communication can consume a disproportionate amount of your time. Work to ensure you respond to all forms of communication in an even-handed manner.

4. The School Site

The school site is a parent's main source of information. Always have copies of school newsletters or special mailings forwarded to your office for you to read. Include them in the board's weekly packets. This also applies to all student publications. Superintendents and board members need to be as informed as parents as to what is happening in the schools.

Sometimes teachers or the principal at a school do not effectively communicate with parents and staff. You will receive comments and perhaps complaints about this. Likely your board will know about it, especially if a board member has a child at the school. In these instances, meet with the principal to review the situation. If needed, provide training for the principal or teacher. Or pair that person with a colleague who is talented in communications.

Your school sites are the links to the community. The goal of each site is to reach every parent. In case of emergencies, have a protocol in place for communicating with school principals and other administrators. In turn require that they have a plan for communicating with the parents and staff. In the case of a natural or manmade disaster, e-mail may be down and cell phones jammed. Have alternate plans in place. Communicating in an emergency is discussed later in this chapter.

5. Engaging the Public

Engaging the public and, in particular, parents can be challenging. Avoid large, routine district meetings where little discussion occurs. Instead, schedule periodic meetings with district groups who share similar interests. For example, quarterly meetings with district parent organization representatives, special education parent associations, immigrant parents, or other special interest groups allow for conversations between and among participants on topics of mutual interest. Even if there are disagreements about issues, these smaller meetings provide you with valuable information. They also provide an opportunity for parents and community members to know you on a more intimate and personal level. Often solutions to what were complex problems arise from these meetings.

Example

One district had a small Hispanic student population. The students' parents believed their children were stereotyped by staff. After an initial meeting, monthly parent meetings were established. These meetings included counselors, teachers, students, administrators, and community members. Hard conversations were held and solutions developed. Both the parents and the district learned to better understand one another and meet the needs of the students.

If the district is planning a large change, such as a grade reconfiguration, school closures, or boundary changes, develop a specific communications plan for that issue. Know the major points to communicate. Develop *talking points* for you, the board, and others involved. Set up meetings around the district. Hold enough meetings at different times and locations so all affected can attend at least one meeting.

At these meetings, explain the district recommendation or position, respond to questions, and engage in dialogue. Listen carefully; often you and the board can use this information to improve the initiative. For example, parents may have a solution to one aspect of a boundary change that simplifies the process while meeting district needs. In addition, plan e-mail and print information campaigns around the issue.

District Campaigns. If you are conducting a bond campaign or asking the community for additional financial support, you may want to retain a consultant to assist the district. Review Chapter 3, where the use of consultants is discussed. In most states, you may use district funds for consultants to convey information to the community on how funds will be used, but not to ask for public support. This is a fine line. Work with legal counsel to understand these differences.

Establish a committee comprised of respected parents and community leaders to run the campaign. Often one or more of your board members will volunteer to take on this leadership role. This committee can raise outside funds to pay for a consultant or run the campaign. Ask your board how campaigns were done in the past and how successful they were. Talk with neighboring superintendents and research how other districts conduct campaigns.

Learn as much as you can about these initiatives and how to run a successful one before recommending one to the board. State associations and national publications can be helpful with this. In sum, every district initiative requires its own communication plan for gathering and responding to public input.

6. Your Broader Community

In most communities, less than 25 percent of the population is made up of parents with school age children. This includes the number of families in the community who choose to send their children to private schools. Include your entire community in your general communications plan. These individuals vote on school issues, run for school board seats, and are in other civic activities that affect the school district.

Reach out to these groups. Join a local service association like Rotary or Kiwanis. At the least, make arrangements to speak yearly to them. Offer to speak at the local Chamber of Commerce and meet on a quarterly or biannual basis with the mayor and chief of police. Attend yearly civic events that are of particular importance to the community, such as a Fourth of July picnic, an arts festival, or a spring parade. The district needs to be seen at these events. Board members should also be encouraged to attend, if they are not already involved.

Four or five speeches a year and attendance at three or four key events makes a significant difference in the way a district is perceived and supported by the local community. Do not expect the help of the community and businesses if you have not reached out to them.

One superintendent spoke and attended events on a regular basis in the three communities in which he served as superintendent. He was able to raise resources and support from these businesses communities to pass very large bond measures.

When you speak or meet with people, tell "the story" of the district.

Include in Your Speeches

- ☐ Relevant Data, Especially Data About Students and Their Achievements and Challenges
- ☐ An Overview of the District's Successes and How You and the Board Are Addressing Challenges the District Faces
- ☐ An Explanation of the District's Funding Model and Expenditures
- ☐ A Description of How the Audience Can Become Involved
- ☐ Most Importantly, Gratitude for Their Support of the Schools

As you attend these events and move throughout the community, you will meet parents and community members who contribute hours of volunteer time each year to the district. These individuals may come from parent organizations or from local community or business groups, or they may be citizens who believe in the efficacy of public education and simply want to help.

A personal note of thanks to these volunteers means more than you can imagine.

Example

One superintendent had note cards made from student artwork. She sent personal notes at the holiday time to these volunteers. These cards often generated a thank you from the individuals receiving them. Some noted they had never before been acknowledged for their work. The superintendent also used these cards to honor the students at the start of a board meeting and gave to the parents several cards made by their children. While it consumed time, the goodwill it gathered for the district far outweighed the time invested.

Each community has other key constituents or groups. These groups may be comprised of former board members who never lost interest in the schools and whose opinions are valued by the community. For example, in communities with colleges and universities there are often groups of retired professors and administrators who meet monthly with influential business leaders to discuss local issues, including the schools.

Learn who these groups or individuals are in your district. Approach one of them and ask to meet. They are permanent members of the community with long histories. Remember, you are a newcomer who may only be there for a few years. Listen to what they have to say and learn all you can. Find out how best to keep them informed about the district. You may not always agree with them on issues, but you will know what is important to them and why. In turn you will better understand the district.

In communicating with parents and the public, be it on the website, in e-mail or newsletters, in speeches, or at meetings, always acknowledge the good work staff is doing and the achievements of students. Every district has good news—make it known. This will build good will and confidence among the staff, students, and community. It will also make it easier to confront difficult issues that inevitably arise.

Local and Federal Legislators. Legislators are more important to communicate with than most new superintendents realize. Local legislators can write or back legislation that either assists or hampers the work of the district. Further, many states control the finances of local districts. Federal legislators have a profound impact on national educational policy.

Understanding this and learning how to effectively communicate with legislators is essential. Respect elected officials. Set up appointments to meet with them and go to their offices. Establish a good relationship with their assistants so you can call and provide information or request assistance.

Realize that support is a two-way street. While you cannot actively support legislative candidates in elections, you should provide them the information they request in a timely manner. You also can share your personal opinion on their candidacy with your close friends. School facilities can be offered for community meetings. Given the magnitude of issues facing schools and public programs, good working relationships are essential.

Local Colleges and Universities. Even if they are private, these institutions can have an impact on your district. If you have them in your district, arrange meetings with the college presidents. Work to develop good partnerships. In districts fortunate to have institutions of higher education, it is possible to set up programs for school district students. To be successful, these programs need to benefit both institutions.

Local Superintendents. You want close working relationships with superintendents in neighboring districts, especially if you share boundaries. It is also important if your district is in a county or region with a long history of collaboration between and among districts and superintendents. If you are a high school superintendent, reach out to superintendents in your elementary feeder districts. Likewise, if you are an elementary superintendent, reach out to the high school superintendent.

You are likely to work more closely with superintendents from districts similar to yours. In many counties, some districts share similar size, grade configuration, or funding models. There are superintendents you like and trust immediately due to similarities of background and experience, or even just "chemistry." Many counties or regions have a tradition of appointing experienced superintendents to serve as mentors or coaches for the new superintendents. This can be helpful.

Some counties have collegial relationships between and among superintendents, while others are more formal, competitive, and even outright hostile. In most counties, superintendents meet on a regular basis. Meetings may range from once a month to twice a year, depending on the county, number of districts, and the leadership of the county. When first meeting these superintendents, avoid dominating the conversation. Attempting to show everyone how good you are and why you were hired is either a sign of your insecurity or marks you as a braggart.

Some counties have a superintendent responsible for a county or regional district. Depending on the state, the county superintendent may be appointed or elected. This person's role is to provide support for local school districts and students. Often county superintendents provide specialized student services for very small districts or coordinate services for all districts.

County superintendents are often political positions. They may exercise substantial power and influence within the county. Work with your board to learn how decisions are made in your county, as well as your board's expectations for your involvement in countywide issues. School board members are often involved in county associations and subsequently in countywide issues effecting education policy. Your board can provide you with needed information and guidance as you become acquainted with the county.

It will not take long to develop professional working relationships with most of your neighboring superintendents. However, not every peer is interested in your well-being or has your best interests at heart. Some might have applied for and interviewed for your job. Others could be close friends with some of your board members or even live in your community.

Common sense calls for discretion with other superintendents. Avoid sharing information about your job, board, or district that you do not want the public or your board to know. It is appropriate to share while participating in organized problem-solving activities. It is not appropriate to participate in "confessional" workshops in which the leader encourages you to share the challenges of your job, including difficulties with board members or your concerns about your performance. Do not assume confidentiality in these situations. There is no such thing.

One superintendent learned to his dismay that the person he confided in had been an applicant for his job and believed himself to be more qualified. The comments he shared about the district's problems soon appeared in the local newspaper.

If there are no formal meetings of neighboring superintendents, set up monthly breakfast meetings or brown-bag lunches and rotate the meetings from district to district. This gives you a sense of what is happening in these districts and an opportunity to talk about local school issues with your peers.

WORKING WITH THE MEDIA

Working with media is challenging. Many newspapers limit their coverage of community news. People increasingly gather information from the Internet or participate in blogs that share perceptions rather than facts. In whatever form it exists, your community media are not in the business of promoting schools. It is in the business of reporting what it considers to be newsworthy. These stories may concern student assessment data, difficult union negotiations, controversial board actions, or student or staff problems.

Sometimes the local media will note staff or student awards or achievements. It may also publicize upcoming board meetings or school community events. Work to maintain positive and open communications with the media. Foster good working relationships.

How to Work Effectively With the Media

☐ Introduce yourself to the editors and to reporters responsible for covering the school district. Do this for all publications, including weekly neighborhood ones.

☐ Respond in a timely manner to information requests.

☐ Respect the deadlines of newspapers and radio and television stations. Return calls or e-mails as soon as possible.

☐ Outline either mentally or in writing what you intend to say on a given topic. This is particularly important if the issue pertains to negotiations, personnel, or a controversial student issue.

☐ Do not negotiate with unions using the media.

☐ If you have a question on how to respond to a particularly sensitive issue, consult with legal counsel before providing requested information.

☐ Whatever you say is *on the record* and can be quoted unless you ask to speak *off the record*. Even then choose your words carefully. In particular avoid jokes, sarcasm, or criticism in relation to the topic you are discussing. Listen carefully to the questions. Be forthright, clear, and positive.

☐ Only answer what is asked, unless you believe additional information sheds important light on the issue.

☐ Do not fight with editorial boards, even if you do not like what they write. Remember the axiom: "Do not fight with individuals who buy ink by the barrel. You will not win." This axiom applies to all media forms.

☐ Accept the fact that you will be criticized. No one has total support for all actions. This is particularly true if you are in the midst of school reforms, difficult personnel decisions, or budget reductions. Develop a thick skin and do not respond in kind.

☐ If you believe the district is being treated unfairly, discuss this with your board president. If the board president supports your concern, then set up a meeting with the editor and the board president. At the meeting, factually present your concerns and provide data to support the district's position.

☐ If there is a problem, acknowledge it. Be concrete and truthful. For instance, if the district's math scores have dropped significantly, acknowledge this and then talk about what is being done to address the problem.

☐ Respect the media and the job they have, and by and large you will receive respect in return.

☐ Learn local, state, and federal guidelines as they pertain to access to public information. Respect the media's right to request documents from the school district and be aware they may quote verbatim from them. No matter what you provide, it may be picked apart and only certain facts listed.

Example

A district was in the midst of deep budget cuts. The media requested copies of the superintendent's and board's most recent expenditures on travel. They also wanted copies of the superintendent's contract, as well internal e-mails between the board members and superintendent on the budget. The superintendent's salary appeared in the next edition of the paper.

Most local media sponsor blogs so community members may state their views on current stories. Often people do not identify themselves on blogs and some statements are diatribes with few facts. If there are controversial school issues, read these blogs. Do not enter the conversation—just read and gather information.

Learn from each encounter with the media. Find time to reflect on how you responded, the effect it had, and what, if anything, you could have done better. If you are the target of the media, the less said the better. Little garners less community support than public officials proclaiming how their actions were misinterpreted. The role of the superintendent is to promote effective student education and do this with the greatest support possible. If that is not possible, it is better to be criticized than fail to act in the best interests of students.

You also will find the media invaluable in case of disaster, as the disaster becomes the news. They are more likely to assist you in communicating with the community during a disaster if you have shown a willingness to work with them.

If you have difficulty working with the media, your state administrators association can provide assistance. Whatever you do, do not simply avoid the media. Doing so can imperil the work of the district.

COMMUNICATING WITH STAFF AND STUDENTS

Do not assume staff knows all that is happening in the district. Usually this is far from true. Staff, be they teachers, secretaries, principals, or custodians, focus on their jobs. These jobs consume their days. As a result, district employees often have little knowledge of the broader context in which the district operates. Simply remember your days as a teacher and reflect on how much you knew about the workings of that district. If information about the district is not provided in a routine and timely manner, then information carried in the media and on the employees' "grapevine" will provide that context—true or not.

1. Websites, E-mail, Twitter, and Print Materials

If possible, have a website devoted to staff. Provide access at each work site for employees who do not have computers and encourage staff to read the information. Use this site to do the following.

❏ Post district activities, including staff development opportunities.

❏ Provide a link to board meeting agendas and materials.

❏ Provide updates on topics of interest to staff, such as deadlines for the annual health care coverage sign-ups or leave-of-absence requests.

In addition, a monthly update to all staff via e-mail and a printed copy keeps them informed of the overall work of the district. Work with your administrative assistant to develop a template for this bulletin, making it easier to produce. Include in it a summary of key board actions, district issues, and reminders of upcoming district events. When a controversial issue arises, staff will be used to referring to this update. Ongoing communication builds trust.

Respond to staff e-mails in a timely manner. If you are comfortable with the medium, do the same with tweets you receive. What is important is that staff know how best to communicate with you. Let them know whether you prefer e-mail, text messages, tweets, or voice mail.

The larger the district, the more difficult it may be for you to personally respond to all communications. Try not to use automated responses. A short, personal response goes a long way. Always remember that your reply may be sent to every member of the staff and even to the press.

2. Accessibility

Respond to staff phone calls and letters using the same criteria noted above for e-mails and tweets. Staff members are entitled to meet with you and should not have to jump through hoops to do so. They deserve care and respect.

Work with your administrative assistant to ensure you are accessible to staff. Good administrative assistants learn when it is appropriate to schedule a meeting for a staff member and when it is more appropriate to refer the staff member to another department. In the beginning, err on the side of more individual meetings.

Teachers, administrators, or support staff may stop by to see you when they are at the district office for another purpose. They may just want to say hello. Accommodate them if possible. You want to be known as a leader who is open and accessible, and who listens. The more you are seen in this light, the easier it will be for staff to accept the hard decisions you make. In addition, you may learn something valuable.

If staff members come to you with concerns or complaints about other staff or a supervisor, listen carefully. In many instances this concern should be directed through the formal complaint process. It is your responsibility to follow up on them.

Staff members often seek out the superintendent to resolve a personal problem, such as an extended leave to visit children or attend a family reunion, or a family issue related to drug or alcohol abuse. Be sensitive and listen. But do not allow yourself to be put in a situation of making a decision or overriding a decision already made by an administrator before knowing the facts. Also, as noted in previous chapters, be aware of negotiated contracts and setting precedent.

Over time you learn when to delegate these issues to others and when to address them yourself. You learn this through taking the time, every time, to gather the needed data with which to make the decision. The head of HR needs to understand your expectations in regard to special circumstances and that you are the only one who makes exceptions.

Employees talk to one another. They share how you responded to their requests. This is why it is important for you to keep an ongoing record or log of each request and your response. Everything you do in these circumstances contributes to how individual staff members and the associations view you as a leader, as a communicator, and as a human being.

3. Teachers and Support Staff

Routinely hold open meetings at school sites for staff. These meetings can be before or after school or during lunch. Set them up a year in advance and make sure staff is notified. Notices can be posted on the staff website and listed in the monthly staff bulletin. Meeting frequency depends on the size of the district and the number of schools. A good rule of thumb is to plan on spending at least two days a week in the schools. This time includes not only meetings with staff but also visits to classrooms or principals.

For small to medium-sized districts, this means you should be able to visit staff at their school sites at least two to four times a year. The purposes of these meetings are to address questions staff may have and to get to know them better. Be sure to invite support staff as well as certificated staff to these meetings.

School Staff Meetings. During these visits thank staff for the work they do. It is something they hear too little. Always take notes so you can follow up on questions. You also may wish to follow up on something you saw or heard. Relying only on memory may let an issue fall through the cracks.

Pay particular attention to issues raised by staff at these meetings. Often you hear concerns not yet raised at the district level. They may be small items but you have an opportunity to address them before they become districtwide issues. Often it is a matter of explaining something in a clear fashion. Avoid taking action on concerns raised at these staff meetings until you have researched the issue with the principal or the appropriate district office administrator. Everyone needs to feel respected, and no one should be subjected to arbitrary actions based on something you heard from one staff member.

Listen carefully to questions and discussions involving curriculum or instruction. Teachers are the key to student learning in the classroom. This is an opportunity to explain district initiatives around student learning and to better understand staff perceptions surrounding these initiatives. Helping them helps students. It also allows teachers to understand better your thinking process and priorities.

Good teachers are invaluable and there are few ways we have to show how much they are valued. Going to their work sites, talking, listening, and following up on their questions is one way to do this. Even if they do not tell you so, they will appreciate this and make it known to others. Even if they do not, being there is the right thing to do.

Classroom Visits. If you want teachers and administrators to value your opinion on instruction, visit classrooms and observe the teaching and learning. In your scheduling, do not forget summer school or other special programs you may have in the district. Being with the students at the site will keep you focused on why you are a superintendent.

Your visits tell the principal and staff you understand and respect the complexities of their roles. It is also an opportunity to validate the work being done as well as to see what may need to be done to improve instruction.

Example

One superintendent noted that he had an elementary principal with an extensive background in curriculum and instruction. After each classroom visitation, the principal quizzed the superintendent on what he had observed. Over the course of several visits, a strong sense of respect developed between the two due to the superintendent's knowledge of and caring for the quality of classroom instruction.

Superintendents who visit schools and classes on a regular basis are more highly respected and appreciated than superintendents who rarely leave the confines of their office. These superintendents are also better informed about what is actually happening in their schools.

How you visit schools, what you do and say, what you see and do not help staff form perceptions about your leadership. Perception is reality for many. Everything you do will be noted and discussed once you leave. This information will then move throughout the school and out to other staff via e-mail and on to the board and public. Do not count on principals correcting any misconceptions. While some will, others see their job as supporting their staffs, and still others may want your job. The following guidelines will assist you in making these site visits positive and productive.

- ✓ Let the principal know when you are coming; mutually agree on the dates for these visits.

- ✓ Leave plenty of time for the visit so you do not appear rushed. You want to stop and talk with teachers, support staff, and students.

- ✓ Upon arrival at the school, stop first at the office and chat with the office staff and with the principal.

- ✓ Ask the principal if there is anything in particular he or she wants you to see. Note that on your first visit to the school, it is always good to have the principal accompany you as you go to classrooms.

- ✓ Stop by the staff lounge, but do not monopolize the staff in the room as this is their break time.

- ✓ Go into classrooms and observe what is happening. If appropriate go to the desks of students and look at their work. Spend enough time in each classroom so that you are aware of what is being taught and how it is being taught. If the teacher asks you to introduce yourself, do so. Smile and be upbeat. A frowning superintendent can leave a wake of concern behind.

- ✓ Do not supervise or correct individual staff members unless the safety of a child is in question. Ask students about their class work, but do not ask students to assess the performance of their teachers.

- ✓ Do not discipline students unless there is a safety issue the teacher cannot control. You are not the teacher and do not know about the student. What may appear to be disruptive to you may be something the teacher has been working to achieve with this student.

- ✓ Avoid nonverbal expressions that can be misinterpreted, especially in a classroom. Teachers and students are very observant when a superintendent is visiting. You may later receive a complaint from a union president or parent about your behavior.

Example

A superintendent visited a high school in early June and observed a female student wearing a skimpy outfit that was in extremely poor taste. He gave the student a disapproving look. Later that afternoon the girl's mother came to the superintendent's office to tell the superintendent that his behavior was unacceptable. He had embarrassed her daughter in front of her friends rather than calling the mother or speaking with the assistant principal who could have spoken privately with the young woman. The next time the superintendent saw the young woman was at graduation where she gave the valedictorian speech.

✓ Avoid disrupting a lesson unless the teacher stops to introduce you or requests that you to do something. When leaving, always catch the eye of the teacher and smile.

✓ At the end of the visit, always stop by the principal's office. Be willing to share your experience and perceptions if the principal is there. Discuss any issues you see. Principals are anxious to hear what you have to say and what you observed. In some instances principals who are effective instructional leaders will be testing to see what you know. Others will want your backing for their school initiatives. Still others lobby for more district resources, such as additional playground equipment. They want your ear and your willingness to share your observations and listening to them is critical. It assists you in better understanding their needs and how to implement district goals.

✓ Do not micromanage or make decisions based on what you see before you leave unless there is a safety issue. Even then do this with the principal and do not put yourself in the position of overruling the principal.

✓ As you visit classrooms, be aware of which teachers are substitutes, probationary, and tenured. Substitutes and probationary teachers are usually uncomfortable with a visit from the superintendent. This is why frequent visits are advised. The more you visit the more staff will become used to seeing you and relax.

✓ As noted in Chapter 3, always stop and talk with support staff. In many districts they are most likely to live within the district. Often they know more than anyone else about the district and schools in which they work.

Ideally you want your visits to be positive and not viewed as negative fact-finding missions. But it is through these visits that you find where improvements are needed. It is certainly far easier to have a conversation with a principal or the administrative team about needed changes when you have concrete examples to share. In essence you are demonstrating leadership by walking around.

After your first round of classroom visits at a school, you may want to visit the classrooms without the principal. This saves the principal time and is often less disruptive to the educational program. These visits demonstrate your interest in the primary work of the district. Either during the course of the visit or right after, note what you observed and whether any actions need taken. Do not forget to e-mail your thanks to the staff or, better yet, send a handwritten one.

4. The Administrative Team

Your administrators, especially principals, work daily with teachers and staff. Their understanding of issues is critical to your success. While everything pertaining to staff communications pertains to administrators, establish additional channels of communication with them. These help you understand their issues, as well as enable you to communicate the reasons for your decisions.

Always respond as soon as you can to administrators' e-mails and phone calls. Have an open door policy so they feel comfortable visiting your office. If you are out of the office or in a meeting, make sure your administrative assistant offers to set up a meeting time. Never assume administrators know they are doing a good job. If they are, tell them and be specific about what you are acknowledging.

Use your administrator meetings to gather timely data. At the end of these meetings, go around the room so that everyone can raise a question, pose a topic for future discussion, or share information that the entire group may be interested in hearing. This information allows you to better understand administrators' issues and assists you in framing future agendas.

Whenever possible, meet with principals at their school sites instead of having them come to your office. The exception to this is when you are delivering bad news, such as failing to get a promotion or disciplinary action. You do not want staff seeing the principal upset after you leave or having to keep a brave face on until the end of the day.

Send a personal note or card to administrators when they are hired, on their birthday, at the holidays, and when a family event such as a birth or death occurs in their lives. Having student-made cards on hand for these purposes makes this easier to do. Personal notes mean more to people than it is possible to convey. While it may take you some time, it is more than worth the effort. It is also easy to manage once you have established a system.

Have your administrative assistant give you all the administrators' birthday cards for a given month five days prior to the start of the month. Complete the cards at one sitting and give them to your assistant to mail at the appropriate time. For holiday cards, finalize your list each October and work on them in batches of ten or twenty starting in November. This makes it easier to complete.

No Surprises. No superintendent appreciates receiving calls from board members or reporters about an event occurring in a school about which they have no information. Communicate to your staff that you expect them to inform you of new or emerging issues. Let them know it's OK to call you at home.

Respond positively when you hear bad news. Some superintendents, either overtly or covertly, convey to staff they do not want to hear it. Principals or managers who feel threatened by sharing bad news are likely to withhold information. As a result, when the problem ends up in your office, as it always does, the problem has festered and you do not have all the background. For example, when a difficult personnel issue arises involving a possible crime, you want to know as soon as possible. If you have a reputation for "killing the messenger," you may not receive the information in a timely manner. This delay could mean you not only have an unfortunate incident, but a surprised board, a less-than-accurate media story, and a confused public.

It is far easier to deal with difficult issues when they arise than after. Even if you decide not to address an issue until more information is available, knowing about it gives you an advantage.

Playing catch up makes an effective response and decision more difficult and more time-consuming. A simple phone call makes all the difference in how you respond to a situation and how you are perceived by your board and the community. Work with your administrative assistant to make certain you receive and respond to these communications in a timely manner.

5. Special Occasions

Prior to major events and holidays, such as the start and end of the school year and winter, spring, and Thanksgiving breaks, send an e-mail or letter to all staff, with a copy to the board. Wish them well and thank them for all the work done on behalf of the students. These do not need to be long, simply heartfelt. Include a quote that fits the occasion; many can be found on the Web. It is amazing how these small touches add to a staff's sense of its professionalism and its sense of being valued.

In addition to the event for all staff at the beginning of the school year, try to hold an annual end-of-year event. It could be a coffee, barbecue, or reception to honor staff members who are retiring. Many staff have provided years of service to the school district. Even though an individual work site may do something to acknowledge this work, having a district-wide event will mean a lot to these individuals. It is another way of demonstrating how important the work of education is. If possible, have a small token for each retiree. It could be note cards made by students, a student book of poems, or a paperweight with the district's logo. If resources are an issue, and they always are, ask for assistance from the Chamber of Commerce, the parent organization, or the school foundation.

6. Students

Students are why school districts exist. Find ways to be with students and to learn their views. You can be a valuable role model to them. They can be a valuable teacher to you. There are a number of ways to do this.

Ways to Communicate and Connect With Students

- Teach a class on a weekly basis or be a substitute once a month.
- Hold quarterly lunches with middle and high school students.
- Arrange for lunches or dinners with student representatives, the board, and the cabinet.
- Attend student events and talk with students whenever you visit a school.
- Meet with journalism classes and elected student officers.
- Observe students in the classrooms, read their publications, and listen to what they say.
- Have student representatives on the school board.

Students are the reason the schools exist. Know what they think and what issues are important to them.

One superintendent held monthly meetings with middle and high school student officers. As a result of these luncheons, the quality of school lunches was discussed. The head of the Student Nutrition department joined these meetings.

Over the course of the year, healthier lunches were made available to students and a student panel was established to work with the nutrition department.

In another district, because students are usually far more knowledgeable about technology and can use it far more effectively than their teachers, the superintendent used texting to communicate with high school student officers. He kept them abreast of meetings they might be interested in and they, in turn, kept him informed of events and issues of importance to them.

The ways in which students learn are different from their parents and teachers. It is critical that educators understand this and use it to their advantage. Reflect on what you hear from the students, learn from observing them, and review assessment data. Use this information to work with your staff. This will assist you as you work to refine the instructional program. Have students be a focus in your communications plan.

FINAL CONSIDERATIONS

Two important aspects of communication are easy to overlook as one becomes superintendent. One is emergency planning and the other customer service.

1. Communicating in an Emergency

Inevitably an emergency will occur. You are expected to demonstrate strong leadership in managing it. It may range from students pulling all the fire alarms at the same time to natural disasters such as fire, flood, hurricane, or earthquake; intruders on campus; a bus or playground accident involving students; a lost child; or the suicide of a student. While you do not want any emergencies, you must be prepared for whatever happens. Since 9/11 many states mandate that districts have emergency plans in place not only for responding to terrorist attacks but also to natural disasters. At the heart of these plans is communication—getting out the call for assistance, notifying those who need to be involved, and addressing the emergency. It also involves working with the media.

Take this responsibility seriously. The consequence for not doing so can be catastrophic. The key question is, "Are we prepared for a serious earthquake, flood, or terrorist event on the first day of school?" If the answer is no or "I'm not certain," then take whatever steps are needed so you feel confident answering "Yes, I'm certain." If your district does not have up-to-date policies and procedures for emergencies, including clearly defined expectations or protocols for administrators, attend to this immediately. Work with the local emergency responders and neighboring districts to obtain assistance in doing this.

If you have a plan in place and it appears comprehensive and usable, then your main task is to ensure it is updated yearly and shared with staff. A plan is not effective unless everyone is aware of it, knows how to use it, and has the resources for doing so at hand. In many states all staff—support and certificated—are considered mandated responders in the case of large natural or man-made disasters. This means they are legally bound to remain on site until released by the individual in charge of the community disaster response.

Example

One district had an unexpected and heavy snowfall in an area known for little or no snow. All staff at one elementary school had to spend the night at the school with students whose parents could not pick them up the afternoon before. Staff had to stay until all students were safely home and the school secure for the four-day closure that followed. This included calling each family to let them know what radio and television stations to listen to for school closures and openings.

Staff members need to be aware of this obligation and the message should be reinforced yearly. This means all staff members, including you, need emergency plans and communication methods for their families. This is difficult for many whose first instinct is to get to their families as quickly as possible. Work with the union leadership to get this message out to all its members. Include this information on the district website.

Each site needs protocols for how to respond to emergencies and staff designated as emergency responders. Sites also need to have supplies on hand to last for a minimum of three days or until assistance can arrive. Good emergency plans and training, along with district emergency oversight by you or a designated administrator, can ensure this is in place.

As you review and revise the plan, remember communication with the people affected by the emergency—students, staff, parents, community members—is critical. You can have an excellent plan on paper that will be viewed as a failure if the people who need to be communicated with in a timely manner are not. Simply put yourself into the shoes of the parent whose child has been in an accident and ask how you would like to be treated. Then do this for everyone. Keep the board informed during this critical time.

Use the yearly before-school management team meetings to review the roles and protocols for emergencies. Have more than one person assigned to each role as someone may be absent or unable to perform the assigned work. Finally, while you as superintendent are ultimately responsible for all that happens, delegate to your top-level administrative staff. In an emergency every hand is needed. In many medium to larger districts, responsibility for the plan and its annual review is assigned to the assistant superintendent for business services. This frees the superintendent to oversee the response, coordinate communications with the board, and address the specifics of the emergency.

The administrator responsible for the district's emergency response usually reviews emergency procedures and any new or revised regulations with the management team. This is particularly important for new administrators. Some districts also provide an overview by local law enforcement or safety agencies on how to respond to fire, earthquake, tornadoes, hurricanes, floods, strangers on campus, or a terrorist threat or attack. Review procedures for school closings and communications to parents, staff, and students. Review how schools communicate with the district office in an emergency. Identify who is in charge should the superintendent or principal be off site or unable to respond.

In the case of a natural disaster, phone lines and cells may be down. Having alternative methods of communication with staff is essential. If possible, have satellite phones available at each work site. They are expensive but placing one at each site allows for communication in the worst of disasters and may save lives.

In an emergency situation you need access to key members of your team, board members, the press, and emergency response agencies. If all lines of communication are not down, your primary source for communication will be phones and e-mail. Require administrators to have cell phones available at all times. Either provide them with a district-paid cell phone or reimburse that portion of their personal monthly cell phone costs that are business related. All administrators need chargers in their homes, car, and offices. They also need emergency phone numbers so everyone can be reached as needed.

Ask your administrative assistant for an updated communications chart including home, cell, and office phone numbers. Review all cell phone expectations at the management team meetings. Also review protocols for using the satellite phones.

Clarify how to respond to media inquiries during an emergency. This includes reporters from TV, cable, blogs, or papers. Normally the school's principal speaks to the press for school emergencies and you speak for district issues. In most states the press cannot simply walk on school sites with cameras or go into classrooms at will. However, as students all have cell phones with cameras and the instant ability to text the outside world, you and your staff must prepare for a quick response. In some situations, student friends and family may learn of a problem before an administrator does.

You hope to never need to use these plans. Having them in place gives you peace of mind that, should something happen, the district is prepared. You owe this to the students, staff, and community.

2. Customer Service

Throughout any emergency or any communications with students, staff, parents, community, and the board, never forget customer service. The community pays for the public schools, including your salary. While the board is your employer, it represents the public. First impressions can be lasting, so ensure every call, visit, e-mail, or meeting is marked by courtesy.

Example

One superintendent always starts her e-mails to upset parents, community or staff members with "Thank you for your e-mail." It sets a tone that was maintained throughout the rest of the response.

Courtesy does not mean you agree with all comments; it means you treat others as you want to be treated. Set similar expectations for all staff. If a mistake is made, go out of your way to call and apologize. Superintendents and staff are not always right.

Do not take abuse and do not be abusive. Simply state that you may not offer assistance until the verbal abuse stops. Explain that you will either hang up or leave should it continue. This can be done with grace and often results in the abusive person calming down. Instruct staff to do the same. You may be surprised how courtesy and civility can turn difficult situations around.

A district marked by customer service is one that is respected by its community. You cannot buy this respect; it is earned. That is done one meeting, one e-mail, and one encounter at a time.

SUMMARY

Effective communication is central to the work of school districts. It needs to be purposeful, planned, and tied into the goals of the district. Well-thought-out communication strategies help districts respond to challenging situations.

Following are major points you can use as a guide in developing effective communications.

- Understand the purposes of communications. Know the various audiences with whom you need to communicate and the needs of each group.
- Learn to use various communication tools. Assess the benefits of using print and electronic communications.
- Know that the school site is the main source of information for parents. Work with principals to ensure good communications.
- Engage the public in large and small group meetings on particular topics. Understand each group's needs. Include business and community groups.
- Learn how to work with the media. Be aware of their needs, as well as the local, state, and federal laws governing public information.
- Develop a plan for ongoing staff communications. Include websites, e-mail access, and print materials. Schedule regular meetings with staff and learn how to do successful site visits.
- Establish additional avenues of communications for administrators. Visit them at their sites or in their offices.
- Develop strategies to communicate and interact with students.
- Connect with groups outside the district boundaries, such as county superintendent groups or other state and local organizations.
- Prepare emergency communication plans and revisit these regularly. Know what is expected of you and staff. Have the necessary equipment and protocols in place.

Communication is ongoing. Recognize that everyone must communicate effectively for the public to view the district positively. Be open to new ideas and approaches for improving communications. Where necessary, develop procedures, protocols, and expectations to ensure this occurs.

Looking Ahead

At the end of your first year, take some time to reflect. You may feel both overwhelmed by the work and excited by the challenge. This is normal. By the end of your second or third year, the job will feel more manageable. Each task or crisis is no longer unique, and you know how to respond. You know when to seek assistance and whom to ask.

The focus of this book has been to provide you with tools to become a superintendent and effectively navigate this first year. Unfortunately some first-year superintendents mistakenly believe that once they have the job and make it through year one, each succeeding year is just an easier repeat of the first. Nothing could be further from the truth. In effect, your work does not stop with obtaining the position and setting up the necessary systems; it only just begins. Simply repeating what you did in your first year, over and over, is like the movie *Groundhog Day.* You make no progress.

You must anticipate and think ahead, not just thirty or sixty days, but thirty or sixty months. Do not assume everything is in place. Assess what you have and have not accomplished, and, where needed, make changes and revise. Build on what has been accomplished, and maintain and enhance the working relationships you have established. These systems and relationships allow you to focus on the real work of the district—the education of students. There are also new issues to confront. This is the nature of leadership. As these issues arise, the staff and community will look to you to provide direction.

This chapter addresses those issues, as well as the decision to stay, retire, or move to another position. Even though your career as a superintendent has just started, there will come a time during your tenure in the district when you start to think about what you want to do next. The foundation for this decision is often based on your experiences of the first few years. Some superintendents leave their positions early because they fail to master or respond well to some or all of the challenges addressed below.

THE CHALLENGES

Years two and beyond will bring new challenges—challenges are faced by every superintendent in every district. They affect your legacy goals and may be intertwined with them. For example, it is difficult to meet your goals for student achievement without paying attention to your administrative structure, board changes, and leadership style.

Many of these challenges were discussed in previous chapters. The focus here is building on what you learned so you can use these challenges to effectively meet your goals. Suggestions on how to address them are included. Though this chapter provides an overview of what needs to be done, you need to follow up by doing the work.

1. Focusing on Student Achievement

You became a superintendent to strengthen the teaching and learning process for all students. Now you know how easy it is for your administrative and budgetary responsibilities to consume all your discretionary time. You are working fifty to seventy hours a week and are responding well to crises. Systems are in place and working well. While this is appropriate and even commendable, it does not absolve you from your instructional leadership role.

Do not become a victim of goal displacement. You are responsible for student achievement—it is your number one legacy goal. The remaining goals support this one. Focus your leadership efforts on key aspects of the instructional program.

A prominent superintendent led his district through a three-year facilities modernization effort, culminating in a facilities-modernization bond election. His board fired him the day after the measure was defeated. They said he spent too much time on facilities and too little time on declining achievement scores.

Keep abreast of timely, research-based trends. Identify those that improve your district's instructional programs.

Areas of Needed Focus

✓ Closing the Achievement Gap

✓ Creativity

✓ Critical Thinking

✓ Cultural Competency

✓ Data-Driven Decision Making

✓ Data-Driven Professional Development

✓ Early Childhood Education

✓ Effective and Focused Use of Technology

✓ English Language Learners

✓ Focused Instruction Built on Student Strengths

✓ Gifted and Talented Students and Programs

✓ Professional Learning Communities

✓ Research-Based Teaching Strategies

✓ Special Education and Response to Intervention

✓ Standards-Based Curriculum and Instruction

✓ Student Assessment Data and Accountability

✓ Student Services

✓ Student Wellness

✓ Transformational Schools

Continue meeting with your leadership team to address issues of teaching and learning, assessment and accountability. Continue refining how the district gathers, analyzes, and uses data. Work to develop your principals' instructional leadership skills. Train them to conduct frequent classroom walkthroughs as part of an integrated instructional improvement effort.

Provide the necessary professional development and support to move this agenda forward. Hold teachers and principals accountable to achieve clearly defined accountability standards. Make certain you have the correct technology infrastructure in place and use it.

If you began your tenure visiting schools and classes on a regular basis and now find yourself too busy to get out of your office, reassess your weekly schedule and recommit to ongoing school and classroom visits. If you have a successful practice of visiting classrooms, make certain you continue this practice throughout your tenure in the district. If you spoke in generalities about "closing the achievement gap," now is the time to implement strategies that hold principals and classroom teachers accountable for improving student achievement for all identified subgroups.

Example

A district had high overall test scores, but Hispanic, African American, and low-income students failed to perform at the highest levels, so the superintendent established specific achievement gap goals to improve their performance. When visits to advanced placement, honors, and gifted classes revealed that the vast majority of enrolled students were white, restrictive entrance policies were eliminated and additional support to these other students was provided.

While superintendents must lead in every aspect of school district operations, instructional leadership is the area that counts the most. As you select your professional development opportunities, find those that address instructional leadership. Visit your district's teacher in-service sessions and take time to participate in some of them. Review the in-service provided to your principals and cabinet members. Ensure they are receiving the information they need to be effective instructional leaders in their jobs.

Throughout your tenure, revisit your commitment to instructional leadership. Involve your board in any needed recommitment. If instruction is seen as your focus, it will become the focus of your staff.

2. Implementing Your Legacy Goals

You know the difference between formal district goals driven by the district's strategic plan and goals driven by your internal standards and expectations. You must accomplish the former to meet the board's expectations, as outlined in your annual personal performance goals. You accomplish the latter because they reflect your personal core values, expectations, and even dreams for the district. Your challenge is to integrate the formal district goals with your personal legacy goals.

As noted throughout this book, the primary focus of your legacy goals should be on student achievement. This is what your job is about. Ideally the district goals also reflect a commitment to student achievement. But you may be in a situation in which the district is focused on financial survival or some other crisis. In that case, work to meet the financial challenges, but keep in mind that the ultimate goal is a financially stable district that can provide an exceptional education for students. Always frame the district goal in this light, thereby intertwining both goals and keeping the focus on instruction.

Do not lose sight of your legacy goals. Refer to them periodically when you have time to reflect. Use them as an internal filter when preparing a major report to the board. Consider how best to integrate these goals with the ongoing work of the district. Regularly review your progress.

The direction of the district is a reflection of your personal values and vision, as well as the values and vision of the board and the community. Never forget why you are a superintendent and where you want to take the district. Through your persistent leadership, the board and community may adopt your legacy goals for their own. If you lose your vision, the work will have less meaning for you. Ultimately, the district will note your lack of interest and focus.

3. Refining Strategies to Achieve Goals

Continue refining strategies to achieve the district's goals and your legacy goals. Foremost among these is knowing how fast to move forward. Just because you are committed to a particular program or course of action does not mean everyone agrees with you. Experienced superintendents know, and skillful new superintendents instinctively recognize, that sometimes you need to "go slow to go fast." This is particularly true as you enter years two and beyond.

If you are clear about the end vision or goal, move forward one or two steps at a time. Bring along as many people as you can before taking the next steps. You accomplish more by doing this than by attempting to ram through a major change all at once.

Far too many new superintendents believe they must implement all changes in their first year. They are then surprised when they are undermined by push back from staff, parents, the community, and the board. Successful leaders know when to modify recommendations, extend timelines, and even rescind recommendations due to changing circumstances.

However, in some circumstances you must move quickly. For instance, act with deliberate speed if you are superintendent in a district where the test scores are so low that the state is threatening to take over the district. Move quickly to identify the problems, generate solutions, garner support, and obtain board approval to move forward. People expect you to lead them out of the crises.

A second strategy is learning how to implement change. Most change is not driven by crisis. Change should be driven by the vision and goals for the district. Review the literature on implementing change. Understand how important it is to have the majority of people behind the changes you initiate. For example, inexperienced superintendents frequently believe all they need to implement a change is the overwhelming support of the board. A five-to-zero vote does not guarantee success.

There always will be people who oppose your recommendations. You need a core of enthusiastic supporters to persuade those who are unwilling to go along. Staff, parents, and even students must believe in the change. Target your work to ensure you get this support.

A third important strategy is mastering the art of communication. As outlined in the previous chapter, knowing how to convey and receive information is an essential skill for every superintendent. Your ability to make changes and move the district forward depends on defining clear goals and expectations and building support for them.

Work with your school community to make certain everyone knows the good things happening in the district and the progress you are making in achieving goals. Use your communication skills to keep people informed. Be open to receiving new information and making course corrections. Work with the board and school community to reset goals when appropriate to reflect changes in community values, priorities, and district resources. Leadership requires exercising good judgment as well as courage.

4. Using the Eighteen-Month Planning Cycle

The eighteen-month planning process outlined in Chapter 4 drives the forward movement of a district. Strategic planning, long-range and annual goal setting, resource allocation, program implementation, assessment, accountability, and revision are the hallmarks of this process. Its consistent implementation provides the foundation for the district's progress toward achieving its mission and implementing the strategic plan. Achieving long-range goals takes time. It demands focused and disciplined resource allocation, both human and financial.

Pay close attention to the planning cycle. Make certain all aspects and components are scheduled and completed. Do not let internal and external events divert attention from it. If you let the cycle slip or disappear, the district's forward momentum will falter or movement will become random, not focused. You do not want the whims of individual board members to replace orderly and consistent planning.

Example

A board decided that the eighteen-month planning process was too time-consuming and cumbersome. Instead, it decided each board member would identify one goal per year for the superintendent and the district to implement. At the end of three years, the board complained that the district "wasn't going anywhere" and dismissed the superintendent.

As years pass, new trustees join the board. Help them understand the value of this planning process. Listen to their comments, suggestions, or concerns. Where appropriate, make modifications to reflect their views, as well as changes in the internal and external environments. What is critical is not to lose the major components of the process. Having a systematic, ongoing planning process is essential for the welfare of both the district and you.

5. Working With Your School Board

At some point in your tenure you may lose the board that hired you. This is almost inevitable if you remain in your position for more than a year or two. This initial connection is very powerful. Your first board knows your work. Your success justifies their decision to hire you.

One by one the trustees who hired and supported you during your first years are replaced. New board members who were not part of your selection process and do not know you well, are less invested in your success. They may not share the same values and expectations of your original board. They may be critical of your work and the work of the board. Term limits set by communities for board members only increases the pace of board change.

When the composition of the board changes, board dynamics change as well. One new board member can disrupt a board, change voting patterns, or create doubt about your performance. The addition of just one new member can substantially influence your standing with the board.

It does not take too many changes before the balance of support may switch from *total* to *probable* to *little or no* and and you find yourself looking for a new position. However, if you are fortunate, new board members share the values of the current board and support the work you are doing. In these situations you may have a long and productive tenure.

During this time of transition, work with your board president to facilitate the smooth integration of the new board members. Respect and acknowledge new and possibly differing points of view of these members. Do not rely on your relationships with the old board members and ignore the new ones.

This is true even when new board members share the values and expectations of the board. Many boards actively encourage candidates who share their values to run for seats vacated by long-standing board friends. When elected, they join the "team." Do not take these new members for granted.

Treat new board members, regardless of how or why they become a board member, with the full respect due them. They are elected representatives of the community. Listen carefully to the concerns and expectations of each new member. Pay special attention to one-issue board members or those who ran on an oppositional platform. Help them to understand the complexity of their issues and any unintended consequences these issues may have for the district. Work to promote their success without giving up your vision for the school district. Try to find areas of common ground.

You are obligated to listen to trustees whose interests and opinions differ from yours or from the rest of the board. Do not fall into the trap of believing you "have the votes" and can ignore what new members say. Superintendents who do this often discover that other board members, even those supportive of them, react negatively to their lack of respect for the newcomer.

Board members are protective of their roles as policymakers. While good boards listen to suggestions from their superintendents, they know they ultimately set policy and you implement it. Do not let success lead to arrogance. Superintendents who fail to understand this often lose their jobs. At the least, superintendents who attempt to usurp this role will be reprimanded.

Example

One experienced board member informed the superintendent during a particularly contentious discussion at a board meeting, "We vote. You don't!"

Do not stop informing the board of what you are doing and how you are doing it. Some superintendents who have been in districts for several years begin skipping Friday letters or provide fewer and fewer details to the board about district issues. Do this at your own peril. A board's need for knowledge and data is no less because you are in your second or third year on the job. In fact it may need more information as groups or individuals react negatively to proposed changes or as the board itself experiences changes.

Encourage the board's continuing involvement in local, state, and national education issues. Work with the board and individual members to develop a professional growth plan. Attend workshops with new board members. If they have a particular interest or ability, continue to encourage it. For example, if a board member is interested in state educational policy, encourage that person to meet with elected officials and report back to the board.

You want a governance team fully committed to providing a quality educational experience for your students. This is a key to the attainment of the district's long-term goals and your tenure. Should the board become dysfunctional, seek outside assistance. Often this can be obtained through the state school boards association. As with any relationship, yours with the board needs constant work. Never take the board for granted. You are responsible for helping them succeed.

6. Responding to Your Evaluations

Most new superintendents do well in their first year or two. They receive positive and even enthusiastic evaluations from their boards. But, as new members join the board or the work becomes increasingly challenging and problematic, positive evaluations become less enthusiastic. They contain more recommendations for improvement. New board members often have a different perspective of the district or want to move the district in a different direction. That is why they ran for office. As a result they may be less impressed with you and your work then previous board members.

Listen carefully for subtle shifts in the board's perception of how well you are performing. Some superintendents make the mistake of ignoring the concerns expressed by one board member only to discover that soon other board members are sharing those same concerns about their performance. Treat all concerns with respect, even those expressed by outlying or oppositional trustees.

Do not let key components of your evaluation process slide. You are responsible for notifying the board of key events and dates in your evaluation. Work with your board chair to keep them on schedule. For example, always schedule a mid-year evaluation. Do not let the board cancel it because everything appears to be going well or they are uncomfortable evaluating you. If this occurs, you may find things are not going so well by the end-of-year evaluation, particularly if new members have joined the board. In the long run it is far better to know even the most minor concern as soon as possible.

Take seriously every recommendation on the mid-year and end-of-year evaluations. Develop an implementation or work plan to show you understand the board's expectations for you. Share it with the board. This plan shows you listened and are committed to meeting the board's expectations.

Include a personal performance goal for each recommendation offered in your evaluation. This allows you and the board to focus on specific outcomes. It makes it harder for one board member to say you are not meeting your goals when the next evaluation occurs and the specific outcomes have been reached.

Negative Evaluations. At some point in your first or second year, the board may give you a less-than-satisfactory evaluation. This can occur mid-year or at the end of the year. The board may agree to your serving another year with the expectation that your performance improves. If you determine that your position is tenable and wish to remain in the district, work with the board to develop a very specific improvement plan with target dates and means of assessment. Consider requesting coaching assistance.

Or, the board may inform you that your performance is unsatisfactory. It may want to buy you out, have you leave immediately, or remain only until the end of the school year. This information may be conveyed by the full board, the board president, or the board's attorney. If this does occur, do the following.

- ❏ *Listen carefully to what is being said.* Take notes. Do not betray your emotions through facial expressions, especially ones showing disbelief or disgust. Do not argue or defend yourself, simply listen.

- ❏ *Ask questions to clarify what is being said.* If no examples are provided, ask for them. Do this politely. No matter how disagreeable one or more of the board members are, be calm and courteous.

- ❏ *Thank board members at the end of the discussion, but do not tell them what you plan on doing.* If a board member asks, simply respond, "I have been provided with a lot of information to think about. I will be in touch with the board president in a few days." Do not specify a specific time or day.

- ❏ *Go back to your office or home and assess carefully what happened and why.* Review your notes. If you think of new questions, write them down but do not ask board members for a response. Even if you believe you have a strong ally on the board, do not talk to that board member at this time.

- ❏ *Call your personal attorney and review the situation in depth.* You may wish also to review this situation with your coach or a mentor. Do not gloss over events that led to this. Be accurate, talk about how you may have contributed to this situation, and be clear on what you would like. For example, you may want to finish out the school year and use the time to look for another position. As a result, you may want a letter of recommendation. Or you may wish to retire, simply to leave, or to be bought out. All of these are momentous decisions for you, your career, and your family.

Do not attempt to work through this with the board without outside assistance. You need the support of an independent objective expert with no personal involvement in the outcome. If you did not see this coming and do not have an attorney, retain one who is skilled in education and contract law. A skilled attorney will prevent the board from taking advantage of you, as the board will have already consulted with counsel.

Do not use your district's counsel for this. Your state administrator association can supply you with names of attorneys. If you have been working behind the scenes with an attorney, that attorney now will provide you with options. Review these options, weighing the pros and cons, and determine what you wish to do.

❑ *Prepare a response to the board.* This response may come from you or your attorney. It may be in writing or done through a phone call or meeting. Whatever the response and the ensuing negotiations and outcome, always be calm, thoughtful, deliberate, and courteous. Even if you leave the district, the manner in which you do it is as important as when you entered it. Just because the situation is disagreeable, you do not need to act in kind.

How you leave the district is as important as how you entered it. Maintain your professional demeanor throughout these negotiations and do your best to fulfill your contractual obligations. Work with a trusted colleague to assess your career status and determine your next steps.

Some new superintendents, despite receiving good evaluations, decide they are not a good fit for the district, or they do not like being a superintendent. If you are in this situation, inform the board of your decision and work out an amicable departure. Meet all your contractual obligations. You want to leave the district as positively as possible.

7. Managing Your Contract

You are responsible for managing your employment contract. This responsibility begins before you become a superintendent and continues throughout your entire career. As discussed in Chapter 1, keep abreast of changes in contract law and current practice by attending workshops, reading professional journals, and conferring with your counsel, knowledgeable peers, or state administrative association consultants.

Review your contract annually, paying close attention to any recent changes in state law. Bring requests for modifications to the board as needed. In some districts the board appoints one or two board members to serve as an unofficial subcommittee to work with you on contract management issues. These board members are likely to be those who negotiated your original contract on behalf of the board. In other districts the board chair and one other board member compose the subcommittee.

Bring your contract concerns or recommendations for change to these board members for discussion well in advance of the annual anniversary date of the end of the contract term. This gives you the opportunity to test your proposals with the subcommittee before determining if you want to submit the proposals to the full board. This also provides the board sufficient time to review your proposals before the end of the school year.

New, inexperienced superintendents often accept contract language at the time of hire that may not be in their best interests. They assume that they can change the less favorable terms in future years. This can be a successful strategy if your performance is outstanding and the board wants to do everything possible to keep you in the district. However, if your performance is not outstanding, or one or two board members are new or now less enthusiastic, you may find it far more difficult to remove the unfavorable terms.

The three major contract provisions that most new superintendents want to change are the term of the contract, the conditions for termination, and compensation.

Term. Most boards initially hire a new superintendent for a three-year term. As mentioned in Chapter 1, many contracts have an *evergreen clause* that provides for an automatic one-year extension based on a satisfactory evaluation. If your contract does not include a provision for an automatic extension, you must ask the board for an extension.

After one or two years of successful performance, you may wish to add an evergreen clause or request a two-year contract extension. Most states limit the term of a superintendent's contract to no more than four years, and many states are now questioning the use of evergreen clauses. Know your state law before you ask for this clause to be added. Also be aware that your board may not be receptive. Just as you would like more security, board members may want to keep more flexibility, even if your performance is outstanding.

Some successful superintendents elect to run out their contract. They work through the full three or four years of their term without seeking an extension. They prefer to wait until the contract is about to expire before negotiating an entirely new contract.

An advantage to running out the contract is that it forces the board to compare your contract provisions and compensation to what a new superintendent would receive. You may catch up to what new superintendents are earning in comparable districts. A disadvantage is that changes in the board, combined with perceptions of lower performance, can greatly reduce your leverage. Again, this strategy forces you to direct attention to your contract versus the goals you want to achieve. Ongoing contract revisions take time and may consume substantial political capital.

Conditions for Termination. Boards with recent experience with an unsatisfactory superintendent often insist on dismissal provisions that provide the district the broadest possible control. New superintendents, faced with an "all-or-nothing" contract proposal want to soften the provisions but, in the end, accept the language. After two years of successful performance, they often request more accommodating language.

You are more likely to succeed in changing the contract if you have a record of exemplary performance and are still working with the board that hired you. There is also a possibility that asking to change this provision signals to the board that you have concerns about your performance or the composition of the board. As with any change there may be unintended consequences.

Compensation. Most superintendents expect an increase in their compensation if they receive a satisfactory evaluation. Some contracts have clearly prescribed provisions for compensation increases, while others are silent on the details. The former strategy works best to reduce the political fallout from an increase in compensation but may limit your ability to remain competitive with other superintendents. This limitation can be counteracted by the way the provision is written. It also allows you to focus on the work of the district, knowing your salary needs have been met.

The latter strategy has greater political risk but can be rewarding. The downside is that boards are often reluctant to give large raises to their superintendents, even if they are deserving and the district has the resources. If funds are available for salary increases, assess your status with the board and the political environment. Develop recommendations and include a clear rationale for the requested increase, along with comparable data.

Most boards recognize that they must compensate their superintendent well if they wish to keep the superintendent in the district. They also realize that the superintendent's compensation is always of political interest to staff, parents, and the community. If the superintendent's compensation is greater than superintendents' in comparable districts, or if the percentage increase is greater than that received by teachers, support staff, and management team, then the likelihood of a negative push back is great, even if the superintendent should deserve the increase.

If you negotiate yearly for compensation increases, determine the level of political risk you are willing to experience. Some superintendents ignore the comments, the newspaper articles, and editorials. Other superintendents are crippled by the criticism and attention. Once burned in the press by a salary increase, they elect to stay within a safe compensation zone. As a result, they may fall further and further behind other superintendents. They resent their situation and may decide to seek a position in another district to increase their compensation.

Do not take action on your compensation before negotiations are completed for all other groups. Superintendents who put themselves first are resented by employees. Unions will use your increase as the model for their raises: "If it's good enough for the superintendent, it's good enough for us." This is especially true in hard times.

Many superintendents refuse to accept the guaranteed compensation increases built into their contracts if other employees are not receiving an increase. Superintendents close to retirement may take the raise and then return the dollars to the district through a payroll deduction. This allows the amount to be credited to their retirement accounts while not actually taking the raise. If you do this, be aware of your state's laws and review your decision with an attorney. Also, be aware that other retiring staff members may want similar treatment.

After three or four successful years as superintendent, you may wish to conduct a thorough review of your contract and compensation with your board. Inform the board of your needs and expectations. Experienced boards expect this and will try to address your needs if they want you to remain in the district.

As you continue in your career, weigh the pros and cons of these approaches and determine what works best for you. Some superintendents skillfully negotiate contracts that meet their needs throughout their entire tenure. Usually these superintendents are in their second or third districts, have excellent reputations, and are extremely effective in their work. They are clear on what they need and want, and they dislike revisiting the contract on a yearly basis.

8. Strengthening the Administrative Organization

The administrative organization supports the work of the district and your vision. You need an organization designed to meet the challenges of the next five years, not one that reflects the work of the past five years. As so clearly stated in *Good to Great* (HarperBusiness, 2001), this means having the right positions for the work and the right people in each position.

It is considered a best practice to conduct an administrative audit every five years. The purpose of the audit is not to evaluate the performance of individual staff members—that is your responsibility. Rather, the audit reviews the work of the district and determines if administrators and support staff are appropriately assigned to do the work.

In the mid to late 1990s, many districts randomly assigned various aspects of technology management to different staff. These assignments were based on the particular interest and skills of the administrator or teacher. These districts lacked a coherent understanding of what they were doing or even needed. As districts invested more in technology, it became apparent that decentralizing responsibility was not effective.

Districts that conducted audits clearly understood this. Soon a new category of administrator emerged: Director of Technology. Districts that recognized the need for focused technology leadership hired highly motivated and qualified people. These people wanted to work in districts that understood and valued their unique skill sets. As a result, these districts improved their use and application of technology for both administrative and instructional purposes. They also discovered that centralizing technology leadership was cost-effective.

Audits provide a unique opportunity to identify and address personnel needs and allow for a more efficient use of district resources. The audit may address or identify the following.

✓ Outdated or Nonexistent Job Descriptions

✓ Positions No Longer Needed

✓ Positions Needed but Not in Place

✓ Too Many or Too Few Support Staff

✓ Outmoded or Nonexistent Chains of Command

✓ Overcompensated or Undercompensated Positions

✓ Excessive Costs

Retain the services of an outside consultant to conduct the audit. Choose one who has experience with audits and assisting districts in implementing the recommendations. A consultant can allay the fears of staff who are concerned that their jobs are in jeopardy. It also protects staff from accusations of favoritism if the recommendations are not liked.

Work with your cabinet, your leadership team, and the board to clearly delineate the goals of the audit. Prepare an outline of the steps in the process and include a timeline. Identify how the district will use the recommendations. Everyone should be reminded that the recommendations are advisory. Meet with employee groups to review the audit expectations. In some situations, changes will involve negotiations. Where feasible, introduce the consultants to the district before the start of the audit.

The audit is in addition to the administrative review and any reorganization you may have undertaken in your first year. Your experiences as a first-year superintendent help you better understand and use the results of this study.

Annually review your administrative structure between audits. Make adjustments as needed using the audit recommendations as a guide.

9. Providing Dynamic Leadership

The board hired you because it believed your leadership skills best met the needs of the district. In turn, you used these skills to move forward the work of the district. But you may find that circumstances necessitate modifying some aspects of your leadership style. This may happen as early as your second year.

Example

> When a new superintendent arrived, the district was facing an immediate financial crisis. She quickly assessed the situation. Working with the board, she implemented a series of policy changes and returned the district to solvency. Once the crisis was over, she recognized the need to be more collaborative and less directive.

Once your staff has seen you under fire, they know you can manage a crisis. But crisis management is not a viable day-to-day management style. It is exhausting. If you fail to adjust your style to changed circumstances, you face an increasingly unhappy cabinet, leadership team, and board.

Conversely, imagine you have entered a district that was satisfied with its status quo. The board and staff saw no need for change. But you saw that change was necessary in order to move the district's instructional program forward. Building on the knowledge you gained about the district and the trust you built with the board during your first year, you suggest a strategic planning process. Your style remains collaborative, but more assertive than the previous superintendent's. Change becomes acceptable.

Strong superintendents recognize that they must adapt to changing organizational circumstances. Leaders who do not recognize this put themselves at risk. If you pride yourself on being a change agent, do not be surprised that over time the district comes to need a leader who is more collegial. Or, if you were hired to pull people together and have done so, do not be surprised that the board then wants you to be more of a change agent.

Pay close attention to changing district dynamics. You may have to change or modify your leadership style. You do not want to be stuck doing things "your way." Despite your past success, you may become less relevant to the work at hand.

Resistance. Another aspect of dynamic leadership is managing push back. At one time or another, all superintendents face this. This may be more of an issue for new superintendents who were particularly effective in their first year. As a result of your work, by the start of year two, you may have new administrators in place, new training programs for teachers, new methods of communication, and more accountability for student learning. You are feeling good. Your staff, however, is tired.

Adjusting to a new leader adds to everyone's workload. Staff members are responsible for accomplishing their previous work as well as meeting your new expectations. By year two, many successful superintendents find the staff, and even the board and community, begin to resist your ideas, suggestions, and recommendations. You hear comments such as, "That will be difficult to implement," or "The teachers will not like this new direction." People ask resistant questions such as, "Why does this program have to be revised?" or "Are you willing to hire additional staff to get this done?"

Once staff or community members begin to trust you, they soon become more comfortable expressing concerns and contrary views. Individuals who went along with changes made in year one have now experienced the consequences of these changes. They may be less enthusiastic.

Recognize that people may need time to integrate the first round of changes before accepting additional change. Just as you cannot always be in a crisis mode, neither can you always be in a change mode. Going slow may get you farther in the long run. That is the value of the eighteen-month planning process.

Make the necessary changes in year one. Use year two to assess the impact of each change and to integrate these changes into the culture of the district. Validate contributions that were made. Recognize the positive benefits of listening and responding positively to people's concerns. Use the staff's energy to deepen the work you started.

An exception to this is a district in true crisis. If student learning is not progressing, the district is in dire financial straits, or there are unrelenting infrastructure needs, you will need to continue making changes. Under these circumstances, you probably will receive less push back. But even if you do, you must do what is right by the students and the district and not what is easy. Ultimately this is what effective leadership is about.

10. Committing to Lifelong Learning

All superintendents, irrespective of their years of experience or success in their current position, must continue to develop their knowledge and skills. Without this, your effectiveness diminishes. Knowledge is not static. Commit yourself to lifelong learning and be open to new ideas.

Always include personal professional development as one of your annual performance goals. Ask your board to support your attendance at educational conferences and workshops. If times are hard and resources are scarce, pay for these experiences yourself. Under these circumstances, some boards will pay registration fees if you pay for travel and living expenses. Do not use lack of resources as an excuse not to grow. In addition to attending conferences and workshops, you can do the following.

- ❑ Read books and professional journals.
- ❑ Engage in online seminars or discussions.
- ❑ Enroll in college or university courses.
- ❑ Teach a college course.
- ❑ Attend professional development activities in your district or county.
- ❑ Invite outside speakers to county superintendent meetings.
- ❑ Deepen your involvement in local, state, or national educational organizations.

Look at your career as an educational experience. Remain intellectually curious. Model professional development behaviors for your staff to emulate.

At some point you may leave your current position. If you apply for another superintendent position, prospective boards will expect you to be knowledgeable and familiar with current trends. If you have abandoned your own education, why would a new board want to hire you to lead the education of its students?

11. Maintaining Your Physical and Emotional Well-Being

Serving as a superintendent is demanding work. You work long hours, often six or seven days a week. You are on call 24/7. You need to maintain your emotional and physical health to remain effective under these conditions. This includes maintaining a balance between your personal and professional life. Your personal well-being requires this.

Far too many superintendents are divorced, estranged from children who barely know them, or too involved in their work to have close personal friends or a close-knit family. They suffer from high blood pressure, stroke, or heart disease; have substance abuse problems; and are seriously overweight or underweight.

Example

A highly regarded single superintendent was so overcommitted to the work in his district that he rarely took a day off, even on weekends. His staff, board, and colleagues all liked him and respected his work. But he had high blood pressure, and in his mid-fifties, at the height of his career, he suffered a devastating stroke.

Some Indicators of Concern

- You find yourself always drained and unable to recharge.
- You no longer discern between big and small issues; everything looks like a big issue.
- You lose patience and interest in your work.
- Your doctor warns you about the negative effects of your work habits on your health.
- Nothing in your job is exciting or fun anymore. You lost your sense of humor and cannot laugh at yourself.

All superintendents experience the negative effects of pressure. How you respond depends on the severity of the situation and your ability to recognize the symptoms. The signs may indicate a need to revisit your legacy goals or reorganize your work.

Or, these may be signs of something more serious, like depression. In these situations, changing how you do your work will help. But you may need assistance. Do not be afraid of asking for help from your mentor or coach. Seek medical care and assistance when appropriate. Following are two different ways superintendents responded to similar signs in their lives.

Example

One very successful superintendent in his mid-fifties realized he was no longer having, as he put it, "fun" in the job. He had spent almost twenty years in two districts as superintendent. He was respected for his work as an instructional leader and was appreciated by his board and community. He knew that moving to another district would not solve his problem. He wanted to do something different. As a result he took early retirement to lead a nonprofit educational organization, a position he is in twelve years later and still finds challenging and enjoyable.

Another superintendent realized that after five intense, stress-filled years she needed a break. She had brought the district through difficult financial times, reorganized the district staff, and significantly raised student achievement. The board and community wanted her to stay. She worked with her board and arranged to take six weeks off during the summer to travel. She returned recharged and remained in the district for an additional five years.

The best way to maintain your emotional and physical health is to start with good habits. Review and recommit to them each and every year.

If you find yourself stuck in unhealthy work habits, make a determined effort to move toward a healthier life style. Again, talk with your board about what you need to do to be effective in your work.

12. Remaining in or Leaving the District

At some point during your tenure you start thinking about your future. This is normal. This may occur at the end of your first or tenth year. It will occur if you are doing well or not so well. You find yourself asking, "Should I remain or leave?" Many factors may influence your decision.

Whatever triggers your thinking, the decision you make is a critical one for your professional career. Do not make it lightly. Be thoughtful and consider the consequences. Every superintendent faces difficult times. These are not easy jobs; they are complex and challenging. They are also the most rewarding positions anyone can have because of the positive influence they can have on the lives of students.

Sorting through your feelings to determine what is the best course of action takes discipline. The best decisions are made with rational thought and planning. Just as you do not want to stay in a position where you no longer believe you can be effective, neither do you want to leave a position because of a few setbacks. Nor do you want to be viewed as someone who jumps from one position to another each time difficulties arise.

Superintendents prefer to make their own decision about when to leave or retire. But in certain instances you have no choice. As noted earlier in this chapter, you may need to leave the district to avoid a possible dismissal or nonextension of your contract. This could be due to the election of a new board majority or your failure to perform. You must be prepared to leave with grace and dignity.

Conversely, you may find at the end of several years that much remains to be done and you have strong board and community support. You may even decide you want to stay in one district for your entire career. If you decide to stay, be prepared to make the necessary changes to ensure that the successful direction of the district continues. This means revisiting the district's goals and your legacy goals, as well as examining the kind of leadership you need to exert to move the district forward.

Questions to Ask. Chapter 1 provides a series of questions to help you determine whether you want to be a superintendent. Similarly, you need to ask questions before you make a decision to stay or leave.

- Am I receiving positive evaluations? Do I have the support of my board? Do I like working with this board?
- Have I achieved my legacy goals? Do I have a vision of where I can lead this district for another three to five years? Can I commit to achieving that vision?
- Does this position permit me to improve teaching and learning for students?
- Does remaining here meet my physical, emotional, personal, and family needs?
- Does remaining meet my financial goals? Is the board offering to extend my contract?
- Does remaining here help me achieve my long-term career goals? Or, is there a new and challenging career opportunity? Do I wish to retire from this district?

If the answer to most of these questions is a resounding no, start planning for your next position. Or, it may be time to consider retiring and using your knowledge and skills in another capacity. But be certain you understand the reasons why you wish to leave. Finding a second superintendent position can be as challenging as finding your first. The reasons for your leaving will affect how other districts view your application.

If the answer to questions above is a resounding yes, you may have no reason to leave. Trust your instincts. In this situation your challenge is one of recommitment and renewal to your work.

Remaining in your district does not mean continuing to do as you have in the past. It poses a different set of challenges. This is especially true if you serve more than four years. The longer you remain, the more you become a part of the system and the less you see the organization with fresh eyes. Your challenge is to take a long hard look at yourself, what you have accomplished, and what you want to accomplish over the next five years.

The district is not the same as when you first arrived. You made changes, and the district adjusted to these. You now need to lead the district forward for the next three to five years. Begin by carefully examining what needs to occur to make this happen. This reexamination or renewal is a challenging process. It is difficult to let go of what made you successful to try new, more challenging strategies. However, if you continue leading as in the past, you are likely to be less successful in the future. As the organization has changed, so must you.

Example

A successful superintendent completed her first four-year contract in the district. She was a strong superintendent and had moved the district through difficult financial times and challenging negotiations. However, her skill set did not include an understanding of the use of technology to support instruction. She continued to underfund technology applications despite concerns expressed by the cabinet and the board. She let her board know that she "just wasn't a techie." Halfway through her second contract, a newly constituted board gave her an unsatisfactory evaluation because the district was not narrowing the achievement gap. The board said that, unlike neighboring district superintendents, she failed to make assessment data available to classroom teachers.

Preparing to stay in a district as superintendent requires as much planning and focus as did planning for your first superintendent position. Renewal requires recognizing your strengths, identifying areas of weakness or needed growth, and committing to making changes. Renewal means looking carefully at your legacy goals and making revisions there as well. Your goal is to develop a personal plan for the next four years.

Whatever you decide and whenever you make the decision, know your decision requires the same careful thought as your initial decision to seek a superintendent position.

SUMMARY

Successful first-year superintendents cannot plan on simply repeating the first year over and over. The work may appear to be the same, but certain nuances and issues make each succeeding year different and more complex.

Following are the major points covered in this chapter that will assist you in your long-term professional growth and development.

- Learn the challenges you face in year two and beyond. Focus on student achievement through effective use of the eighteen-month planning cycle and implementation of the district's goals.
- Focus on how to work effectively with a changing school board. Learn how to respond to your evaluations and manage your contract.
- Develop an administrative organization to support the work of the district.
- Understand why your leadership style must evolve to meet the changing needs of the district.

- Commit to lifelong learning and maintaining a healthy lifestyle.
- Address the issue of whether to remain or leave the district. Understand the new challenges that await you no matter what decision you make.

Years two and beyond are rewarding years as you see the results of your work and the positive effect they have on students. The knowledge you gain through this experience helps inform future decisions you make regarding your career.

FINAL THOUGHTS

Today we face challenges more severe than any faced in recent memory. Our country is more diverse with greater needs, more students, and fewer resources. We need the talents of all our children. We need a well-educated populace to preserve our democratic values and institutions.

Use this book to become a superintendent. Use it to support your success as a new superintendent. Most importantly, use this book as a foundation for providing an outstanding educational experience for each and every student in your care.

We are committed to supporting our readers in this endeavor. We would like to hear about your experiences and how this book may have helped you. Contact us at achievingsuccess1@yahoo.com.

Resources

Throughout the book we emphasized the importance of intellectual curiosity and a commitment to lifelong learning. We also referred to the necessity of keeping current in all areas of educational leadership. What follows is a listing of some resources that may be of assistance to you. The list is by no means exhaustive. Your intellectual curiosity and continued learning will lead you to other sources.

ORGANIZATIONS

American Association of School Administrators (AASA) www.aasa.org

Membership is open to superintendents and assistant superintendents, both retired and active, as well as those in affiliated roles. Membership includes a subscription to the *District Administrator* and discounts to conferences. AASA is active in lobbying for K–12 education, coordinates activities with its state affiliates, and provides other services to members, such as liability insurance and legal counseling.

State School Administrator Associations

Each state has a school administrators association, and you can find yours on the Web. Most of them include periodicals with their memberships. Often these are the best source of educational job vacancies for the state. Many sponsor meetings, conferences, or workshops for members. Some may offer access to limited legal counsel or other general advice services, such as employment contract review. Like the AASA, they may advocate for districts at the state and federal level.

National School Boards Association (NSBA) www.nsba.org

This organization is comprised of state associations of school boards. Many districts across the country hold affiliate memberships for the superintendent and board members. NSBA sponsors an annual conference, supports state affiliates, produces publications, and lobbies Congress on behalf of its members.

State School Board Associations

As with state administrator associations, you can find the state school board association in your state by searching online. Services offered by these state associations may include hiring superintendents, reviewing and revising school board policies, school board training, individual school district consultants, communications, periodicals, and limited legal advice. They also usually offer annual conferences and workshops, as well as advocate at the state level on behalf of school districts.

Educational Records Bureau (ERB) www.erblearn.org

ERB offers an extensive array of tests for independent and public schools. Its Writing Assessment Program (WrAP) and Writing Practice Program (WPP), as well as other subject area tests, are helpful to public schools as the data is both disaggregated and benchmarked. ERB is developing computer adaptive tests. In addition to an annual conference, regional workshops are held across the country.

American Educational Research Association (AERA) www.aera.net

While this organization primarily focuses on university and college research in education and related fields, its publications can be of great assistance in learning about current trends in education and successful practices. Nonmembers may purchase its periodicals. Often superintendents, curriculum and instruction directors, or assessment directors in K–12 either belong to AERA or at least subscribe to its publications.

Association for Supervision and Curriculum Development (ASCD) www.ascd.org

ASCD focuses its membership services on best practices and policies for student learning. It is open to all educators, including board members. ASCD provides periodicals and sponsors conferences and workshops. It is an excellent source of staff development resources.

**Association of School Business Officials
International (ASBO) www.asbointl.org**

ASBO is open to individuals employed in a business or administrative function in public or private schools. It provides a wide array of services, including workshops, publications, and career assistance. Most state school business organizations are ASBO affiliates.

PERIODICALS AND NEWSPAPERS

In addition to publications offered through professional organizations, we recommend you read other journals and periodicals. Also, visit the websites of major colleges and universities that have educational programs to view their publications. Following are a few suggested periodicals.

Education Week www.edweek.org

Education Week is a weekly paper that contains up-to-date information on all facets of education. It calls itself "American education's newspaper of record." It provides job listings for vacancies across the country, as well as a yearly list, by month, of all education related conferences. It is part of Editorial Projects in Education, Inc., which also publishes other materials of interest to superintendents and educators. Its website contains information on all of its publications.

Harvard Business Review www.hbr.harvardbusiness.org

This monthly publication is available in print or online. It often contains articles in fields related to education. Its articles on leadership are particularly useful. For example, the authors of *Disrupting Class: How Disruptive Innovation Will Change the Way the World Learns* (McGraw-Hill, 2008) recently wrote an article titled "Meeting the Challenge of Disruptive Change" that discusses why so few companies can effectively innovate. This article provides a perspective that can apply to education.

Harvard Educational Review www.hepg.org

Harvard Educational Review publishes educational research, as well as opinion about what is happening in the field. It hosts a blog on which current topics are debated. *Harvard Educational Review* is published quarterly and reaches a broad audience. It is frequently quoted by policymakers.

Marshall Memo www.marshallmemo.com

This weekly memo is the equivalent of a nationwide clipping service for its readers. The articles come from a wide variety of publications. But do not forgo subscribing to other publications because you read this.

Daily Publications

Read a wide array of daily publications. Include local community and regional newspapers. Many can be accessed online. Depending upon their political points of view, superintendents often subscribe to either the *New York Times* or the *Wall Street Journal*. If possible, read both so you can gather news from an array of view points. Even in communities that are predominantly liberal or conservative, there are people with differing or contrary views.

BOOKS AND AUTHORS

Reading is one way to stay current in the field of education and develop your knowledge. This means not only reading journals, periodicals, books, and articles on education, but also reading widely outside of education. Books on leadership, poetry, writing, psychology, philosophy, history, business, biographies, and even novels provide insights valuable to any leader. Lists of books often appear in the journals or publications of the organizations to which you belong. Newspapers like the *New York Times* contain extensive book reviews in the Sunday editions. What is important is to find those books or periodicals that help you better understand the context in which you work and assist you in that work.

What follows is not a traditional listing of books. Rather it is a listing of some of our favorite authors and sources that you may find helpful. All of the works mentioned can be found by going to the websites of publishers, booksellers, or authors. We have grouped them under general headings. Use these as a starting place for your own exploration.

Education

The journals mentioned previously in this section contain book reviews and suggestions for reading. In addition, most every major university with a department of education has publications. For example, Harvard University Press (www.hup.harvard.edu), Stanford University Press (www.sup.org), and Teachers College Columbia University (www.tc.columbia.edu) are some of the preeminent publishers in education. Visit their websites and browse.

In addition, Corwin (www.corwinpress.com), Jossey-Bass (www.jossey bass.com), McGraw-Hill (www.mcgrawhill.com), and Sage (www.sagepub. com) are some of the major educational publishing companies. Often these sites provide detailed information about the author or book. For example, McGraw-Hill, the publisher of *Disrupting Class: How Disruptive Innovation Will Change the Way the World Learns* (2008), has information on its website about podcasts with the main author, Clayton Christensen. Amazon.com is also another wonderful source to find books. One can browse the website for hours, moving from subject to subject.

There are also authors like John Dewey, Michael Fullan, Jonathan Kozol, Gene Maeroff, Robert Marzano, Debra Pickering, and Harry Wong whose books continually remind us how to be good educators and why we are in the field.

Outside of education we also have recommendations by areas of interest.

Writing and Speaking

If you want to improve your writing and speaking style read Christopher Lasch's *Plain Style: A Guide to Written English* (University of Pennsylvania Press, 2002), Peggy Noonan's *Simply Speaking: How to Communicate Your Ideas With Style, Substance, and Clarity* (Regan Books, 1998), and Edwin Newman's *Strictly Speaking: Will America Be the Death of English?* (Warner Books, 1975). These are some of the best books written on the subject. Writers and speakers often refer to them and the influence they have had on their work.

Quotes and Inspiration

If you are looking for good quotes and inspirational stories read poetry. W. H. Auden, e. e cummings, T. S. Eliot, and Walt Whitman are good places to start. You can also search the Web for inspirational quotes and find annotated books of quotes from numerous authors for specific occasions. Often biographies yield wonderful quotes, as do the speeches or writings of individuals like Maya Angelou, Marian Wright Edelman, or Eleanor Roosevelt.

Sometimes you will find a unique book on your travels. One, *I Have Not Seen a Butterfly Around Here: Children's Drawings and Poems From Terezin* (The Jewish Museum in Prague, Tenth Edition, 2006) is a beautiful and inspirational work that provides new insights into children faced with unspeakable horror.

Leadership and Conflict

Books abound on this subject. Many come from the field of business, and what is in one year may be out the next. This is an area where reading biographies and history can be important. Try authors like Thomas Friedman, Doris Kearns Goodwin, and Bill Moyers. Their writings on the contemporary scene often provide better insight to good and courageous leadership than do books specifically addressing the topic.

In John O'Neill's *The Paradox of Success* (Penguin, 1993) and *Leadership Aikido* (Harmony Books, 1997), O'Neill writes from the perspective of an educator, businessman, and psychologist. Jennifer Abrams's *Having Hard Conversations* (Corwin, 2009) talks about how to successfully discuss difficult issues with colleagues and subordinates. Finally, look to the classics. William Shakespeare's plays still hold wonderful insights into human nature, leadership, and conflict.

Contemporary Issues

Some books also provide different perspectives on the world and, ultimately, the youth with whom we work. Read Robert Putnam on the growing isolation in society, Neil Howe and William Strauss on the generations and the needs of each in the workplace, Glenn Singleton or Fred Brill on equity issues, or Malcolm Gladwell, who provides interesting insights that apply to education and leadership.

Other sources of information include art and natural history museums, movies, documentaries, concerts, and children's literature, including graphic novels. Availing yourself of these learning experiences will develop your contemporary cultural literacy. It will allow you to connect with a wide number of constituents and better understand students' learning needs. We also recommend you talk to superintendents—both experienced and new—and find what books they consider of interest.

CONCLUSION

These listings are but a brief overview of sources available to you. Once you begin exploring, you will find others that enrich and guide you. Enjoy the time you spend doing this. As the educational leader of your district, you are the model for lifelong learning. It is also a wonderful way to relax and place your work in perspective.

Index

CORWIN

A SAGE Company

The Corwin logo—a raven striding across an open book—represents the union of courage and learning. Corwin is committed to improving education for all learners by publishing books and other professional development resources for those serving the field of PreK–12 education. By providing practical, hands-on materials, Corwin continues to carry out the promise of its motto: **"Helping Educators Do Their Work Better."**